Studies in Modern History

General Editor: **J. C. D. Clark**, Joyce and Elizabeth Hall Distinguished Professor of British History, University of Kansas

Titles include:

Bernard Cottret (*editor*)
BOLINGBROKE'S POLITICAL WRITINGS
The Conservative Enlightenment

Richard R. Follett
EVANGELICALISM, PENAL THEORY AND THE POLITICS OF CRIMINAL LAW REFORM IN ENGLAND, 1808–30

Philip Hicks
NEOCLASSICAL HISTORY AND ENGLISH CULTURE
From Clarendon to Hume

Mark Keay
WILLIAM WORDSWORTH'S GOLDEN AGE THEORIES DURING THE INDUSTRIAL REVOLUTION IN ENGLAND, 1750–1850

William M. Kuhn
DEMOCRATIC ROYALISM
The Transformation of the British Monarchy, 1861–1914

Kim Lawes
PATERNALISM AND POLITICS
The Revival of Paternalism in Early Nineteenth-Century Britain

Marisa Linton
THE POLITICS OF VIRTUE IN ENLIGHTENMENT FRANCE

Nancy D. LoPatin
POLITICAL UNIONS, POPULAR POLITICS AND THE GREAT REFORM ACT OF 1832

Marjorie Morgan
NATIONAL IDENTITIES AND TRAVEL IN VICTORIAN BRITAIN

James Muldoon
EMPIRE AND ORDER
The Concept of Empire, 800–1800

W. D. Rubinstein and Hilary Rubinstein
PHILOSEMITISM
Admiration and Support for Jews in the English-Speaking World, 1840–1939

Lisa Steffen
TREASON AND NATIONAL IDENTITY
Defining a British State, 1608–1820

Lynne Taylor
BETWEEN RESISTANCE AND COLLABORATION
Popular Protest in Northern France, 1940–45

Studies in Modern History
Series Standing Order ISBN 0–333–79328–5
(*outside North America only*)

You can receive future titles in this series as they are published by placing a standing order. Please contact your bookseller or, in case of difficulty, write to us at the address below with your name and address, the title of the series and the ISBN quoted above.

Customer Services Department, Macmillan Distribution Ltd, Houndmills, Basingstoke, Hampshire RG21 6XS, England

The Politics of Virtue in Enlightenment France

Marisa Linton
Senior Lecturer in History
Kingston University

First published 2001 by
PALGRAVE
Houndmills, Basingstoke, Hampshire RG21 6XS and
175 Fifth Avenue, New York, N. Y. 10010
Companies and representatives throughout the world

PALGRAVE is the new global academic imprint of
St. Martin's Press LLC Scholarly and Reference Division and
Palgrave Publishers Ltd (formerly Macmillan Press Ltd).

ISBN 978–0–333–94959–7

This book is printed on paper suitable for recycling and
made from fully managed and sustained forest sources.

A catalogue record for this book is available
from the British Library.

Library of Congress Cataloging-in-Publication Data
Linton, Marisa, 1959–
    The politics of virtue in Enlightenment France / Marisa Linton.
        p. cm. — (Studies in modern history)
    Includes bibliographical references and index.
    ISBN 0–333–94959–5
    1. Political ethics—France—History—18th century. 2. France–
    –Politics and government—1715–1774. 3. France—Politics and
    government—1774–1793. I. Title. II. Studies in modern history
    (Palgrave (Firm))
    JA79 .L56 2001
    179'.9'094409033—dc21
                                                          2001021609

10   9   8   7   6   5   4   3   2   1
10   09 08 07 06 05 04 03 02 01

Transferred to Digital Printing in 2010

For Peter
Who dare say that virtue is not rewarded?

Contents

Acknowledgements

It makes me very happy to be able to acknowledge the many people who have helped me so much in the writing of this book. I would particularly like to thank Colin Jones and John Burrow who gave so much valuable time and careful thought to the reading of the entire manuscript and proferred such excellent advice. Mike Sonenscher also read earlier versions of the text and made invaluable suggestions for its improvement. I would also like to thank the series editor, Jonathan Clark, and the anonymous reader for Palgrave for their enthusiasm for the book. Despite the best efforts of these readers, there were some things I could not, or would not, change and, naturally, no one but myself must bear responsibility for any shortcomings in the finished work.

I benefited greatly from the research ethos and environment of the History Group at the University of Sussex, particularly the informed discussion of the seminars for work in progress. I also owe much to the stimulation and animated meetings of succeeding generations of graduate students who attended the Gender and History Group at Sussex. It was only possible to rethink the relationship between language and politics in the context of the kind of interdisciplinary approach that thrives at Sussex. For animated discussions, suggestions, references I am indebted to a number of historians, though I would particularly like to acknowledge the help of Tom Crow, Dena Goodman, Mark Ledbury and Julian Swann. A special mention is due to Dale Van Kley who contributed many insightful comments and enlivening ideas on a memorable series of walks, talks and meals in Edinburgh.

Money and time are two essential commodities without which no book, even on so elevated a subject as virtue, could be written. I would like to acknowledge with much gratitude the financial support extended to me by a number of institutions. The British Academy granted me a major studentship which supported me (and my son) whilst I carried out the initial research. I was also the grateful recipient of the Royal Historical Society's Centenary Research Fellowship in 1991. As a student I was also given bursaries by the Owen Taylor fund and the Society for the Study of French History, which helped greatly in the research stages of the project. No less importantly, in 1999 the Arts and Humanities Research Board gave me a semester's leave to complete the writing of the book. I am also grateful that Kingston University gave me a semester's leave in 1998.

I am grateful to my children, to Harry, Elena and Sophia. They did not exactly speed the process of writing along, but they made life happier on the way. Above all I want to thank Peter Campbell. If I had a talent for writing eulogies of heroes of public and private virtue I would write one to him. Luckily for him perhaps, despite having read so many such formal eulogies, I have no skill in the art, and so will spare him the attempt. But I will say that he has been a constant source of unwavering help and support, both intellectually and emotionally, in everything from critical reading of the manuscript to child-minding whilst I wrote it. He has certainly suffered the vicissitudes of virtue every step along the way, and for that reason this book is dedicated to him.

A Note on Translations

Except where specifically stated, all translations are the author's own.

Introduction

Virtue alone is happiness below.

Alexander Pope, *An Essay on Man* (1733–4)

If the mainspring of popular government in peacetime is virtue, during a revolution the mainspring of popular government is both virtue and terror; virtue, without which terror is baneful; terror, without which virtue is powerless. Terror is nothing more than speedy, severe and inflexible justice; it is thus an emanation of virtue; it is less a principle in itself, than a consequence of the general principle of democracy, applied to the most pressing needs of the patrie.

Maximilien Robespierre, speaking to the
National Convention, 5 February 1794

Virtue as happiness, virtue as terror: two more contrasting statements could scarcely be imagined than those made by the English poet and the French revolutionary. Yet the concept of virtue encompassed within itself both these ideas, and much more besides. It was at the very heart of eighteenth-century political, social and moral thought. It had a multiplicity of meanings, applications and resonances, some of which were interconnected, whilst others were distinct and appeared in sharp contrast to one another. Of the many meanings that virtue had, one in particular was to cast a long shadow. This was the idea that the political organisation and the social ordering of society should be based on virtue. It shaped the Revolution that ended the eighteenth century – and consequently continued to inform the world which that Revolution itself precipitated, still to a degree our own world.

Writers in the eighteenth century regularly asserted that virtue was necessary in political life, by which they meant that anyone who

1

engaged in politics ought to be motivated solely by the desire to promote the general or public good rather than by their own self-interest and personal gain. The idea that virtue was necessary in political life was an old one; it derived from the classical republican tradition and the political thought of the classical civilisations of Greece and Rome. But alongside this powerful and egalitarian concept grew another one in the eighteenth century which was also to be far reaching in its implications. This was the contention that the possession of virtue entitled people to participate in public life and eventually, by extension, to exercise political rights. By being those of 'virtuous citizens', that is, moral public-spirited beings, people's voices were legitimised, the people became a moral force with a right to be heard, even before the Revolution of 1789 made them citizens with explicit political rights.

The debate on virtue involved fundamental questions such as what the aim of politics should be, and how it should be conducted; questions which are no nearer to acquiring definitive answers now than they were in the eighteenth century. The problem of whether either political leaders or ordinary citizens should be obliged to display public or private virtue raises problems and tensions between public duties and private aspirations which still haunt modern political life. Thus the ways in which people in the eighteenth century thought through these problems and conceived of a moral politics are still of considerable interest to us. It is the aim of this book to arrive at a better understanding of how people at that time began to use the notion of virtue in order to arrive at a new way of conceptualising politics. We need to consider not only political theory in the abstract, but also its dynamics and practical applications. 'Virtue' is a fundamental concept which offers us a key with which to explore such ideas and strategies.

The notion of a politics based on moral abstractions may seem to our eyes naive and possibly faintly ridiculous. It may even appear dangerous and redolent of coercion. Today we are acutely aware of how manipulative politicians may seek to justify violence and oppression in the name of an imposing but empty rhetoric of 'the public good', 'the general will', or 'liberty and equality'. The very word 'virtue' has been long since drained of almost all effective meaning, and now signifies little more than a vague notion of sentimental morality, or a quaint, almost comically outdated, word for the chastity of women. It is only with an effort of historical understanding that we can, from our vantage point at the end of the twentieth century, comprehend what was meant in the eighteenth century by the idea of moral politics, the politics of virtue. Yet such an effort is indispensable if we are to reconstitute the meaning of politics at this key period in the development of modern political thought.

The history of concepts and of political culture in France has been virtually rewritten in recent years. The debate over the origins of the French Revolution is at the heart of much of this work: historians such as Keith Baker and Roger Chartier have returned with new energy to the problem set out by Daniel Mornet in the 1930s: was there a direct relationship between the ideas of the Enlightenment and the outbreak of Revolution and, if so, how can it be characterised?[1] The social and cultural history of the Enlightenment is now as vital as the ideas themselves to any account of the nature of the Enlightenment. No longer are historians content to consider the Enlightenment as a set of ideas viewed in isolation from their readership: they are also engaged in assessing the effect of the growth in an audience for intellectual works, particularly amongst the bourgeoisie. The cultural expansion in eighteenth-century France – with the ever-growing market for books, plays and artworks – is now recognised as a compelling subject in its own right. Historians such as Robert Darnton have uncovered the publishing history of this period and have shown that the impact of the Enlightenment needs to be assessed as much through the study of its readership and of the minor writers who operated at its fringes, as through the classic repertoire of its major thinkers.[2] Thanks to the pioneering work of Habermas, the eighteenth century is now seen as the crucial period in the formation of a bourgeois public sphere. This in turn has led to a radical rethinking of the implications of the expanding and self-conscious audience for cultural works.[3]

Gender is now seen as a major concern for historians of political culture. No current work on the politics of virtue could remain unaffected by the growing awareness of the part played by distinctions based on constructions of gender in shaping political rhetoric, particularly for this simultaneously most public and yet most private of terms. This is one area in which the concept of virtue in eighteenth-century France has been the subject of a significant reevalution in recent years – by Outram and Blum, amongst others.[4] My fuller consideration of this issue is available in another place: unfortunately, the economics of modern publishing intervened to preclude it being given its due in the present work.[5] Here there is only space to offer a summary of the main points of my research. The discourse of feminine virtue provides a thought-provoking counterpoint to the mainly masculine discourses of political virtue. Nowhere do we see more clearly that the same discourse that could be used to empower and bestow a right to participate, could also condition and entrap the speaker. The rhetoric of virtue was double-edged for women, certainly, and not without its problems and ambiguities. But it provided strategic possibilities which could be exploited. Although virtue in its civic sense left little space for women in the public sphere, women were not completely passive agents in this discourse. They could, and did, employ notions of moral virtue and *bienfaisance* to justify arguments that women could play an active role in society through virtue to improve public manners and morals. Models of women's virtue which appeared may seem very limited now, but represented a considerable step forward in the way that women were represented during the eighteenth century. The language of virtue was employed within the social confines of what was possible for women at that time. But at its more radical edge it challenged the political and social conventions and provided a voice for women who, hitherto, had been voiceless.

The relationship of the legal profession and legal cases to the political culture of the later eighteenth century has recently been brought to light by historians such as Maza and Bell.[6] There has not, until now, been a general study which focuses on the concept of political virtue in France, but the English-speaking world of the eighteenth century has been subject to a number of works on the rhetoric of political virtue particularly in the context of classical republicanism.[7] Led by Pocock and others, studies of British politics and political theory have shown how such classical-republican terms as 'virtue' and 'patriotism' were key words used to justify dissent from government policy, and thence to legitimise the idea of political opposition and transform conceptions of the nature of politics. On the other hand, studies of the politics of virtue in France have tended to focus on the ideas of individual *philosophes*, most notably Rousseau.[8]

It may be that studies of the concept of political virtue in France have not yet been undertaken precisely because our view of this subject cannot but be affected by the cataclysmic events of the French Revolution and this makes the subject much more sensitive and contentious than for Britain. The revolutionary project after the fall of the monarchy was, in the words of Robespierre, to bring about literally a 'republic of virtue' on earth.[9] What began as a vision of universal happiness and goodwill descended into a nightmare. In the name of virtue, a policy of terror was instituted against the enemies of the virtuous republic. It was a traumatic experience which, more than anything else, served to discredit the politics of virtue, so that the word subsequently vanished from political vocabularies and has never since been effectively revived.

The link between virtue and terror remains a compulsive and terrifying one – as we can see from Robespierre's speech cited at the start of this introduction – such an incongruous juxtaposition of words still retains its power to horrify. Many commentators have since argued that the step from virtue to terror was, despite the apparent paradox, an inevitable one, and that the employment of moral absolutes in political rhetoric will necessarily result in the use of violence against those whose moral and political allegiances differ from those of the dominant political group. Such was the view put forward by J. L. Talmon and other writers of the Cold War period, who saw in the French Revolution the origins of twentieth-century Stalinism, and even of the racial policies of the Nazis. Talmon looked at the ideas in isolation, thus enabling him to see a linear development from Rousseau's 'general will' to Robespierre, Marx, Lenin and ultimately Stalin.[10] It was a viewpoint which found little favour with historians of the period, who were sceptical of the extent to which the context and events of the French Revolution could be understood in twentieth-century terms.[11]

In recent years the 'totalitarian' thesis has been reanimated by one of the foremost historians of the revolutionary period, François Furet. Influenced by post-modernist thinking, Furet has put the study of revolutionary language, rather than social or economic history, at the forefront of debate. He depicts 1789 as the moment of the invention of a new 'political discourse'; one which for the first time conflated politics and morality: 'When politics becomes the realm of truth and falsehood, of good and evil, and when it is politics that separates the good from the wicked, we find ourselves in a historical universe whose dynamic is entirely new.'[12] He argues that this juxtaposition of politics and morality was both novel and inherently unstable and that these very instabilities led directly to the revolutionary Terror. Thus it was the new revolutionary moral politics (the politics of virtue although Furet does not use the term) which made the Terror not only possible, but inevitable from the moment the Revolution broke out. This interpretation has had an immense and important impact on the way in which modern historians perceive both the Revolution and the politics of virtue. Whatever the values of Furet's approach for revolutionary historiography – and he has attracted both adherents and critics – it is predicated upon the essential novelty of the political language of the revolutionaries and downplays the continuities which existed between the political ideas of the *ancien régime* and those of the Revolution.

Influential though this approach has been, it by no means offers the only explanatory framework within which to situate the complex relationship between revolutionary politics and eighteenth-century thought. An alternative method, and one which is less historically anachronistic, is to explore the continuities between revolutionary politics and the political language of the eighteenth century. As Alfred Cobban argued long ago, the idea that 'fundamental moral principles in government was the only cure for political evils' was a commonplace of eighteenth-century thought: virtue, patriotism and popular sovereignty were all dominant political ideas long before the Revolution.[13] The French Revolution was indeed to prove a springboard for modern conceptions of politics, but revolutionary conceptions of the nature of politics themselves emerged out of the context of ideas which were already familiar in the eighteenth century. The example of Robespierre's terrifying statement that virtue and terror are interlinked is helpful here. It was a revolutionary statement in every sense. Yet Robespierre's basic understanding of political virtue derived from Enlightenment thought.[14] And Rousseau was by no means the sole influence in this respect. The revolutionary concept of political virtue was in fact derived from a much broader body of ideas than those of Rousseau alone. Thus, Robespierre's speech on that occasion contained a definition of virtue in terms which paraphrased the famous explication given by Montesquieu – a definition which was itself derived from Italian classical humanist writers, and which had influenced political theory in France throughout the second half of the eighteenth century. In Robespierre's words:

> What is the fundamental principle of democratic or popular government, that is to say, the essential spring that supports it and makes it work? It is virtue; I speak of that public virtue that worked so many wonders in Greece and Rome, and which should produce even more astonishing ones in the French republic; of that virtue that is no other thing than love of the *patrie* and of its laws.[15]

Conceptions of politics gradually and painfully took on new forms within the unprecedented context of the revolutionary experience. The idea of political virtue provided a key point of continuity: it was already a concept of crucial importance long before the Revolution itself broke out. Revolutionary rhetoric, however, would add new resonances to the classic notion of political virtue. Most significantly, it was in the context of the unprecedented political situation of 1793 that it became thinkable for the first time to juxtapose the word 'virtue' with the word 'terror'. It would be in the conjunction between these two such disparate words, not linked by pre-revolutionary thinkers, that the language of political virtue took on a truly revolutionary significance and proved definitively its break with the customary patterns of eighteenth-century political thought.

The current historiographical trend has been to see the eighteenth-century concept of political virtue in terms of the Revolution and to overlook the legacy of Enlightenment thought in this respect with the exception of Rousseau's specific contribution. But if we consider the concept of virtue solely in terms of how it relates to the Revolution, the temptation is to view its development teleologically and assume that the evolution from pre-revolutionary to revolutionary virtue was a necessary one. As an approach this seems to me to be potentially misleading, since it encourages the assumption that the politics of virtue already constituted a revolutionary language before the Revolution broke out. The evidence suggests the contrary. Although political virtue had a particular affinity with radical arguments, it was a rhetoric which both political conservatives and radicals could employ. Indeed, it was a rhetoric familiar to members of the educated classes throughout much of Europe and in North America – anywhere, in fact, where a classical education was standard practice at secondary level.

This book considers the eighteenth-century concept of political virtue as a subject in its own right. On the whole, eighteenth-century writers expressed their ideas with striking sophistication and showed much adroitness in their active manipulation of rhetorical strategies in a variety of circumstances and contexts. Most of the writers whose works figure in these pages appear to have been well aware of what could and could not be said in a given situation and the consequences of adopting a certain mode of rhetoric. Far from them giving much indication of having been manipulated by a discourse whose real significance they were unable to comprehend most seem to have had as least as clear an understanding of what they were doing as we can have in piecing together their meaning. The historian, of course, always has the final advantage of being able to say 'what people meant' and to impute to their subject matter ideas and intentions, without their subjects ever having the chance to reply or to repudiate such claims made on their behalf. It seemed to me safer (as well as more just) to hesitate before making any judgement, and to try to allow space for the complexity and subtlety with which eighteenth-century writers used, understood and thought of the language of virtue. This does not imply adopting an uncritical attitude towards the texts under examination. But it does mean that we need to exercise caution and seek to understand the nature of the texts before venturing to criticise them.

Why virtue was so important to the eighteenth century

Throughout the eighteenth century a positive obsession existed with the idea of virtue: not only in political terms, but in all its manifestations. During this time virtue never loosened its hold over the public imagination: indeed, that hold simply intensified as the century progressed and the concept developed further and more radical implications. Part of the reason why the rhetoric of virtue exercised such a degree of influence lies in the fact that it imparted power through the force of its moral authority. It gave power to those who employed the rhetoric: it gave them a voice, an alternative moral authority to the traditional arbiters of society, church and state. And it gave power to people who formed the audience for the rhetoric and could see themselves transfigured by it into virtuous citizens. An extraordinary range of people, including writers, artists, government ministers, radical journalists, priests and philosophers, who had little else in common, were brought together by this obsession. Rousseau is the best known to us, but he was far from being the first to situate virtue at the heart of human endeavour. He was one amongst many, albeit extraordinarily eloquent and influential. The rhetoric of virtue pre-dated him, and would have existed without him, although it would possibly have lost something of its wider influence and certainly some of its most eloquent expression.

The impact of the rhetoric of virtue reached much further than those who actively wrote about it, to those people who absorbed the literature on the subject. Readers sighed and wept over novels in which the virtuous heroes – and above all, heroines, of whom Richardson's Clarissa was the archetype – suffered endless vicissitudes whilst remaining admirable figures and true to themselves. More prosaically, atheists such as Helvétius and d'Holbach devised theoretical models for societies which would be ruled not by God but by virtue; priests from their pulpits extolled the joys of virtue and doing good to others (an idea known as *bienfaisance*). Even the marquis de Sade, who spent his literary energies swimming against the tide of virtue, did not feel himself able simply to ignore the subject; he too was obsessively engaged with virtue in order to refute it. He regarded the idea that virtue was rewarded as one of the most nauseating lies to which mankind was subject. Thus, the theme of his most notorious novel, *Justine*, where virtue is not rewarded, but punished, was set up as a deliberate refutation of the moral framework of Richardson's *Pamela*. One way or another, it was difficult to avoid the notion of virtue in the eighteenth century. Indeed, even the somewhat contradictory marquis liked to think of himself as in some sense a man of virtue, a philanthropist (*bienfaiteur*) in his personal life, if not in his literary endeavours, disclosing in private letters that he had helped the poor of his neighbourhood.

These self-consciously innovative eighteenth-century writers were also drawing upon the past for their inspiration: the word virtue itself dated back to classical antiquity. Private and public virtue were familiar themes throughout a long tradition of European ideas. Influential figures, from Marcus Aurelius to Boethius to Montaigne, had discussed at length the need for virtue in order to live a proper life. But why did this idea emerge with such unparalleled intensity in the eighteenth century? It may be that part of the answer lies in the phenomenon characterised by Paul Hazard as 'the crisis of the European mind': that is, the growing uncertainty from the later seventeenth century about the nature of the world and of man's place within it. This crisis was precipitated by the dawning conviction that whilst God as the source of moral authority had not disappeared from the world, he was nevertheless increasingly remote from human affairs. It appeared necessary to find some alternative source of moral authority which could effectively take the place of God – or at least of that version of God which belonged to the established churches. People were increasingly thrown back on themselves, unable to accept the Bible as a literal truth, but not satisfied just to exist. They wanted to know and understand the moral order of the universe, and to reassure themselves that such a moral order existed. Philosophers began to elaborate theories of the moral basis of society whose authority derived from 'nature', rather than from the God of revealed religion as the source of order in the universe. Virtue itself was seen as a manifestation of the natural world: a natural phenomenon. Few thinkers rejected God altogether; instead they tended to characterise human virtue as an emanation of God made manifest through nature. But to all intents and purposes the locus of virtue was humanity itself. Virtue provided a source of moral authority in a world beleaguered with uncertainties. It was the means by which mankind could forge a moral pathway, and establish some kind of moral certainty, in the face of an unknown and unknowable universe.

Virtue was thus an ideal which represented human morality, with or without God. But its meaning was not fixed into a single inflexible form. It was a living word, loaded with a heavy weight of polemical and often contradictory interpretations. It was used strategically, as a weapon in debate, providing moral justification for a contrasting range of philosophical and political meanings. We need to comprehend this fluidity of meaning through observation of the many ways in which the concept of virtue was enlisted in different debates about the nature of politics and of society. Virtue was much more than just a political catchword. The ideas it invoked reflected profound and persistent questions about the meaning of existence itself. For those people who wrote or read the rhetoric of virtue it could operate on many levels at once – moral, political and philosophical. They saw no inconsistency in this multiplicity of meaning, and neither should we.

Approaches to the subject

The study of the history of a word demands particular methods. The study of linguistic meaning in a specific cultural situation presents many problems and pitfalls because language loses so much of its meaning if examined in isolation from the context in which it was produced and the specific circumstances in which an author wrote. The notion of a discourse, that is, of a group of linked words by means of which a speaker gains authority and power, offers an invaluable means for uncovering the nature of language and linguistic strategies. Keith Baker, in particular, has employed this concept to powerful effect to illuminate the political languages of the last years of the *ancien régime*.[16] Opinions differ, however, on the ways in which this concept should be used by historians. The philosopher Michel Foucault, for example, to whom the development of the study of discourse owes so much, employed the term in a fairly specific sense whereby the concept of discourse necessarily exerts a very schematic relationship to authority and power. Personally, I have found it more helpful to enlist the notion of discourse in the rather more flexible sense favoured by, amongst others, Pocock.[17] I have employed the term 'discourse' simply to indicate groups of loosely-linked words and concepts from which a writer could draw in order to justify and substantiate a variety of arguments. Whilst the terms 'theory' and 'ideology' seem more appropriate for describing *specific* beliefs and arguments, discourses are much less fixed or pre-determined in their meaning: thus, a particular discourse could provide the building blocks to construct a particular theory, but it might also be employed to justify quite a different ideological edifice. A less contentious linguistic term than 'discourse', and one which I have frequently used, is that of 'rhetoric' and rhetorical strategies. Rhetoric is the art of selecting the most persuasive arguments with which to convince an audience to share one's opinion. This expression has the added advantage of being a term with which contemporaries themselves were familiar and is more indicative of the extent to which their choice of language was part of a conscious strategy, whereas 'discourse', particularly in the Foucaultian sense, suggests that speakers and writers were essentially the mouthpieces of a language over which they had little control.

The students who attended the *collèges* received a grounding in rhetoric along with a basic level of classical education. They were thus familiar with such seminal works as the declamations of Cicero, in which the process of law was frequently depicted as the struggle of virtue against despotism. It seems that eighteenth-century writers were generally very well aware of what they were doing in employing a discourse of virtue, but none the less, one must be wary of assuming that we know what those intentions were. People's 'true' motives are both complex and elusive and we can never be confident that we know what these were without a lot more evidence than the texts themselves can disclose. On the other hand, we can learn much about how people thought at a given time by asking why a particular form of rhetoric was the one selected in a specific historical situation and what made it so effective in that context.[18] Nor would it be wise to reject Foucault's premises entirely. Time and again we can see that discourses have unintended consequences, and exert influences and direct the thoughts of others in ways that are often very far removed from those that the original author would have wished. This book is as much about the reception and strategic use of ideas about virtue as it is about the original contribution of well-known thinkers.

One way in which the concept of virtuous citizenship made itself felt in ways far beyond the original intentions of men such as Montesquieu was in its contribution to the development of the idea of a legitimate public opinion. Habermas's concept of the bourgeois public sphere has generated much interest amongst historians and has greatly affected our conception of eighteenth-century political culture. According to Habermas, the bourgeois public sphere developed during the eighteenth century as a conceptual space between civil society and the state, within which recognition and legitimation could be provided for that social class which had previously been excluded from political life. The bourgeois public sphere crystallised in the idea of 'public opinion'.[19] 'Public opinion' itself was a phrase used frequently in the later eighteenth century – contemporaries referred to it as a sort of impartial tribunal to which one could appeal for judgement and whose moral authority was superior to the traditional authority of monarchy. But it is a term which eludes easy definition. It has been variously characterised as a sociological reality arising from the growth in numbers of the reading public, and as a political construction or abstract conception of authority.[20] The idea of 'public opinion' is highly relevant to the present work, for as an abstract political construction it is closely linked with the concept of political virtue, which could provide a moral justification for public opinion as a source of authority (based, of course, on the assumption that the public was virtuous and had only the common interest at heart). What is less clear, however, is that 'public opinion' was a particularly bourgeois phenomenon, if only because so many of the writers who wrote in criticism of the authority of absolute monarchy were themselves noble rather than bourgeois. The rhetoric of political virtue as it developed in the eighteenth century was not confined to any one social class, but was indicative of an egalitarian attribute to which anyone (at least in theory) might aspire, regardless of their birth.

In order to appreciate the significance of a politics of virtue we need first to consider what 'politics' itself meant in this period. Under the autocratic government of the *ancien régime* there was no legitimate provision for any form of participatory politics. 'Politics' as it was understood by contemporaries meant something altogether different from what we now understand by the term. In so far as the concept of 'politics' (or the public welfare of all) had an official existence it was deemed to be the king's business alone. The only people who therefore had a legitimate right to concern themselves with the conduct of politics were the king himself, and those officials and ministers whom he designated to see that his wishes were carried out. In effect, this meant that the court was the centre of political life – a subject which has been much illuminated by a series of important new historical works.[21] But the court was also seen as a source of intrigue and jostling for position. The politics of the court were framed in terms of the pursuit of self-interest. Patronage, clientage, family connections, institutionalised 'corruption', and the purchase of public office were all recognised means by which *ancien régime* politics functioned. Only the king himself was supposed to be above the pursuit of self-interest and to embody in himself the politics of public interest. But since he dwelt at court and amongst courtiers he was seen as being himself vulnerable to the corruption of his political duty, whether this resulted from his being misled by those around him, or was due to his own weakness.

In contrast to the *realpolitik* world of court politics there existed an alternative – an idealised concept of politics, based on ideas of society as it *ought* to be. This conception derived from the classical republican tradition. This was drawn originally from the classics of antiquity, with which all educated men were thoroughly familiar, and was further refined by Italian renaissance humanists and later by British and American contributions of the seventeenth and eighteenth centuries. Virtue in its classical sense of 'love of the *patrie*' or 'love of equality' was an essential ingredient of this political ideal.[22] Virtue was that sustaining quality which was vital for citizens to carry out their public duties, a selfless devotion to the public good: it was seen as incompatible with the amassing of private wealth and the pursuit of luxury.

Despite their contrasting positions, for the most part these two very different understandings of politics, the pragmatic and the ideal, co-existed with little friction. There was no reason why the officials and administrators of the *ancien régime* should not continue to admire classical political forms whilst continuing to promote rather more pragmatic policies in their day-to-day lives. Even Montesquieu, who, more than any writer of his time, did the most to popularise the idea that the ideal form of government was a republic based upon political virtue, did not consider this view to be incompatible with furthering his career and increasing his family prestige by means of venal office in the accepted manner for one of his class and social station. One must live, he conceded, in the real and not an ideal world.

A profound theoretical gulf nevertheless persisted between two such different modes of formulating politics. The starkness of the contrast made it more difficult for a political theory of compromise to gain ascendancy in France as it had done across the Channel. Political theory in Britain was much affected by the fact that here a form of participatory politics (albeit strictly limited) was accepted as legitimate, in which the interests of a small minority of society including the nobility and more affluent bourgeoisie were given official representation in government. Reflecting the compromise in the British system of government, political theorists in Britain also developed a more flexible concept of political virtue in a set of arguments, originating with Mandeville and further refined by Smith, which mingled political theory with economic self-interest. Here the argument was that one need not deliberately act according to the public interest in order for one's activities to have public benefits by generating economic expansion and national wealth. On the contrary, self-interest (namely the pursuit of personal profit) could result in public virtues, and one could be a virtuous citizen even whilst dedicating one's efforts to the pursuit of material gain. In France, by contrast, the rhetoric of civic virtue had little connection with the actual business of governing. This separation of theory and practice resulted in the rhetoric of virtue according to the French tradition keeping much more of its classical austerity. Here the belief that the virtuous citizen was one who devoted himself to the public good was argued much more emphatically than by British theorists and a closer connection was maintained between the notions of personal luxury and political corruption. Since civic virtue had little legitimate place in the French conception of politics a greater degree of virtue in terms of devotion to the public good was therefore expected of the state, in the person of the king himself.

Thus, we cannot clearly define the boundaries between the political and the non-political in eighteenth-century France simply because there was no legitimate space in which politics might exist outside the very limited sphere of royal policy. In addition to this lack of theoretical space for participatory politics, the systematic censorship of any discussion which might question the authority of monarchy or church was a constant fact of cultural life in the *ancien régime*.

Since there was no pre-existing legitimate space for the discussion of politics in *ancien régime* France, this book is about the process of construction of such a space through the legitimating discourse of virtue. We are concerned here with politics in its broadest sense as the conduct of relations between people on a collective scale. Virtue imparted moral authority to the contention that ordinary citizens could play an active public role. Virtue provided people with a voice that had a right to be heard. In so far as a politics of virtue existed in the eighteenth century, it was a linguistic and notional politics. This did not become an explicitly political right until the outbreak of revolution brought down the system of absolute monarchy and formalised civic rights into new legislation. In exploring the eighteenth-century discourse of virtue we are looking at a process of linguistic negotiation, and the strategic application of language to create new concepts of the relationship of man to the rest of mankind. By the concept of virtue, wrought into a linguistic unity, men could be brought together as virtuous citizens.

There are several key points to be made. The first is that there was more than one way of thinking about the political and social organisation of society in terms of categories of virtue. One could think of this in terms of a field of discourses (or models) of virtue which had particular relevance for ideas about the nature of political organisation. We will trace different discourses of virtue that had particular implications in the field of political ideas and show how they could be enlisted to support very diverse views about the nature and conduct of political authority and the social organisation of society. Virtue could be associated with particular social groups – such as military nobles, or judicial nobles in the *parlements*. It could be used to reinforce the authority of an individual – in absolute monarchy this was the king himself, and the discourse of kingly virtue was one of the oldest, but also one of the most ambiguous, ways of conceiving politics. It could be used to legitimise vociferous minorities, such as Jansenists, or even to give moral authority to a largely silent majority – women. In addition, it could be applied in terms that were at once vaguer and broader, as a notional defence of the moral integrity of ordinary 'citizens'.

Of the traditional discourses of virtue, the most significant were those of kingly virtue, noble virtue and the civic virtue of classical republicanism, and this book will begin by an evaluation of these languages and their dynamics in the first half of the century. Of these, the most explicitly political as well as the most egalitarian in its implications, was classical republicanism. Equally important for the eighteenth-century mind were traditional Christian ideas about virtue. These ideas had a political dimension, although this was often a negative one which emphasised the futility of virtue without God, and which was in marked contrast to the faith in civic virtue of classical republicanism. Jansenism was to bring forth new ways of conceptualising politics and whilst many Jansenists were sceptical about virtue, others incorporated its rhetoric into their ideas. From about the middle of the century a new discourse of virtue came to the fore which would be of dramatic importance in revitalising traditional ideas of the place of man in political life and society. This was the concept of natural or sociable virtue, which came via English philosophers such as Shaftesbury and Hutcheson and was seized upon by the French *philosophes* and adapted to their own concerns.

The second point we need to bear in mind is that the meaning of virtue was not static: rather it was used polemically and in particular contexts. In French society the negotiation of censorship was an everyday fact of life. Writers sometimes needed to be adept at finding permissible ways to express themselves, even when touching on such dangerous subjects as the authority of the Church and absolute monarchy. The very fluidity of the idea of natural virtue made it in many respects a more useful way of talking about the dignity and value of the ordinary citizen, who stood on his own merits, his virtue. Above all, the virtuous citizen had the right to participate fully in discussion and actions relating to the public good. This proved a more flexible and effective way of conceptualising the worth of the citizen than did the more traditional and rigid political formulations derived more exclusively from classical republicanism. But it can be very difficult to pinpoint distinctions between different discourses. Writers did not confine themselves to rigidly defined concepts of virtue. On the contrary, they selected those aspects they wanted from different models of virtue, and adapted them to the particular circumstances in which they found themselves and the kinds of points that they were trying to make. Nevertheless, writers had to work within the constraints and limitations of the language. The discourse of virtue could empower them, but it could also condition their meaning, and entrap it. It had a certain dynamic of its own, and could contain implications far beyond the intentions of a particular writer.

The third point to note is that one model of virtue in particular was to gradually to come to the fore and begin to dominate the others, and even to subsume them into itself. This was the model of virtuous citizenship, which was based partly on the older traditions of classical republicanism, but which drew even more deeply on the idea that came to the fore from the mid-century, that mankind is naturally virtuous and sociable, bound by loving fellowship. This was the model of virtue which would prove so compelling for the revolutionary generation. In their hands the radicalism and egalitarianism always potentially present in this idea of virtue would explode into an explicit language of political rights. But the model of virtue that the revolutionaries would take up was one of several in a field of discourses available to them. We need, therefore, to ask how we should go about uncovering the various discourses of virtue that formed the repertoire of ways of using language to conceptualise the spheres of power, civic rights and political participation in the eighteenth century.

The field of possible sources for exploring the politics of virtue can be extended far further than overtly political treatises. A wide variety of cultural forms served in the self-conscious creation of a 'public opinion' amongst the literate classes, and aided the formation of a 'public sphere' wherein current issues were debated. It was not uncommon for political discussion to appear in apparently unlikely places. At a time when most categories of people were effectively excluded from political participation, plays, novels, exhibitions of paintings, law cases and even pornographic or scurrilous literature could all constitute political texts: they could all be used to criticise, implicitly or overtly, the actions of government and even to question the assumptions on which absolute government rested. Nevertheless, this blurring of categories of political and non-political writings does not mean that all texts are consequently of equal value and significance, or that we should dissolve the differences between various forms. A political treatise and a work of fiction should not be treated as of undifferentiated value since they were written with particular intentions, and for a specific kind of audience who had certain expectations. These were distinctions of which contemporaries were themselves well aware, and ones which we need to respect if we are to reconstitute the meaning of eighteenth-century political writing.

It should be apparent by now how difficult – and in some ways artificial – a task it is to attempt to make rigid distinctions between political and non-political discourses of virtue. Virtue was a central concept in several quite different sets of ideas, amongst which were moral philosophy, debates on the social role of women, and the notion of sensibility. Some of its meanings were overtly political, while others were more concerned with social relations or with individual morality, but these might be given an oblique political resonance by a writer in a particular context. Therefore, whilst we can isolate and define some specifically political meanings of virtue, its political resonances are by no means confined to these limited areas.

The vocabulary of political virtue as derived from classical republicanism was familiar to anyone who had shared a higher-level education in Europe at any time since the Renaissance: it was part of a common elite culture. In political thought the principal meaning of 'virtue' was the definition derived from the classical republican notion of devotion to the public interest rather than self-interest. The rhetoric of virtue brought an explicitly moral dimension to the heart of political thinking. It expressed the idea that the basis of political power was, or at least ought to be, moral integrity both in public and in private life. 'Virtue' was, with 'nation' and *patrie* (or 'fatherland'), one of a series of interconnected key words which reinforced and legitimised each other. Virtue was that facilitating quality which enabled all the other attributes of good government and good citizenship to exist. Without virtue the whole political edifice would collapse into atomism. It was widely believed that both private and public virtue were indispensable for the good regulation of politics and for the well-being of society. Enlightenment thinkers stressed that government, whatever its form, must be virtuous if society was to be healthy. But it was not necessary for everyone in a society to have political virtue – only those who had the responsibility of government. Thus, for a monarchy to fulfil its public duties the king must be virtuous, whilst a republic depended on the virtue of all its citizens. But not everyone was necessarily a citizen, for under the ancient classical republics inferior men (slaves) and all women had been excluded. Similarly in eighteenth-century France, the ideal of a virtuous republic did not necessarily encompass all the people who dwelt there, but only those who were deemed capable of being active citizens. Active civic virtue was both the highest and, by definition, the most demanding political quality. It was an ideal so demanding that, almost by definition, it was seen as all but impossible to sustain. Political theorists, even while they idealised civic virtue, generally acknowledged that, given man as he was rather than as he might be, it could never be fully attained.

Political or civic virtue was, however, much more than an abstract political theory. During the eighteenth century it became a polemical weapon which was employed to give moral force to contentious debates. It is this use of virtue as a strategy which most concerns us here. The rhetoric of civic virtue provided a model against which the actions of participants and would-be participants in political life could be measured. Virtue was the voice of defiance, the rejection of corruption, factionalism, political compromise – and yet this challenge to the old order was drawn out of the familiar eighteenth-century language of politics. The rhetoric was employed to impart moral justification to a wide variety of political positions, taking on different inflections of meaning depending on how it was used in a particular context. For example, civic virtue carried, as has been said, connotations of equality: although citizens might not be equal in wealth or status, they could all possess virtue. It did not, however, follow that a speaker who enlisted the rhetoric of virtue must have radical and egalitarian sympathies – just as the Christian doctrine of equality of souls did not make all Christians political democrats. The rhetoric of virtue was not confined to political radicals or future revolutionaries. On the contrary virtue was part of a broad conception of politics, spanning a number of political perspectives – and in this lies its greatest power. It was an official and acceptable language, which was radical at one end of its spectrum, and could be used to make opposition legitimate, but which could be used to defend virtuous monarchy.

As well as examining the theoretical development of the concept of political virtue through the works of the acknowledged 'great thinkers' of the period, we must cast our net wider and consider some of the now half-forgotten writings of lesser figures whose works were possibly less profound than those of the major philosophers but which were avidly read by a voracious and rapidly growing audience. Many such works, though mostly forgotten now, exerted a greater degree of influence on their contemporaries than that of some of the works now best known to us. Nor should we confine our inquiries to those people who were won over to Enlightenment ideas. The concept of political virtue was not the exclusive preserve of a few progressive and intellectual thinkers: its influence was felt throughout the mainstream of political culture. It is possible to learn as much by looking at people who were hostile to the rhetoric of political virtue, as from those who were receptive to it.

In the course of this work we will assess the extent to which virtue, along with such related terms as *patrie*, 'nation', and 'popular sovereignty', became a key political term during the eighteenth century. One could trace the history of the word 'virtue' in many different ways, but a principal aim here will be to show why this word in particular proved to be so powerfully evocative and effective as part of a rhetorical armoury of growing political criticism and even outright opposition to absolute monarchy. Older concepts of kingly virtue and noble virtue were gradually superseded by the more egalitarian rhetoric of civic virtue, making possible both a sustained critique of *ancien régime* government, and a growing self-confidence amongst the politically articulate classes. We will ask how it became increasingly acceptable for people to speak publicly on political matters, and how they justified this participation using arguments based on their claim to possess civic virtue, so that the insistence of the autocratic government that French citizens should be denied a political voice came to be seen as a glaring injustice.

With such a wide brief, the process of tracing the rhetoric of political virtue in the eighteenth century must necessarily be a carefully selective one. The first chapter of this book will examine the prevailing discourses of political virtue as they existed at the beginning of the eighteenth century, notably the codes of kingly, noble, and classical-republican virtue. Subsequent chapters will explore the ways in which the discourse of political virtue changed in character and emphasis during the course of the century. We will look at the rise of new philosophical concepts of natural sociable virtue and how these mingled with and modified the classical republican tradition of civic virtue. We will consider the ways in which traditional concepts of kingly virtue began to change under pressure from these new ideas. We will then take the example of the most powerful political force in the *ancien régime* next to that of the monarchy, that is the *parlements*, and examine the ways in which *parlementaires* and their supporters employed the rhetoric of virtue in their polemical disputes with the monarchy and how this use of rhetoric was taken up in turn by a wider reading public eager for new ideas and conceptions of political life. Lastly, we will examine the escalating use of the rhetoric of political virtue in the crucial last decade of the *ancien régime*, when a positive explosion of this rhetoric appears to have seized the consciousness of the reading public.

A book on this subject cannot hope to be comprehensive and it would be foolhardy to try. Let me at this point therefore say a few words about what this book is *not* about. It is not an attempt to chart the philosophic view of virtue. It is not a study of the high Enlightenment. So, many writers do not feature here despite having had important things to say about virtue. Nor does this book set out to impose a meta-narrative on the multiple discourses of virtue in the eighteenth century – a task beyond the capabilities of most historians, and certainly beyond the abilities of this one. There are innumerable books waiting to be written on the idea of virtue in the eighteenth century. This is only one of them.

I have confined myself to an analysis of specific areas which illuminate key moments in the development of ideas about political virtue; and I have sought to show how such ideas were used in polemical debates. Likewise, it has been essential to narrow down the range of sources to be considered. I have concentrated on two types of source. The first of these consists of works which in themselves brought about significant and original changes in the way virtue was used and understood in the eighteenth century, and this category includes some of the major philosophical and intellectual works on virtue and political theory. Some of them derive from the accepted 'canon' of political thought, such as Rousseau, Diderot and Montesquieu; others include names with which we ourselves are no longer so familiar, but which were in their time well-regarded – such as Toussaint, Duguet, and Thomas. The second type of source is that which serves to illuminate the ways in which polemics of virtue were constructed and how the strategic use of such a discourse could work in practice. This broader category is represented in this book by several hundred documents. It includes: works which influenced ideas in France, from the classics to works of the English and Scottish Enlightenment; contemporary dictionaries, through which we can explore shifts in linguistic meaning; treatises and prescriptive works on happiness and the role of natural virtue and sociable virtue; novels and plays which explored the joys and griefs of virtue and citizenship; sermons and eulogies which set out the ambiguous relationship of virtue with Christian theology; conduct books, popular works of history, and essays written for prizes for academies, all of which set out prescriptive models of heroic and virtuous behaviour; documents relating to the periodic contests between monarchy and *parlements* for moral authority, including pamphlets and remonstrances from the crisis of 1770 to 1774; and finally, developments in a wide range of literature during the crisis of absolute monarchy in the 1780s.

The problem of where to begin and where to end a discussion of so nebulous a subject as the language of political virtue is a formidable one in itself. Few of the theoretical claims made about political virtue in the eighteenth century were altogether without some historical precedent. Therefore, what we are searching for here is not so much the emergence of an entirely unprecedented *language* of virtue, but rather, for new *uses to which that language was put*, new contexts in which it was used, new juxtapositions of discourses which shifted the meanings and implications behind the language of virtue, and, perhaps most importantly, the dissemination of that language on a much wider scale then anything that had been seen previously. Baker has claimed that the elements of the political culture from which revolutionary language would emanate, 'began to emerge in the 1750s and 1760s and that its essential elements were already clear by the beginning of Louis XVI's reign'.[23] It appears that certain elements of the political culture of opposition to absolute monarchy far pre-dated even this period. So this work will begin much earlier, in the later seventeenth century. It ends in August 1788, when the pre-revolutionary political situation had so drastically altered the stakes in the contest of political virtue that an altogether different book would be needed to explore the changes which were then taking place.

1
Concepts of Virtue before 1745

Alas! Alas! Alas! The misery and worthlessness of the man who has
nothing better to rely on than virtue.

Bossuet, *Oeuvres oratoires*

The years from 1745 to 1748 were to witness a striking change in the ways that virtue was conceptualised. But well before that date several key models or discourses of virtue were already flourishing. In this chapter we will go back to the earlier period and examine these models and see how they were related to complex patterns of power and political authority. Long before the eighteenth century the word 'virtue' already possessed a venerable history, a history which was built upon by succeeding generations of political thinkers. Changes in linguistic meaning are gradual, cumulative and hard to date with precision. Thus, the word 'virtue' was gradually wrapped around with added layers of significance and emphasis which clung, like successive onion skins, around its original core of meaning. During the latter years of the reign of Louis XIV and into the first part of the eighteenth century it is possible to trace a slow process whereby traditional concepts of political virtue took on a new emphasis and expansion of meaning. Above all, there was a perceptible shift from elitist notions of kingly and of noble virtue to a greater emphasis on civic and egalitarian virtue.

By the last years of the seventeenth century, 'virtue' already contained a multiplicity of meanings, some of which were in direct conflict with each other. Three models or discourses of political virtue encapsulated conflicting notions of power and political authority: these may be designated respectively as kingly virtue, noble virtue and civic virtue. In a moment we will examine these concepts and see how virtue served as a basis for legitimising quite different sources of political authority. But in order to understand how virtue fitted into political thought, we need first to consider some of its wider linguistic meanings.

Dictionaries provide an initial means of recovering shifts of meaning. The word virtue (*la vertu*) was originally derived from the Latin word for a man, *vir*. From *vir* came the Roman word *virtus*, meaning literally 'that quality which befits a man'. This manly quality was often identified as 'moral courage'. From this association there emerged two principal clusters of meaning which focused around the concepts of 'courage' and 'morality'. Sometimes these concepts converged, as in the original meaning, and sometimes they diverged and came to be associated with quite differing qualities. Virtue retained its meaning of courage, with the associated meanings of fortitude, energy and daring.[1] An additional primary meaning of 'virtue' was that of a quality or property which a thing possesses, for example, the medicinal attributes of a plant, or the ability of a fire to give warmth.[2] Virtue was also used as a generic term to comprise all qualities worthy of praise, and which included within it specific 'virtues'.[3] Moral virtues might be characterised as either pagan or Christian. The four pagan or cardinal virtues were 'prudence', 'justice', 'temperance' and 'fortitude', and the three Christian virtues were 'faith', 'hope' and 'charity'. The Stoics had believed that true virtue lay in self-mastery. This theme was still powerful in the seventeenth century, though often linked with Christian austerity rather than the ancients.

For the most part, moral virtue was seen as limited in scope and was treated with a certain degree of suspicion. It was variously described in dictionaries of this period as a quality dependent on the suppression of 'the passions', as 'a habit of the will governed by reason', as 'moral rectitude' or as 'probity'.[4] La Rochefoucauld, the sceptical moralist, considered an excess of virtue to be a positively dangerous quality comparable with excessive vice, symptomatic of inverted pride masquerading as moral purity. His cynical view of virtue was often cited approvingly, especially in the earlier dictionaries which reiterated the idea that virtue was in conflict with human nature, and especially with self-love (*l'amour-propre*) and could never be attained in its entirety. 'True' virtue was thus moderate in character and avoided extremes.[5] According to these seventeenth-century dictionaries, virtue and honour were closely linked. To illustrate this point the story was often recounted of the Roman Marcellus who built a temple to 'virtue' and a temple to 'honour' in such a way that the only entrance to the temple of honour, or public renown, was via the temple of virtue or moral probity. The moral of this story was that only those who merited it by their virtue would win glory and public recognition.[6]

Chastity was a relative late-comer to the vocabulary of virtue. There was no reference to it in Richelet's 1680 dictionary, for example. By 1690 it had made a brief appearance, but in a non-gender-specific form, where it was linked to 'continence', probably having been adapted from the older meaning of 'temperance'.[7] By 1704, virtue was being more specifically used to signify modesty (*la pudeur*) and chastity (*la chasteté*), qualities associated mostly with women, though 'chastity' was also a fundamental requirement for the clergy, male and female.[8]

Virtue was associated both with the idea of an exclusive heroic elite, and with the idea of egalitarian citizenship, ideas between which there was a potential for incompatibility. The Roman *virtus* and its Greek equivalent *arete* were both associated with the ethos of an elite warrior caste, from which originated the idea of stoical virtue, as the heroic fortitude with which an individual hero could withstand the blows of adversity.[9] As a quality denoting strength, martial prowess and valour, virtue in early modern France retained an association with this original warrior ethic. But 'pagan' virtue was also a key term in classical-republican thought, at whose heart was the ideal of the virtuous citizen, devoted to the public good. The tensions between these two meanings, virtue as warrior courage and virtue as civic morality, were to continue to affect the subsequent history of this word.

In the late seventeenth century three distinct forms of political theory can be identified which drew on some of these meanings of virtue. They were concerned with the basis of temporal authority and power, which were located respectively in kingship, nobility and citizenship. Although each theory advocated a different source for authority, they were all based on the premise that political authority must be considered as a moral issue: those who wielded power had to be virtuous. The concept of virtue thus provided a moral legitimacy which gave authority and legitimacy to very different theories of political right. According to these theories, virtue was depicted variously: as an attribute associated with a single person, as in kingly virtue; as an attribute of a caste, as in noble virtue; and as an attribute of the people or citizens, as in civic or classical-republican virtue (although 'the people' and 'the citizens' were themselves flexible terms, which might include or exclude a varying proportion of the population). The divergence of meaning with which virtue was invested in these discourses enabled it to impart moral authority to three quite different ways of conceptualising political authority.

Traditional ideas about virtue and kingship

The theory of absolute or divine-right monarchy differed from other theories of political rights in that it was the official ideology of the kings of France, and therefore provided the legitimising basis for government as it actually existed.[10] According to the ideology of absolute monarchy the source of a king's authority derived from the will of God. Sovereignty was located within the 'sacred' body of the king. In a very real sense the king was the only 'public' person in France; that is, the only person who was supposed to have the public good as his guiding principle. There was no place in this conception of power for a 'nation' to exist as an independent force outside the king's sovereign authority – that is, for a 'nation' in the sense of the people as a collective sovereign body as opposed to the people as individuals or as corporate interests. Authority, law, and justice, all emanated from the monarch as the intermediary of God's will. It was a paternal model of authority: like God the Father, the king's relationship towards his subjects was that of a father: he owed them paternal care and they owed him filial obedience. The power of the king was endorsed by the Church, which at his coronation declared him to be God's representative. The theory of absolute monarchy was thus closely bound up with orthodox Catholic theology.

As we can see from the works of some of the most sophisticated exponents of the theory of divine-right monarchy, such as Louis XIV's bishops, Bossuet, Massillon and Fénelon, the concept of Christian virtue as a limited and rather an uncertain attribute lent support to the idea that only the monarch, with his particular qualities of kingly virtue, was adequately equipped to be the source of political authority. Christian virtue was a very ambiguous idea: in theory it was egalitarian, for all souls were equal and had the same potential for virtue. In matters temporal rather than in the hereafter, however, the orthodox Christian suspicion of virtue as a weak and ineffectual quality reinforced the hierarchical view of society.

There was a fundamental tension between orthodox Christian views (both Catholic and Protestant) of virtue and those of 'paganism' or classical republicanism. The classical republican concept of virtue invoked the dangerous and unorthodox belief that mankind had the power to manage its own affairs and shape its own destiny without divine aid. Christian virtue was, by contrast, at best a weak affair, whilst at worst it led to the sin of pride. The purest and least contaminated expression of Christian virtue therefore was to be found in piety, humility and the love of God rather than of base humanity. According to Bossuet, 'this invisible point in which virtue consists is so small, so difficult to perceive!' that one might well doubt whether it existed at all.[11] Belief in original sin reinforced the idea that people were insufficiently virtuous to govern themselves. True Christian virtue was said to resemble a chaste virgin, who hid herself from the public gaze.[12]

By contrast, kings appeared as the embodiment of masculine virtue, an image which served to emphasise and reinforce their claim to be the embodiment of sovereignty. Kingly virtue was not necessarily a moral quality, for, like other Christians, they too were sinners and might have many lapses in their moral virtue. But in order to be an effective ruler it was not necessary to be morally good, it might even be a serious weakness. This point had been made openly by Machiavelli when speaking of princely virtue, and whilst few apologists for absolute monarchy could bring themselves to condone quite such an open split between political and moral virtue there was a tacit, if regretful, recognition amongst even the strongest advocates of absolute monarchy that, the world being what it was and kings being unfortunately as liable to vice as anyone, it was only to be expected that they would occasionally have moral lapses but that this should not affect their political authority. It was an accepted convention, of course, that kings should be pious, but there was some degree of ambiguity as to what this royal piety should entail. Certainly Christian princes must publicly uphold the authority of the Church if only in order to maintain public order, but excessive personal piety could come dangerously close to excessive weakness, which, for a man in whom supreme power and responsibility were invested, could be fatal. An example sometimes cited was that of Henry VI of England, who was seen as more of a monk than a man; his queen was a better 'man' than he, for she fought on his behalf to keep his throne. His personal sanctity was undoubted but his reign had led to many years of civil war and disaster for his people. By contrast, Louis IX of France (St Louis) combined undoubted piety with admirable strength of purpose. His willingness to lead the armies of France on crusades to slaughter the 'infidels' was depicted as an example of the masculine virtue of courage appropriate to monarchy. Whilst personal morality might not be an essential attribute of kingly virtue, the impartial administration of justice was seen as an essential quality of a virtuous monarch; an idea that went back at least as far as sixteenth-century apologists for monarchy such as Budé.[13] By acting forcefully, but justly, with impartiality, and within the laws which he himself had made, a king mirrored the paternal authority of God and prevented his realm from being subject to the extreme form of monarchy, despotism.

Bossuet's *Politique tirée des propres paroles de l'Ecriture Sainte* (1709) provided the classic account of the principles of absolute monarchy legitimated by religious sanction. Christian virtue entailed submission to a paternal king, whom his subjects were obliged to obey. Royal authority had four essential characteristics: it was 'sacred', 'paternal', 'absolute' and 'guided by reason'. 'Kings must respect their own authority and only use it for the public good.'[14] Absolute monarchy ought not to degenerate into despotism, but no safeguard was to exist to ensure a king's integrity save that of his own conscience. He would be answerable ultimately to God, but if he chose not to rule justly, his subjects themselves had no legitimate recourse but to accept his authority. Bossuet did not base the moral legitimacy of monarchy on the uncertain virtue of the king, but on the firmer basis of God's mandate. An unjust king, a king without virtue, would still have just as much right to be king, his people would have no right to resist him, since it was by God's will that he reigned over them. The only exception to this was where the king's commands contravened those of God. But even then, only passive resistance was permissible, and subjects must accept the king's punishment.

To be a virtuous king was to lead the people to act virtuously even though their natural inclination was towards vice. The most effective way for a king to rule over his unvirtuous people was to appeal to their self-interest and to use it to promote the 'public good'. A king should 'promote, defend, and patronise virtue'. By this means, his own kingly virtue served as a channel through which the self-interest and atomism of his subjects could be processed and made to secure the common interest.[15]

The integrity of absolute monarchy depended in large part on the individual conscience of the king. This presented difficulties for Louis XIV's higher clergy, who were well positioned at Versailles to observe the regrettable moral shortcomings of the king and his court. On appointed days, king and court bustled in their finery into the chapel at Versailles to hear their morals castigated and the incipient judgement of God threatened. As God's official intermediaries, the clergy at court speaking from the vantage point of the pulpit had the traditional right, especially during the Lent cycle of sermons, to criticise lapses in courtly – and even royal – morality. In 1709, for example, after 24,000 people had died that winter of hunger and cold, Massillon preached at Notre-Dame about the pleasure of doing good, appealing to the sensibility of the rich, informing his privileged listeners that they only held their wealth in trust, and that to withhold its benefits from the poor and needy was both 'usurpation' and 'injustice'.[16] Funeral orations were an especially effective means of chilling the blood of even the most frivolous courtiers – temporarily at least. Bossuet, Bourdaloue or Massillon thundered out with impressive eloquence on the fate of a pious – or impious – noble whose body now was food for worms and whose soul had fled shivering to face its Maker. But there was a limit to how much moral castigation a king would tolerate. Even the higher clergy had to be careful not to take their privileged position too far: when they criticised they spoke circumspectly and in general terms.[17] There was also a tacit understanding that these permitted criticisms of monarchy ought not to travel beyond the confines of the court to the wider public. Court sermons under Louis XIV were generally confined within the semi-private world of the court itself: it would not do for the king's subjects to know too many details of what passed between a monarch and his God.

The education of future kings was regarded as a vital means whereby they could be instilled with the principles of virtuous rulership. Prescriptive works on the education of princes accordingly set out appropriate models of kingly virtue. Bossuet, for example, who was privately anxious that Louis XIV's heirs should not perpetuate his shortcomings, took the opportunity when he was given the duty of educating Louis's son, the Grand Dauphin, to write a series of *Lettres sur l'éducation du Dauphin*. The most important of the virtues that needed to be instilled in the young prince were habits of hard work, 'piety', 'goodness' and 'justice' – and also 'chastity'.[18] Bossuet's efforts, by all accounts, met with a singular lack of success: his royal pupil grew to be renowned at court for his ignorance, apathy and depravity, rather than his virtue. When the dauphin died in 1711 Massillon gave a funeral oration in which he praised in perfunctory fashion the dauphin's personal qualities – such as they were – but studiously avoided speaking of the dauphin's sense of duty towards his people, or his virtue, whether private or public.[19] The rhetoric of kingly virtue was at least as significant when it was not invoked as when it was dwelt upon. It was necessary to be circumspect, but simply by avoiding the subject, Massillon made his meaning clear to his hearers.

By contrast, when the dauphin's son, the duc de Bourgogne, died tragically the following year, Massillon, who was again called upon to deliver the funeral oration, spoke at length about the virtues of the dead prince. The duc de Bourgogne had been the great hope of a circle of would-be social reformers aghast at the extent to which Louis XIV had fallen short of expectations, and the portrait which Massillon gave of his virtues reveals the ideal of kingship at the end of the reign of Louis XIV. The 'great virtues' of the young dauphin consisted in his piety and humility; he read pious works, prayed, took the sacraments regularly, mortified both body and soul, and feared God's judgement. Courtiers were the source of vice at court: they were flatterers, serving only their own self-interests, the corrupters of kingly virtue. The prince had avoided the traps set by courtiers, particularly the artificial 'Delilas', those women who tried without success to seduce the prince and thus subvert his virtue in the pursuit of the 'passions'. The speaker dwelt mostly on the prince's private virtues. The prince was charitable, but not excessively so: he enquired into the deserving character of the poor before distributing his alms. In accordance with the early eighteenth-century ideal of kingship, his charity was depicted as a private exercise. It was not a social or public quality by which he might in any way improve the condition of the poor, but a way of exercising his Christian duty.[20] One cannot know to what extent the duc de Bourgogne, had he lived, would have fulfilled the hopes which his admirers held for him: there is no king so virtuous, so full of potential, as the one who never lives to reign, or who dies young.

Even during the reign of Louis XIV, the discourse of kingly virtue was not fixed or static. Bossuet used it to defend the status quo, but the model of virtuous kingship could also be used as a moral basis for criticism of the actual practice of monarchy. Such critiques of Louis XIV's government were more marked during the closing years of his reign. Social disruption, famine, war, and the slow decline of the king himself, all served to discredit the notion that kings necessarily uphold the public good. One of the most influential works to criticise the practice of monarchy appeared in the form of a utopian vision, half novel, half educational treatise. Fénelon's *Télémaque* was originally conceived as a treatise on the education of a monarch, being intended for the young duc de Bourgogne, who was Fénelon's pupil. *Télémaque* in its published form put forward a cogent argument for virtue as a vital attribute of kingship. Without wishing to challenge the basis of the monarchy's authority, or to threaten the system of privilege on which the hierarchy functioned, Fénelon wanted to ensure that the king dedicated himself to the good of his people, and to integrate all sections of society more closely. Fénelon himself is difficult to categorise politically. He had fallen out with Bossuet but this was, initially at least, more over the religious controversy of Quietism than over any particular political issue. As a political theorist, Fénelon combined the conviction that absolute monarchy was the most sensible form of government with his belief in the need to uphold the social and political role of the nobility. But, without seeking to challenge the system of absolute monarchy, he also defended the idea that virtuous citizenship was necessary to the well-being of a nation. The complexity and ambiguity of his political critique helped to keep *Télémaque* an 'open' political text which was still widely read and the subject of some controversy almost a hundred years later. Curiously, it was to exert a far greater influence on the young Louis XVI and on the revolutionary generation, including radicals such as Brissot and Saint-Just, than it had ever done in Fénelon's lifetime. In many ways it was one of the most significant texts of the eighteenth century.[21]

Télémaque is notable for the way in which it combined classical and Christian concepts of virtue. Its mythological, utopian form made it more accessible to contemporary readers, but also permitted Fénelon to express his critique of bad kingship in more vigorous terms. In the utopian country of Salente, Fénelon represented a form of the virtuous republic. Here Mentor, the tutor of kings, instructs Idoménée, the new king of Salente, on the best way for a virtuous king to govern his people. Salente was to be a frugal, rural society, eschewing 'luxury'. A privileged nobility should be maintained, but it would not depend entirely on hereditary right, for its ranks would be open to the children of those who had done virtuous actions: thus it was a nobility based on birth and virtue. A king should raise public buildings and funeral monuments to recall 'all those achievements brought about with extraordinary virtue for the service of the *patrie*'. The king is not above the law: it is his duty to make good laws and create a solid government to make his people happy. The importance of the state's role in education was recognised: children 'belong less to their parents than to the republic: they are the children of the people', and a king should take an active concern in their education and inspire them with 'love of glory and of virtue'.[22] Later, in his journey to the afterlife, Télémaque encounters bad kings, suffering all the torments of hell, because they have been 'insensible to virtue', have brought about the calamity of war, or have simply failed to do enough for their people. Here the artificial values of the court are exposed in all their futility: the damned kings are made to look ceaselessly into a mirror, held up by one of the Furies, in which they see at last their true selves revealed with 'all the deformity of their vices'.[23]

Many themes which we will later encounter were already present in this work: the notion of a king belonging to the republic; the prevalence of the words *patrie* and *république*; the idea that the state should undertake the task of educating the people in virtue. Moreover, many writers would share Fénelon's view that a virtuous republic was not incompatible with a monarchy, provided that the king devoted himself to the public good. Although Fénelon maintained that his work had no subversive intent, few people at the time seem to have believed him. Louis XIV took many of Fénelon's criticisms of bad government, despite their utopian setting, as a personal affront. The account of Télémaque's encounter with former bad kings now suffering torments in hell did nothing to endear the book to Louis and it contributed to Fénelon's subsequent disgrace.

Fénelon's idea of kingly virtue as a duty owed first to the 'nation' rather than to God, extended even to those who were the most staunch defenders of absolute monarchy. After the death of Louis XIV, the first years of the reign of his infant great-grandson were marked by a period of regency, renowned for its corruption, chaos and naked self-interest. The regent himself, the duc d'Orléans, was rumoured to be a man without virtue, whose 'suppers' with his cronies were whispered to be in fact orgies.[24] Such stories were no doubt elaborated upon by disgruntled courtiers, but the dangers of absolute monarchy when invested in the hands of someone less capable than Louis XIV made more than one prelate uneasy with the notion of unchallengeable authority. In 1718 Massillon preached a sermon officially for the eight-year-old Louis XV, but intended for his ministers, which set out the moral code by which a king should rule. Massillon told the infant monarch outright that he ruled only because such was 'the choice of the nation', and that he owed his throne 'to the free consent of his subjects'.[25] It was a conception of the moral basis of regal authority whose implications would haunt the French monarchy for the rest of the century.

Traditions of virtuous nobility

In addition to theories of kingship, virtue also played an important part in a very different kind of political discourse: this was the debate on the definition and social function of the nobility. The nobility was notoriously hard to define with precision, as a social group. It was a hereditary order, but by no means an impenetrable one. The normal means by which nobility was conveyed was through blood, or more literally, through seminal fluid. But there were also many possibilities in the *ancien régime* to acquire noble status through the purchase of venal offices, particularly those attached to legal, financial and administrative functions. Nobility was more than a legal entitlement and possession of a title. It was also a state of mind, bound up with its status and social acceptance. Consequently there was some concern and anxiety over the question of 'true nobility', and the idea was constantly being redefined and reconsidered, both by those who were eager to establish their rights to it, and by those just as eager to exclude others. At different points, therefore, ideas of noble virtue might be used in a defensive manner, to look back nostalgically to a lost social order, or more aggressively, to legitimate the entry into the exclusive ranks of the nobility of new social groups. In recent years important studies of the changing meanings of the nobility in the *ancien régime*, by historians such as Jouanna, Schalk and Huppert, have in their different ways explored the importance of noble virtue as a means by which the nobility staked its claim to being a superior order.[26]

No less than three separate ideas of the nature of noble virtue can be distinguished in the *ancien régime*, each one of which lent itself to a different way of justifying and legitimating the existence of a noble caste. We will consider each concept separately here, although in practice a considerable degree of overlap existed between the ways in which these ideas were understood and applied.

The first concept of noble virtue was that based on the traditional role of the nobility as a warrior caste. It originated with the feudal concept of nobility as the second of the 'three orders' who made up society: those who fought. This was virtue as 'courage' and 'valour'. Works on genealogy such as L'Alouètte, *Traité des nobles et des vertus dont ils sont formés* (1577), emphasised the importance of virtue as an inherited martial attribute; an ideal which corresponded roughly to the traditional 'nobility of the sword' (*noblesse d'épée*). This form of military virtue entailed manly courage. Here the virtuous noble was seen as a warrior and part of a warrior elite. He had public virtue in the sense that he was prepared to die for his king and his country, but as a model of behaviour he was rather rough around the edges. Apart from his fighting prowess and physical courage there were few calls on him to possess moral integrity, though where the warrior ethic was tempered by the notion of chivalry, there was some refinement of the model and some sense that military virtue must be tempered by the demands of the noble code of honour. This form of noble virtue was generally said to be inherited, although there was also the idea that young noblemen's innate propensity for military excellence should be cultivated and reinforced both in their family environment and in their military academies.

The second concept of noble virtue derived from the principle of administrative, especially judicial, service. The focus here was on the nobility, not as fighting for France on the battlefield, but defending it nevertheless by providing it with magistrates. Thus, the judicial nobility could also claim to have a public function as administrators of government, upholders of the truth and defenders of the laws. As described in works such as Ernaud, *Discours de la noblesse et des justes moyens d'y parvenir* (1584), this definition appealed to those who obtained ennobling offices, especially in the *parlements*, and thus corresponded roughly to the category of the *noblesse de robe*. In practice the social divide between these two forms of nobility was becoming increasingly difficult to perceive by the early eighteenth century, as intermarriage blurred the distinctions, but the discourses still retained a separate and powerful identity amongst different sections of the nobility who might choose to identify themselves with one or the other.

The third concept of noble virtue was that associated specifically with nobles of the court. This concept of virtue was based on the principles of politeness, refinement and the art of being agreeable in society. When used in this positive sense the idea could be used to contrast those who had the polish of the court with provincial nobles, who often possessed little more refinement than their own peasants. But it was an ambiguous idea, and one that came increasingly to be used also in a pejorative sense – a theme to which we will return in a moment.

These concepts of virtue served to give moral legitimacy to the power and social prestige of the nobility. Such attributes of virtue meant that the rights of the nobles were not based on the accident of birth or on their wealth alone. Their social function was defined through their virtue, whether this was as military leaders ready to give their lives for their country, as administrators of justice and defenders of the law, or as models of civilised and cultivated behaviour. These concepts were far from static, but were used polemically both to include and exclude members of the noble caste. Concepts of noble virtue were used by existing nobles not only to define and legitimise their own prestige but also to exclude non-nobles, who could not, it was claimed, aspire to possess these virtues. Despite attempts by established nobles to exclude outsiders, these codes of noble virtue were in fact available to social aspirants, as they appeared in written guides to noble conduct. Would-be nobles, therefore, could seize upon these models and use them to shape their own behaviour according to the professed values of their social 'superiors' – much to the annoyance of the latter.

Each of these concepts of noble virtue gradually came under pressure as the social role and prestige of the French nobility was exposed to increasing challenge. By the end of the seventeenth century the concept of virtue as a military noble ethic had already come under considerable strain, partly because of the traumas of the religious wars and partly through the growth in ennobling offices. For many observers, the identification of the French nobility with a warrior elite was beginning to attract critical scrutiny. One indication of a change in attitudes is the way that the word 'honour' began consistently to replace 'virtue' as the customary term used to describe the warrior ethic. Thus, the practice of duelling, the traditional sport of idle military nobles, and one of the ways in which nobles distinguished themselves from non-nobles, was known as the 'mark of honour' (*point d'honneur*) and came in time to be seen as the very antithesis of virtue.[27] The warrior ethic did not disappear altogether, however, and right up until the Revolution, many noble sons were still pursuing a military career as the 'proper path' for a noble, even when the consequences could be perilous and sometimes disastrous, as when the only son of a great house was killed in battle. The Seven Years War was to prove particularly devastating for some of the more military families of the nobility.

The concept of courtly virtue provides a paradox in that it runs counter to the later (and much more popular) tendency to view the court as the centre of vice. Courtly virtue was moderate and seemly in character, lending weight to social appearances. It was closely linked to the notion of the *honnête homme*, which might roughly be translated as 'the man worthy of respect'. The ideal of the *honnête homme* originally derived from the courtly Italian renaissance model of which Castiglione's *The Courtier* is the most renowned version. In France this ideal was well established by the mid-seventeenth century. Courtly values were not confined to the court itself. They were as much a guide to social aspirants as to those who already held the status of court nobility and appeared in a series of prescriptive books on courtly codes, offering advice on the best way to 'get on' at court. One such work was Faret's *L'Honnête homme, ou l'art de plaire à la cour*. Virtue, he said, was more attractive and more effective when it was met with in a person 'of good condition and quality' rather than in someone 'badly-formed and of low condition'. Faret qualified this statement somewhat by stating that, on the other hand, if 'the greatest prince in the world' was 'depraved' and without virtue he would be subject to even greater derision for having misused the advantages of his birth. Virtue in the discourse of the *honnête homme* was a quality primarily associated with social prestige and the pursuit of glory. Faret declared that glory 'is the mother of virtue'.[28] According to these courtly values virtue was little more than another quality to be given public recognition.

The ideal of the *honnête homme* provided as great a contrast with the 'virtuous warrior' as the warrior himself did with eighteenth-century notions of the 'man of virtue'. The *honnête homme* was gracious, pleasing and civil, whilst never forgetting what was due both to his rank, and to the rank of others. He was at home in the salon, was gracious to women, and was familiar with all the codes of polite society. He was literally 'respectable' in its non-pejorative sense. For the *honnête homme*, luxury was a boon which led to greater refinement and the cultivation of a studied politeness to facilitate social ease. Excessive virtue in society was tedious – and even embarrassing. Philinte, in Molière's *Le Misanthrope*, is the quintessential *honnête homme*. It is he who points out to the anti-social Alceste the dangers of virtue:

> What is needed in society is an accommodating virtue. It's wrong to be too high principled. True reason lies in shunning all extremes; we should be wise in moderation. This rigorous passion for the antique virtues runs counter to the age and customary usage. It demands too much perfection of mere mortals. We need to move with the times and not be too inflexible, and it's the height of folly to take upon oneself the burden of the world's correction.[29]

Although the *honnête homme* was 'virtuous' it was a very different kind of virtue from that which was to emerge in the mid-eighteenth century: indeed, the ideal rested on a fundamental mistrust of self-conscious or self-righteous morality. La Rochefoucauld, like many of the Christian moralists, took a pessimistic and sceptical view of human nature. He took the position that to say that you were virtuous meant that you were almost certainly a hypocrite: 'The word virtue can serve one's self-interest as effectively as does vice.'[30] The *honnête homme*, despite his conscientious solicitude for the well-being of those with whom he came into contact, did not see himself as having excessive social responsibilities towards his fellows. He did not make extreme claims for his own morality; nor did he bore others by taking himself and his own self-righteousness too seriously; rather, he conformed with the ways of the world, and was agreeable, polite and reasonable. He did everything that was required of him by Christian laws, secular laws and the code of polite society – that much and no more. He regarded his own soul as his primary concern rather than the putative well-being of his fellows. He dispensed charity to the poor, but was careful not to 'reward' the indigent by excessive largesse.

In dramatic contrast with the picture of the virtuous courtier was the notion of the court as the fount of vice. Such was the viewpoint of La Bruyère's *Les Caractères*. These succinct but biting sketches of the moral shortcomings of society's most privileged members were based on his first-hand observations of 'the great nobles' at Versailles, seen from the vantage point of his position as a tutor in the household of the Condés. La Bruyère himself was from a relatively humble background and was familiar, not only with the world of the courtiers at Versailles, but also with the lives of those who lived beyond its walls. To his mind the morals of the former did not always bear up well in comparison with those who led far less privileged lives. Like Fénelon, he was appalled at the contrast between the excesses of the court nobility and the poverty in which so many of Louis XIV's subjects lived. In *Les Caractères* (first published in 1688), luxury and wealth led to greed and moral corruption, whilst the studied politeness of the court and of Parisian high society formed masks behind which lurked intrigue, duplicity and artificiality. La Bruyère deliberately inverted the conventions of the virtuous courtier: 'You can hardly pay a man a greater compliment than to censure him for not knowing the ways of the court: that single phrase implies the possession of every sort of virtue.' He looked instead to 'the people' as a better source of uncorrupted morality: 'The people have no wit, and the nobility have no soul; the former are basically good, and lack veneer; the latter have veneer, and nothing underneath it. Am I to choose? I'll not hesitate; I'll belong to the common people.'[31]

That staunch defender of the integrity of the French nobility, Boulainvilliers also deplored the values of the court, but for him the rot originated from the very pinnacle of that society. He located the source of court corruption in the principle of absolute monarchy itself. If courtiers were corrupt, it was because they had been reduced to dependence on the monarchy for favour and position. For Boulainvilliers it was not the 'people' but the nobility which was the source of true virtue, the real nation. He drew on ideas of noble virtue derived from both the military and the service ethics in order to formulate his *thèse nobiliaire* – a political theory which sought to justify the institution of the nobility as an authority that could challenge the autocratic rule of the monarchy and bring about a moral and political regeneration of French society. The political authority of the nobility was founded on its virtue. His concept of noble virtue drew not only on the old idea of a warrior elite, but, more importantly, on the idea of service. Boulainvilliers argued that the courtly system obliged the nobles who came under its sphere of influence to become dependent on the patronage and favour of the king and his favourites.[32] Courtly nobles had been largely corrupted by their proximity to the corruption and luxury around the monarchy. By contrast the provincial nobility had retained their independence and integrity. He argued that a regenerated nobility, by reviving the ethic of noble virtue, could refashion the French nation and undo much of the harm done by the tyranny of the monarchy. He stressed the importance of education, genealogies and histories in inspiring a new generation of nobles with the desire to emulate the virtues of their forebears. The *Essai sur la noblesse* and the *Lettres sur les parlements* put forward a reworking of the history of the French 'nation' in which it was claimed that the legitimate authority of the Frankish nobility and of the *parlements* had been undermined by the usurpations of the monarchy. Boulainvilliers's view of the past was of a nostalgic golden age, but it was soon to be a powerful image for the *parlementaires* to use against the monarchy. Theorists of the *parlements* from Montesquieu to Le Paige would build on the argument that the nobles of the *parlement* possessed virtue and so were serving the best interests of the 'nation'.

Boulainvilliers's challenge to the monarchy, in the name of a virtuous nobility, offers something of a paradox. In his deeply-held desire to oppose an autocratic monarchy he put forward an alternative 'democratic' view; but it was to be a democracy that existed only within the ranks of the nobility itself, for it was only within their ranks that the virtue of the French 'nation' was located. It is this paradox which has caused him to be referred to as the 'gentilhomme citoyen'.[33] For Boulainvilliers, virtue kept its egalitarian overtones, but since only a small group in society were deemed to possess such virtue, only they had a right to democracy and to sovereignty. Boulainvilliers's paradox was to be reiterated in various forms in the future, most notably in the question of how far the *parlementaire* disputes of the later eighteenth century were inspired by a virtuous devotion to the 'public good'.

The classical republican concept of civic virtue

The most important, sophisticated and internally coherent discourse of political virtue was that of the classical-republican concept of civic virtue. The classical-republican framework of thought, or 'civic paradigm' as Pocock termed it, has been the subject of many important studies.[34] The corpus of classical authors provided a common culture to anyone who enjoyed a level of education beyond that of basic literacy. Familiarity with the classical concept of virtue was thus shared by all those boys educated by tutors or in the colleges, be they noble or

bourgeois. Girls, on the other hand, were not taught the classical languages and were unlikely to have much knowledge of the culture of the
classics, though some might learn about it from private tuition or from
their own reading as was the case with the future Madame Roland. On
the whole their familiarity with, and consequently their self-identifica-
tion with, the mentality of classical culture, mythology and histories
was likely to be far less substantial than that of their male contemporaries.

In France the basic curriculum as taught in the colleges derived from a
very limited range of the classics which was largely fixed before 1650,
and went through relatively few changes right up until the Revolution.
The majority of eighteenth-century thinkers were more familiar with
the Roman authors than with the ancient Greeks, although many of the
ideas of the Romans on political virtue had been adapted originally from
the Greeks. The main corpus of Latin works studied included works by
Livy, Tacitus, Cicero, Sallust, Virgil, Horace and Ovid. Of the Greeks,
Plutarch was by far and away the most influential. Although relatively
few schools taught Greek authors in the original language, he was often
read in translation.[35] The principal aim of a classical education was not
to teach history, and certainly not to make republicans of the pupils, but
to instil individual moral values. Above all, the role of the classics was to
teach virtue, by which was meant probity, dedication and selflessness, in
both private and public life. To this end the works studied were selectively chosen, and expurgated versions of texts were sometimes used.[36]
An important secondary aim was to use the classics to impart a knowledge of the principles of rhetoric, that is, the art of selecting the most
persuasive arguments with which to convince an audience. Rhetorical
practice and strategy was particularly necessary for anyone who was
going to take up a public career. Future lawyers and magistrates spent
a substantial amount of time familiarising themselves with the rhetorical strategies of the most renowned writers of antiquity, above all the
declamations of Cicero.[37]

The teachers in the colleges were themselves clerics. Up until their
expulsion from France it was the Jesuits who formed the principal
teaching order. Thus the political ideas of classical republicanism were
imparted to young minds through the filter of the Catholic Church. It
was not to be expected that clerical teachers would see classical republicanism in a positive light, and their interpretation of antiquity tended
to emphasise the weaknesses and limitations of the pagan political ideal,
with its reliance on such unreliable human qualities as virtue, rather
than on the wisdom of God. Some clerics preferred to avoid the repub-

lican model of the classical past as far as possible and spent a preponderance of their time on those classical authors who either were not
interested in politics, or were not supporters of the republic. Bossuet, for
example, had stated that the Dauphin should be taught the Augustin-
ian, rather than the republican, account of classical antiquity.[38] In this
way, most students, even while they received a grounding in the elements of the political culture of classical republicanism, learned to think
of this as a pagan and outmoded political form.

Where students were exposed to the writings of the classical authors
on the idea of virtue as a political concept, they were imbibing from
a past culture which itself showed a complex and often ambiguous response towards political virtue; a response which then had to be further
mediated through the preoccupations and modes of thought current in
the eighteenth century. Many of the meanings, as well as the inflections
and potential conflicts, of eighteenth-century discourses of virtue were
already present in some form in the original writers of antiquity. The
historical role played by classical republicanism shifted over time, but
virtue, however interpreted, was always at the heart of its meaning. The
basic definition of the classical republican concept of civic virtue was
clear enough, although its implications and ramifications were anything but simple. Virtue was the love of the *patrie* beyond one's own
self-interest. Virtuous citizens who were to be active in public life, must
bring their private moral virtue into their political life and hold themselves above corruption, bribery and intrigue.

Classical authors such as Livy and Tacitus depicted republicanism as
the ideal form of politics, but they also considered it to be an inherently
unstable political system, precisely because it depended on civic virtue.
Virtue was a pure quality, but relentlessly demanding. Heroes, like the
Gracchi, were prepared to die for it, but for most citizens it would mean
an unsustainable level of integrity. Idleness and greed undermined virtue: luxury and corruption inevitably brought about the decay of republics. The idealised aura of the republic was heightened by the way in
which classical historians had themselves conceptualised it. As Harold
Parker showed in his classic work on *The Cult of Antiquity and the French
Revolutionaries*, the ancient authors themselves made no attempt to
present the Roman republic in an 'objective' or historical sense. Livy,
Sallust and Tacitus wrote their histories after the Roman republic was
already a remote memory. They wrote of the 'republic of virtue' as an
ideal time; a quasi-mythical golden age. They used the image of the
Roman republic as a means of contrasting that time when virtue held
sway with the corrupt vices of their present.[39] Men of their own time

appeared as weak, corrupt, grasping and selfish and of an altogether lesser stature than the virtuous heroes of the past.[40] At its very inception then, the virtuous republic was a fading dream of a heroic past, to be held up against the diminished 'present' whether that 'present' was Imperial Romen or France under the Bourbons. The virtuous republic was more than a political system: it was an ideal community. The classical republic, especially in its Spartan incarnation envisioned by Plutarch, was as a lost world, a society in which individuals were no longer isolated and atomised but at one with their community, fulfilled and complete.[41]

The interconnectedness of private and public virtue was a constant feature for the classical authors as for the eighteenth century. From the Stoics, Cicero took the theme 'On Moral Obligation' that integrity was necessary both in public and private life. Moral propriety is necessary for virtue and expresses itself as a form of 'reverence towards all men'. Not all acts are justified by the claim that they are for the public good, for 'there are some acts either so repulsive or so wicked, that a wise man would not commit them, even to save his country'.[42] Thus, Cicero's denunciation of Mark Antony in the 'Second Philippic' focused on his drunkenness and debauchery as much as on his political corruption.[43] Factionalism and private interest were an anathema in the classical republic. The virtuous citizen avoided 'avarice' and 'luxury', both of which were seen as 'effeminate' qualities.[44] Politics, when carried out with integrity, was simply the highest moral virtue. Plutarch stated: 'Questionless, there is no perfecter endowment in man than political virtue,' an idea he sought to illustrate through his *Lives.*[45]

Tensions between the egalitarian principle of civic virtue and the hereditary principle were never far below the surface. Thus, Sallust recounted a speech by the populist leader Marius, speaking against the patricians in the senate: 'These proud men make a very big mistake. Their ancestors left them all they could – riches, portrait busts, and their own glorious memory. Virtue, they have not bequeathed to them, nor could they; for it is the only thing that no man can give to another or receive from another.'[46] Cicero clearly had himself in mind as a virtuous man of humble origin when he wrote that the Romans had 'taken in as citizens brave men from every country, and have very often preferred merit [*virtus*] without birth to nobility [*nobilitas*] without energy'.[47] Plutarch took this point further when he contrasted Coriolanus' abundance of patrician 'martial virtues' with his lack of 'civic virtues' and deplored the Romans' willingness to use the same word *virtus* to describe two such different qualities. For Plutarch, Coriolanus' temper and pride in his noble birth were symptoms rather of effeminacy than of masculine virtue.[48] Thus, many of the themes which were to resurface in the very different context of eighteenth-century political ideas were already present in the classical meanings of 'virtue': the idea of politics as a conflict between love of the *patrie* and personal interest; the intimate relationship between public and private virtue; and the tensions between civic and noble virtue.

One of the most hard-fought conflicts between concepts of virtue in the eighteenth century, however, was to become apparent only with the re-emergence of classical antiquity within a world now dominated by Christian theology. This was the conflict between the concepts of political or civic and Christian virtue. The writers of the Italian Renaissance, who had revived Aristotle's concept of the political nature of man, found it difficult to resolve many of the tensions between this idea and the Christian view that there could be no possibility of secular fulfilment in this world. Machiavelli reacted to this conflict by making a distinction in his writing between political virtue and Christian virtue. He went further, by denying the link with morality and virtue made by the classical humanists such as Cicero. Every necessary measure was acceptable for the defence of the *patrie*. No other moral value could exist for the man of public virtue. He depicted virtue (*virtù*) as a political quality, distinct from morality, and which provided the masculine force with which a man could seize fortune (*fortuna*) and bend her to his will. Machiavelli's separation of political and moral virtue was fairly widely known in the eighteenth century. But it remained a declaration which few other thinkers on classical republicanism could bear to contemplate in its entirety. Montesquieu, for example, thought that Christian and political virtue were separate concepts, but this was because he, like the classical authors, saw political virtue not as amoral, but as the highest form of moral virtue.[49]

The Italian renaissance concept of civic virtue had spread to France only slowly. Even Montaigne, who immersed himself in the classical literature on virtue, was interested primarily in virtue as the stoic quality of self-control and mastery of the passions. His concept of virtue was principally a matter of secularised morality, the development of individual human potential, the importance of private conscience and the control of the passions. Although, particularly in his later years, he became more preoccupied with the sociable aspects of virtue as it related to others (*autrui*), this was a quality akin to friendship; he did not explore its more political manifestations and he remained suspicious of extremes of virtue, arguing that public virtue led to too many expediencies and compromises of private virtue, so that the latter was finally corrupted.[50]

Conflict between the classical republican concept of virtue and the moral authority of the Catholic Church increased during the seventeenth century. By acknowledging the existence of virtue as an autonomous quality the Church would have undermined the need for the presence of God in human affairs, and therefore its own authority. One of the first moves to detach morality from any specific religious doctrine came from the Protestant thinker Pierre Bayle. In the *Dictionnaire historique et critique* (1697) he contended that it was possible to conceive of a society of virtuous atheists, an idea which predictably provoked outrage in some quarters.[51] Bayle himself was staunch in his loyalty to the Calvinism of his birth. But some argued that his ideas launched the unwary on the slippery slope that led to 'free-thinking' in religious matters, or even to atheism. There was not, however, a simple and automatic connection between Protestantism and attraction towards the idea of political virtue, although there were moments at which the Calvinist idea of Grace appeared quite close to a self-conscious assumption of moral virtue. But the close connection between the French state and the Catholic Church could have the effect of pushing religious minorities such as Protestants and Jansenists into taking up theories of civil rights based on a notion of civic virtue.

The development in Britain of sophisticated political theories based on civic virtue was to exert considerable influence on the French *philosophes*. These theories escalated under the impact of political upheavals in the later seventeenth century and reached a peak in the early eighteenth century with the emergence of the 'country' party. Under the unlikely leadership of a disaffected Tory, Lord Bolingbroke, attempts were made in the 1720s and 1730s to make the 'country party' into a more cohesive force for opposition to the ruling Whig oligarchy, to create a 'patriot party' in effect, many years before such a group emerged in France. Bolingbroke and other opposition leaders argued that Walpole's ministry was involved in the corrupt promotion of commercial and financial interests, and that the ministers were using overtly the advantages of their position in government to promote the financial speculations and business investments of themselves and their associates. In works such as his journal *The Craftsman*, and in *The Spirit of Patriotism*, Bolingbroke used the language of classical republican civic virtue and of patriotism (a language drawn from the same political ideology previously developed by the Whigs) in order to give a legitimate basis to political opposition. Bolingbroke was far from being a political democrat. As Skinner has shown, it was Bolingbroke's political isolation, and his need to find an acceptable language in which to express political opposition and rally opinion against the government, that drove him to adopt a political discourse whose implications were far more radical than he himself was prepared to be.[52]

The debate around the 'country' party is important for two reasons. First because it shows us that the language of civic virtue was not necessarily confined to the world of abstract political theory: it could be adapted into specific political disputes, where it legitimised opposition. Secondly because of the influence of these ideas on Montesquieu's political theory during his stay in England from late 1729 to 1731. He seems to have been on the fringes of the circle around Bolingbroke, but it is known that he regularly read the polemics in *The Craftsman*. The question of how far the British version of civic virtue influenced the French is complicated, however, by the fact that during Bolingbroke's first period of exile in France from 1715 to 1725 he himself had been subject to French influences. He met with the ageing Boulainvilliers, and his ideas may have contributed to the concept of a patriot party for moral regeneration derived from an enlightened gentry. Bolingbroke also met with Voltaire and Montesquieu, and attended the meetings of the *Club de l'Entresol*, a group of which little is known for certain, but which discussed ideas for political and social reform. Those who attended it included the abbé de Saint-Pierre, the marquis d'Argenson, and Montesquieu himself.[53]

Whilst the language of civic virtue was so central to the ideas of Bolingbroke and his contemporaries, ideas of political virtue in England and in the Scottish Enlightenment began to develop along different lines. A particularly influential train of thought was set in motion by Mandeville's *Fable of the Bees*, where private vices (the pursuit of financial self-interest) became public virtues, by the generation of commerce and wealth, which were increasingly argued to be of benefit to society. What had been 'luxury' and 'corruption' for classical republican vocabulary, became 'commerce' and 'civility' as Hume and Smith redefined virtue in terms of manners and civilised society.[54] Nevertheless, even in Britain, the division between civic virtue and the oblique virtues of self-interest were not as clear-cut as has sometimes been suggested. Smith and Hume retained an ambiguity in their attitude towards virtue: both remained uneasy about self-interest taken to extremes and they retained the idea of a 'moral republic' even when they were at their most materialist, though this was based increasingly on the conception of virtue as sympathy and sociability, rather than on the classical-republican tradition.[55] Ideas about virtue were not fixed, and it would be hard to maintain that they were all 'tending in one direction'.

In contrast to Britain, in France the classical-republican tradition continued throughout the eighteenth century to be central to notions of political virtue. For the development and popularisation of the classical-republican concept of virtue in France, Montesquieu must take a great deal of the credit. His greatest work, *De l'Esprit des lois*, did not appear until 1748 and will be dealt with in the following chapter, but his ideas about the politics of virtue had matured long before that date and merit attention in their own right. Montesquieu's attitude to politics was complex and full of apparent contradictions. He declared that the most ideal form of government was the republic, based on virtue; yet he is often seen by historians as a pioneer of liberal and constitutional thought, in contrast to the 'totalitarianism' of Rousseau's concept of virtue. Yet this portrait of Montesquieu as a 'liberal' is somewhat anachronistic, and it does little to explain why his contemporaries often evinced a rather ambiguous response both to the man and to his work. They admired him and learned much from him, but few did so without some reservations. In order to understand this we have to see his works in the context of his life and his social position. He was extraordinarily well-read and well-travelled, cosmopolitan, fascinated by other cultures, and in many ways open-minded; yet he enjoyed a venal office as a *président à mortier* in the *parlement* of Bordeaux and politically he was in many ways a 'conservative'.[56] Montesquieu was not only a *philosophe*: he was also very much the *ancien régime* noble. Like Boulainvilliers and Bolingbroke, in terms of political affiliations he was an advocate of the rights and responsibilities of an enlightened nobility. His greatest concern was to ensure that absolute monarchy was checked by the power of the nobles and could not degenerate into 'despotism'.

Clearly Montesquieu presents a problem, the resolution of which must lie, as Venturi argued, in the gap between the classical-republican ideal and the reality of existing European republics, which seemed by the eighteenth century to be an outmoded and declining political form.[57] Montesquieu, like so many of his contemporaries, read the classics as a vision of a world peopled by heroes, in which citizens dedicated themselves to the community. Modern republics were a very different matter. His travels in the Dutch and Italian republics contributed greatly to his disenchantment. Corruption and artificiality were as much a way of life there as in Versailles. In Venice, the very architecture reflected for Montesquieu the falsity behind its republican status: he described it as a series of crumbling façades – like the masks which the

Venetians affected. The only 'liberty' to be found in Venice was the liberty to visit prostitutes openly. It was this *openness* (rather than the prostitution itself) which struck him as indecent.[58]

Like Diderot and Rousseau, Montesquieu was before all else a moralist. Virtue for him entailed moral goodness and love of one's fellows. As early as 1725 in a speech before the *parlement* of Bordeaux he referred to 'this general affection for the human race, which is the virtue of man considered as a thing within himself'.[59] Political or civic virtue represented morality on a higher level, since it extended to the rest of the community the love which was usually confined to one's family and friends. But 'love of the *patrie*' – the virtue which kept faith with the many – sometimes broke the laws of individual or familial morality. In the *Considérations sur les causes de la grandeur des Romains et de leur décadence* (1734) Montesquieu described as 'divine' the virtue of Marcus Brutus, when he killed Julius Caesar who was his reputed father, but who threatened the existence of the republic:

> It was an overriding love for the *patrie* which, passing the bounds of ordinary rules about crimes and virtues, followed only its own voice, and made no distinctions between citizens, friends, philanthropists or fathers: virtue seemed to forget itself in order to surpass itself; and an action that one could not at first sight approve of, because it seemed so terrible, virtue made one admire as divine.[60]

The sublime nature of civic virtue made it painful, difficult to sustain and inherently unstable. In the *Considérations* he saw the decline of republican virtue as a contributory factor in the overall decline of the Romans. Military prowess led to conquest and rapid expansion, but with this expansion came avarice, luxury and growing inequality, which had the effect of corrupting the Romans' martial qualities.[61] A similar theme had been used in the earlier story from the *Lettres persanes* (1721) of the Troglodytes, a myth which epitomises both the attraction of the republic of virtue for contemporaries and their conviction that it would not work. Here Montesquieu contrasted a pessimistic Hobbesian view of human nature with an optimistic view of a virtuous community which recalls both Fénelon's utopias and Shaftesbury's concept of natural virtue. The Troglodytes, after a disastrous experiment in the pursuit of self-interest, in which most of them perish, decide to live for virtue. This was both a political and a philosophical concept: the virtuous Troglodytes embodied a civic ideal, but they were also happy since they were at one with the natural humanity in themselves. But the responsibility for being virtuous placed the unremitting duty on each Troglodyte citizen of bearing responsibility for the others. As the Troglodytes grew more numerous they gave up their commitment to civic virtue, and chose the most virtuous man amongst them to be king and to bear the burden of virtuous government for the rest of the Troglodytes. Weeping for their weakness, he did so.[62]

Classical republicanism was not the only influence on Montesquieu's political theory of virtue. In the milieu of the law courts or *parlements* in which he led his professional life, the idea of political virtue began to assume increasing importance. As the most powerful source of authority after the king himself, the noble magistrates of the law courts (or *parlements*) had a long history of challenging the limits of royal authority. For some historians, such as Carcassonne, the struggle in the 1730s was already essentially about constitutionalism. Recent research, however, suggests that the *parlementaire* crises of this period were more a matter of the defence of jurisdictional, corporate privilege, combined with religious concerns, than a genuine constitutional challenge to the authority of absolute monarchy.[63] The language of the *parlements* was couched in a grandiloquent constitutional language of 'ancient liberties'. We need not, indeed should not, take this language at its face value, but it is indicative of the way in which *parlementaires* articulated issues of power and jurisdiction, combining ideas of noble virtue as judicial service with classical republican rhetoric. For example, d'Aguesseau, the *Procureur-général* of the *parlement* of Paris, later to be Chancellor, declared before the *parlement* in 1715 that 'love of the *patrie*' was 'an almost natural' virtue, which is known by 'sentiment', 'a sacred bond between the authority of kings and the obedience of peoples'; but one which flourished only in republics.[64] D'Aguesseau himself was by no means a bold or pioneering thinker: Carcassonne called him vacillating and half-hearted.[65] Here he was speaking only to other magistrates who would understand both the language and the limited application which he intended for it. In taking up a rhetorical pose as patriotic virtuous judges, *parlementaires* may well have had Cicero in mind, but were unlikely to have shared Cicero's anti-aristocratic sentiments. As Bolingbroke had done, nobles in the *parlements* drew selectively on the corpus of available words from the classical-republican vocabulary for what were essentially power struggles within the ruling elite. But this does not alter the fact that over thirty years before the publication of *L'Esprit des lois* the linguistic repertoire of the *parlementaires* had already forged links between the terms *patrie*, 'virtue', 'republic' and 'sentiment' which were to reappear in far more radical documents and contexts.

Parlements and Jansenism

A new development in the language of political virtue in the early
eighteenth century, and one which was to affect the rhetoric of the
parlements in particular, emerged from the growing politicisation of
the Jansenists. Jansenism had begun life as a purely theological movement, as a particularly austere and quasi-puritan branch of Catholicism,
with little interest in worldly matters. Jansenist beliefs about virtue
varied greatly and are often ambiguous and difficult to categorise. Jansenist theologians of the seventeenth and early eighteenth centuries,
such as Pascal, Nicole and Esprit, looked upon virtue with even greater
suspicion than Bossuet had done, regarding it as a manifestation of pride
(*amour-propre*) and self-interest.[66] Like La Rochefoucauld, Jansenists
claimed that virtues were often vices in disguise. But they went further:
Pascal's concept of virtue could not have been further from the eighteenth-century idea that people were naturally virtuous. People were all
miserable sinners: 'The true and unique virtue is...to hate oneself'.[67]
The so-called virtues of the 'ancients' were inspired by pride; only
through God's grace could true virtue exist.[68] The notion of 'Christian
virtues' was also suspicious, for to believe in the existence of one's own
virtue only put one deeper into sin. But there was a further ambiguity
about this question for, since all virtue came from God, those people
who were possessed of God's grace (as Jansenists hoped they were) must
in fact be virtuous, but only if they continued to deny even to themselves that they were anything other than worthless sinners.[69] This
involved Jansenists in the paradox of simultaneously denying their
virtue, whilst believing that God had given them the gift of virtue
which was not vouchsafed to others.

   As a political idea, Jansenist virtue might not appear to have had a
great deal of potential. But the belief that supposedly virtuous actions
were inspired by *amour-propre* did not prevent Jansenists such as Nicole
from arguing that this false virtue could, nevertheless, have beneficial
effects on others in society, since the result of an action motivated by
false virtue would be the same as if it were inspired by true virtue.[70] The
very difficulty of attaining true virtue in Jansenist theology had the
effect of returning the debate to the political and social, rather than
the spiritual, arena. The social and political applications of Jansenist
concepts of virtue were not to be so far removed from Helvétius's materialist conception of virtue as socially utilitarian. Ironically, Jansenists and
materialists were both drawn to utilitarian concepts of social virtue:
Jansenists, because spiritualist and transcendent values were at once so

important to them, and yet so mysterious and unknowable; and materialists, because they simply denied the existence of such transcendent values.

Jansenist accounts of virtue also had a significant political influence in *parlementaire* rhetoric from the early eighteenth century. The Jansenism that had begun as a purely spiritual movement became political mostly through state persecution, and especially the refusal of the sacraments, and therefore the effective denial of the right to private conscience. From about 1731 the *parti janséniste*, composed of priests, lawyers and magistrates in the Paris *parlement*, felt driven into contesting the rights of the monarchy, whose registration of the Bull *Unigenitus* (1713) as a law of state was the basis of the persecution. This political involvement of some Jansenists tended to split the movement; as other Jansenists avoided worldly politics, and retreated into mysticism, convulsionism and belief in 'miracles', for example those at the tomb of the Jansenist Pâris, at the cemetery of Saint-Médard.[71] In the most recent study of the relationship between religious thought and political ideology, Dale Van Kley has noted that in the purest Jansenist discourse there was little place for the idea of political virtue. It is in 'hybrid' works, where Jansenism mingled with other influences such as classical republicanism and patriotic discourse, that a more unconstrained appeal to political virtue can be found.[72]

The *parlements* contained a significant number of magistrates who were Jansenists, as well as many who, like Montesquieu, whilst not being Jansenists themselves, were sympathetic to their desire for toleration from the State and Church. Consequently, theological struggles gave a new impetus to more traditional jurisdictional disputes between *parlements* and monarchy. This combination of concerns began to be articulated through the formulation of a new discourse of political virtue, realised in such works as that of the Jansenist theologian Duguet's *Institution d'un Prince* (said to have been written in 1713 though published in 1739), where the duty of the prince is described in terms of his obligations to the republic. Here the theoretical basis of kingship had shifted considerably from the orthodox notion of divine right. It is not an explicit theory of national sovereignty, but it is very close to one. According to Duguet it is the king who serves the nation, which exists outside himself and is independent of him. Duguet's concept of a 'republic' is compatible with monarchy, providing that the monarch serves the 'public good' (*bien public*), dispenses justice, maintains equality, rewards virtue and punishes vice, defends his people, and keeps them happy.[73] A prince 'must inspire in his subject the love of all the virtues on which the good of the State depends', the first and foremost of these virtues being, 'love of the *patrie*'.[74] From this Duguet concludes: 'It is therefore the same thing to be for the Republic and to be king; to be for the people and to be sovereign. One is born for others, since one is born to command them; because one must not command others except in order to be useful to them.'[75] Many of the words which would play so prominent a part in discourses of virtue later in the century, such as *patrie*, 'republic', 'citizen', 'equality', 'public good', *bienfaisance* and 'nation', were already present in this work; whilst the word 'virtue' itself was given a new prominence. Duguet gave the term 'moral virtues' to what in the language of classical republicanism would have been called 'political virtues' (such as 'love of the *patrie*'), and because of his need to defend the right to worship of Jansenists, he took the important step of distinguishing these 'moral virtues' from Christian virtues. It was the first duty of a prince to teach these 'moral virtues' to his subjects: orthodox piety would come later:

> not that I think that the moral virtues are absolutely different from those which have religion as their principle and goal; on the contrary, I see the former as a rough draft of which the latter are the perfection; and in fact it is because I see the former as being like a joyful preparation for the latter that I think that they need great attention.[76]

These moral virtues are shown to be the civic virtues of 'the Pagans', and he quotes Saint Augustine to show that these civic virtues are not opposed to Christianity, but are an earthly echo of 'the true Religion'. By learning to love their *patrie* and by being virtuous citizens in this life, people prepare themselves to 'become citizens of another *patrie*'.[77] Virtue and *patrie* have become here a form of religious, almost messianic, thought, but one which was explicitly independent of conventional Catholic theology. But this new form of religious virtue was also political in the sense that it dealt explicitly with the role of government and the rights of citizens. These developments in the language of virtue paralleled the transformation of the 'general will' from a theological belief (particularly a Jansenist one) into a political belief, a change which has been shown by Patrick Riley.[78] Jansenists explicitly maintained that they were not attempting to overthrow the social order but trying to win for themselves the right to individual conscience. Nevertheless, by developing a vocabulary which combined elements of civic and moral virtue they helped to prepare the ground on which others might later build when challenging the authority of the political system.

The implicit threat was clearly recognised as such: Duguet's book was banned in 1740 by Louis XV's chief minister, cardinal de Fleury.[79]

Long before 1745, therefore, several distinct and complex discourses of virtue existed that could be used to justify and legitimise power and political authority. The concept of virtue had been appropriated as a means of giving a moral legitimacy respectively to the power of the monarchy, the nobility and the 'citizens' – though as yet civic virtue was very limited in its application and could hardly be said to be a democratic force. Issues of religious toleration and judicial jurisdiction also contributed to new formulations of political virtue. Political theorists and opposition writers made strategic and selective use of these ideas and their linguistic repertoires according to the context in which they wrote. These meanings and uses of virtue were not, therefore, fixed and immutable, but were subject to strains, and realignments. The years after 1745 were to see many changes in the way virtue was understood and used. One thing that we shall examine is the extent to which the discourses of noble virtue and kingly virtue were thrown on the defensive, even in many cases subsumed into a new discourse of virtuous citizens who had the right both to formulate opinions and to participate in defence of the public good. This new model would draw both on classical republicanism and on the new discourse of natural or sociable virtue. The emergence of this new discourse, together with the revitalisation of classical republicanism that took place in the mid-century, will be the subject of the following chapter.

2
Sociable Virtue and the Rise of Secular Morality, 1745–54

> *Therefore I have called* political virtue *love of the patrie and of equality. I have had new ideas; it has been necessary to find new words for them, or to give new meanings to old ones.*
>
> Montesquieu, 'Foreword', *De l'Esprit des lois* (1748)

From about the middle of the century a kind of intellectual ferment began in the climate of ideas. Changes in a climate of ideas are notoriously difficult to pin down to a particular date. Daniel Mornet was the first person to set out the intellectual map of the eighteenth century and draw out its political implications. He dated from 1748 the opening of what he termed an open warfare between the forces of Enlightenment and the French establishment as represented by the twin pillars of Church and State. It is clear that contemporary observers themselves were aware of a change about this time: some spoke of a revolution of ideas, others of a 'republican ferment'.[1] Most of the ideas which contributed to this change of climate had their origins in earlier periods; but they were taken up anew, reappropriated and remodelled into polemical tools whereby the society and politics of the *ancien régime* could be considered and criticised. The refashioning of virtue was a central part of this transformation. Virtue had long been a way of defining and legitimating political power. But now there was heightened awareness, both of the power of the word, and of its polemical potential. It began to be wielded across a wide range of public forums. Voltaire remarked on this phenomenon in 1745: 'The word virtue resounds across the earth; one hears it at the theatre, in the law courts, in the pulpit.'[2] Virtue rapidly became part of the linguistic weaponry with which the forces of the Enlightenment began to do battle with the assembled armies of established authority: the Church and the absolute monarchy.

Daniel Mornet argued that the year 1748 marked the emergence of the Enlightenment as a self-consciously polemical movement, because this was the year in which two extremely influential, though very different, works were published: Montesquieu's *De l'Esprit des lois* and Toussaint's *Les Mœurs*. For both these writers, virtue was central to their conception of politics and social relations.[3] I would argue that, in addition to these two books, another slightly earlier work was to exert a profound influence over the way in which the social implications of virtue were understood and interpreted. This was the translation by Diderot in 1745 of Shaftesbury's *An Inquiry Concerning Virtue or Merit*.

These three texts drew on different concepts of virtue, including those drawn from classicism and Christianity. Montesquieu's concept of virtue remained largely within the classical republican tradition, which he refined, developed and revitalised. But Diderot and Toussaint unfolded an idea which was to have an extraordinary new impact, the concept of natural virtue. Despite their different preoccupations, each of these three men explored the role of virtue as a form of secular morality. They shared the assumption that social and political order was best to be understood by framing it in moral terms. Through their conceptions of politics they were thus attempting to resolve the classic dilemma of eighteenth-century moral philosophy, a problem which obsessed their contemporaries and which still retains its relevance for the twentieth century: if morality was not a set of assured principles, given by God via the Church, on what certain basis could it rest? If one could not be certain that God was indeed going to intervene to punish the guilty and reward the good in the next life then what incentive was there to act well in this one? To answer this question, the classic Enlightenment response was, as Locke had formulated it, to draw on some form of the theory of natural law, that is, the idea that there was a natural order in the universe which reflected and made manifest the will of God. Through nature itself one could trace God's law, which set the basis for the organisation not only of the scientific world but also of human society. But this idea in itself launched more problems and uncertainties. Was 'nature' any more fixed and certain than was religious doctrine? If one accepted that the 'laws of nature' as they related to people and society were not as fixed and universal as scientific laws, and if one then conceded the relativism of moral values, then the way lay open to a long and winding path that would lead ultimately to the despairing country of the marquis de Sade, in which no values existed. Nowhere would the successive twists and turns of this path be better illuminated than in the development of Diderot's ideas as he came to reject the

Christian beliefs in which he had been brought up, and yet persisted in arguing that society needed a moral code by which to live. In his shifting ideas about the need for virtue is expressed the whole philosophical and moral dilemma present in this word.[4]

Diderot and the translation of Shaftesbury's *An Inquiry Concerning Virtue*

At the time at which he translated Shaftesbury, his first major work, Diderot had adopted with enthusiastic wholeheartedness the idea that there was a moral order in society which existed irrespective of religious doctrines. Shaftesbury wrote in the tradition of natural law, that is, the belief that there was a rational order in the universe which could be observed through nature. It was an idea which, like much else, could be traced back to the ancients. Versions of it existed in the works of Plato, Aristotle, and the Stoics. In *De Republica* Cicero had written that there existed a moral order which was based on nature, and conformed with reason. This concept was not confined to 'pagans'. It was taken up by some medieval theologians, notably Thomas Aquinas, who combined the idea of a natural order with Christian dogma, accentuating its divine origins. But these ideas were given a more prominent and schematic form in the seventeenth century when they were developed into a basis for legal theory by the theorists Grotius and Pufendorf. Natural law had also been incorporated into political theory, most notably by Locke, who argued in the *Two Treatises of Government* (1690) that the best form of political government could be discovered by its conformity with nature and with reason. These ideas were largely known in France through translations of the works of Grotius and of Pufendorf by Barbeyrac. A Genevan, Burlamaqui, contributed several works in French including the *Principes du droit naturel* (1748) and the *Principes du droit politique* (1751), whilst Locke was fairly widely known in intellectual circles, in part through the efforts of Voltaire. Familiarity with the rhetoric of natural law extended through many circles in contemporary France.[5]

For Diderot and his contemporaries, Shaftesbury's originality and importance lay in the prominent role he accorded to the notion of natural virtue. Shaftesbury had been inspired by theorists of natural law and the assumption that there was a moral as well as a natural order in the world. But he refined and developed the idea into the centrepiece of his theory. In this respect, Shaftesbury's ideas diverged from those of his mentor, Locke. In *An Essay Concerning Human*

Understanding (1690) Locke had challenged the notion of innate ideas, and argued that a child's knowledge of the external world was conveyed to it by means of its senses. This idea was at the forefront of the Enlightenment debates on 'sensationalist' psychology and the importance of education. Taken to its conclusions, in the hands of Helvétius, for example, this idea could lead to an extreme environmentalist and mechanistic position, where people were seen as being entirely the products of their environment, whose sense of morality was entirely plastic and malleable. For many observers the materialist and pessimistic implications of Locke's ideas proved unpalatable. Shaftesbury, once the disciple of Locke, rejected this aspect of his former mentor's ideas and particularly his pessimism. He argued instead that people did possess an innate moral sense and an innate attraction towards virtue, an idea which he appears to have adapted from the theories of the Cambridge Platonists, such as Henry More. The concept of original sin was abandoned. Virtue was described as 'natural'. It was a form of natural religion rather than a manifestation of any particular religious doctrine. Although Shaftesbury himself believed in a benign form of deism, his concept of virtue was that of an essentially secular form of morality, at the heart of which was humanity itself. Religious beliefs, particularly in an afterlife, encouraged people to develop their natural virtue, but were not absolutely essential to it. It was certainly possible for an atheist to be virtuous, although it would be difficult, for their outlook would be affected and their virtuous impulses sapped by a sense of fatalism and of melancholy. It was better to believe in some kind of a God, but God was not directly essential to Shaftesbury's ethical system.

Of more immediate relevance to the human condition was his belief that human nature had an innate impulsion towards virtue. Virtue's attractiveness lay in its manifest goodness, truth, and beauty. It was apparent that human goodness towards one another was at one with the rightful ordering of the universe. Mankind was essentially sociable, and virtue was a sociable impulse, born of the natural sympathy of individuals towards their fellows. The feelings, or sensibilities, of individuals caused them to feel 'benevolent' towards their fellows and to desire to act virtuously towards them. Shaftesbury went against pessimistic and orthodox Christian views of human nature by arguing that the passions could also be benign in effect since they were susceptible to sympathy for others, so that individuals would feel pleasure in working towards the good of others, rather than for self-interested motives. The reward of virtue was happiness; the happiness of others, to which virtuous persons contributed by their actions, and the joy felt by the virtuous persons themselves, in contemplating the happiness which they had brought about in others.[6] It was a harmonious social vision, in which private and public virtues were essential aspects of the same interconnected network of humanity, in which each person was touched by the pains and joys of their fellows. Individual morality was thus closely related to social responsibility. People should have a balance of 'natural' affections (which were concerned with the good of the community as a whole) and 'private' affections (which represented self-interest). Excessive self-interest, where this conflicted with the public interest or 'general good', was selfishness. Only by promoting the general good could a person be truly virtuous and truly happy:

> Thus the Wisdom of what rules, and is FIRST and CHIEF *in Nature*, has made it to be according to the *private Interest* and *Good* of every-one, to work towards the *general Good*; which if a Creature ceases to promote, he is actually so far wanting to himself, and ceases to promote his own Happiness and Welfare. He is, on this account, directly his own Enemy: Nor can he any otherwise be good or useful to himself, than as he continues good to Society, and to that *Whole* of which he is himself *a Part*. So that VIRTUE, ... *that* which is the Prop and Ornament of human Affairs ... *that single Quality*, thus beneficial to all Society, and to Mankind *in general*, is found equally a Happiness and Good to each Creature *in particular*; and is *that* by which alone Man can be happy, and without which he must be miserable.[7]

Diderot followed Shaftesbury in emphasising the novelty of this perspective on morality: 'This subject', he wrote, 'is almost entirely new.'[8] His translation followed the original text fairly closely. Most of his changes had the aim of sharpening rather than altering the argument, whilst his own more risky speculations were mostly confined to the footnotes. For example, he made the social aspect of virtue more explicit by frequently translating Shaftesbury's phrase 'natural affections' as 'social affections' (*affections sociales*).[9] The translation reinforced Shaftesbury's belief that people who claimed to possess moral virtue should not devote themselves exclusively to private life, but must also actively desire the good of their community: 'there is no moral virtue, no merit, without some clear and distinct ideas of the general good'. Diderot added that the person of virtue must possess 'a considered understanding of that which is morally good or bad, worthy of admiration or of contempt, just or unjust'. Without this disinterested quality of moral, social judgement it was impossible to be 'virtuous'. One could be 'good', in the sense that an animal may be 'good', but not 'virtuous'.[10]

The second part of Shaftesbury's treatise set out to show, in Diderot's words, 'that the particular interest of the individual is inseparable from the general interest of his kind; in short that his real happiness consists in virtue and that vice will not fail to make him miserable'.[11] Shaftesbury's work marked the furthest point of optimism about the nature of virtue and its benefits to society through happiness.

The extent to which Shaftesbury's work was known in France before Diderot's translation is uncertain.[12] Several of his works had appeared in translation in journals, but if anything he appears to have been more forgotten than remembered by 1745.[13] Knowledge of his work appears to have been confined largely to a select few amongst the *philosophes* who read him in the original. Montesquieu had clearly read him; as had Voltaire, who had wavered between Shaftesbury's deist optimism and Locke's near-materialism for many years before inclining in favour of the former. Shaftesbury also seems to have been known to the members of the *Club d'Entresol*, including the abbé de Saint-Pierre, many of whose ideas about peace and acts of kindness, and much of whose vocabulary closely parallel Shaftesbury's. Shaftesbury's idea that natural sociability formed the basis for civil society had found a place in Bolingbroke's concept of patriotism, and so reached the French via this indirect route.[14] Diderot's translation of Shaftesbury was not nearly so well-known or widely read as *De l'Esprit des lois* or *Les Mœurs* were to be, but it played a vital role in bringing Shaftesbury's ideas to the attention of a new and much wider readership in France, amongst which were members of the network of young *philosophes* to which Diderot himself belonged, including Toussaint and, of course, Rousseau. They in turn were to diffuse these ideas amongst a much wider readership. Rousseau appears not to have read Shaftesbury in the original, and he did not cite him in any of his major works, but then he was often selective in owning to influences upon him. He possessed a copy of Diderot's translation in which Rousseau wrote that the author himself had given it to him in 1745, and it would have been extraordinary indeed if Rousseau and Diderot had not frequently discussed the idea of natural virtue at this time.[15]

Diderot's translation, though published anonymously, since it put forward deist beliefs, was well received in France – even the Jesuit *Journal de Trevoux* found the idea of natural virtue a harmless enough concept.[16] The following year Diderot published his *Pensées philosophiques*, which was also much influenced by Shaftesbury. In an unpublished document written at that time he declared that 'The passions always inspire us rightly, for they inspire us only with the desire for happiness. ... Ah! what would morality be, if it were otherwise? What would virtue be? We would be insane to follow it, if it took us from the road to happiness.'[17] Already, although he denied it, Diderot could see virtue taking a divergent path from happiness. By this point he was rapidly making the transition from the optimistic deism of Shaftesbury towards atheism. In 1749 he was imprisoned in the château de Vincennes for his *Lettre sur les aveugles*: an experience which curtailed his desire to confront the authorities of the *ancien régime* head-on, and in his later published works he showed considerable circumspection. Even his atheism, however, was informed by the religious values of the society in which he lived. Later he would grow disillusioned with Shaftesbury's smooth optimism, and emphasise, instead, the pain that accompanied the pursuit of virtue, a pain to be endured stoically. But he would never abandon his commitment to the principle that virtue was fundamental to society's well-being.

Toussaint's *Les Moeurs*

Diderot's youthful enthusiasm for virtue was in turn to inspire his friend François-Vincent Toussaint to write his own study of natural and social virtue, *Les Mœurs*; a book which in its day enjoyed great success. Toussaint has been consigned by posterity to the category of the 'second rank' of Enlightenment writers. Few people are now aware of Toussaint's contribution to eighteenth-century ideas and the extraordinary impact of *Les Mœurs* on its many readers.[18] In terms of originality, the account of natural virtue contained here added little to that of Shaftesbury. But *Les Mœurs* presented one of the first systematic accounts of the social benefits of natural virtue as a legitimate basis for a moral society, and set the tone for the way in which the connections between moral and political virtue would be conceptualised throughout the second half of the eighteenth century. The explicit and recurrent social dimension of *Les Mœurs* distinguished it from earlier popular 'conduct' guides to virtue such as Lemaître de Claville's *Traité du vrai mérite de l'homme* (1734) and Levasque de Pouilly's *Théorie des sentiments agréables* (1747), which had concentrated on the pleasures of individual morality and had kept within a fairly orthodox religious framework, linking natural virtue with Christian doctrine. Toussaint's work, by contrast, deliberately eschewed any link between natural virtue and any specific 'exterieur cult'. It also contained much more polemical social criticism than was apparent in Shaftesbury's high-flown but rather vague rhetoric of universal sympathy and benevolence. Toussaint made a more conscious distinction between those who were virtuous and those who were not. Generally, the richer one was, and the more powerful in the eyes of the world, the less likely one was to be virtuous. This account of the corrupting effects of wealth and privilege echoed La Bruyère's harsh criticism of the morals of 'les grands'. But La Bruyère and other seventeenth-century moralists had largely confined themselves to a pessimistic account of the corrosive effects of worldly success. Instead, Toussaint combined social criticism with the theory of natural virtue in order to present a positive alternative moral framework posited on the merits of the less affluent classes, and founded on their superior virtue. This has caused at least one historian to see *Les Mœurs* as the first expression of a new self-consciously moral theory of the bourgeoisie.[19] There may be something in this, but it is not easy to make simple class distinctions: many of Toussaint's readers (like Rousseau's) were by no means bourgeois themselves.

Toussaint also took much further than Shaftesbury had done the claim that one did not have to adhere to any specific religious doctrine in order to be virtuous. He began by saying that, inspired as he was by 'the love of virtue', he would discuss only 'morals'. He would not consider formal religion at all but would confine himself to 'natural Religion': 'I want a Moslem to be able to read me as well as a Christian.'[20]

Toussaint's strongest social criticism was saved for the 'honest man' (*honnête homme*), that courtly ideal of the seventeenth century, hero of Molière's plays and La Rochefoucauld's *Maxims*. Toussaint posited the *honnête homme* as the antithesis of those moral qualities he equated with virtue:

> Let us leave the quality of *honnête homme* to him who is content to be just that: such a title is acquired at too low a price for any elevated soul to envy it. Very comfortable circumstances, a large fortune, praise for one's vices, that is what makes an *honnête homme*: virtue does not enter into it at all.[21]

The *honnête homme*'s wealth and noble title, once marks of his virtue, his superior status and education, here indicated only the depth of his corruption and indebtedness to vice. Toussaint used scathing language to depict the social and moral hypocrisy of the *honnête homme* as inferior to the ways of the 'more honest' thief:

An unfortunate man, driven by poverty, stops a passer-by at a cross-roads, takes his purse or tries to: that is the dishonest man [mal-honnête homme]; and if you have any doubts about it, the scaffold will make it plain.

But, lodged in a magnificent town house, is a fortunate financier who has made his pile in the service of the state; give him his own Swiss guard, livery for his lackeys, a landed family name, he benefits from public misery, his house is built on the ruins of five hundred families: it does not matter in the least, he is an *honnête homme*, because he is rich and because he breathes.[22]

This hostile portrait of a financier – a traditional target for all – was an attack on conspicuous consumption, exploitation and excessive wealth rather than a straightforward 'bourgeois versus noble' argument. Toussaint was not attacking the nobility as such. He did, however, challenge some of the traditional theoretical justifications for nobility. The implication was that the nobility, in order to retain the right to social pre-eminence, should adopt more 'bourgeois' values such as virtue. His ideas shook traditional concepts of noble virtue, founded on valour, education, blood or service. In the same year that Montesquieu was to separate 'virtue' and 'honour', associating the former with republics, the latter with monarchies, Toussaint also differentiated between them. He put the contrast in less abstract terms, however, than Montesquieu would do; for Toussaint the issue was one of overt social criticism. Toussaint expressed this distinction as the contrast between 'l'honnête homme' and 'the virtuous man': 'All the honest men together are not worth a single virtuous man.' The 'honour' of the rich was based on 'their fortune'. He sought to draw out the differences in meaning of these two words. 'Honour' was associated with social appearances and wealth: 'The same term in French is used to signify both an unfortunate man and a dishonoured man,' whereas virtue was built on the solid foundations of 'good morals'.[23]

True virtue was defined as 'public service', rather than self-aggrandisement or the pursuit of 'glory'. An ideal minister, for example, would devote himself to the *patrie* rather than to his own advancement, but Toussaint suspected that his portrait of such a disinterested minister was 'an imaginary being'. True heroism could not exist without virtue: 'every man without virtue is, at the bottom of his soul, a coward'. Sometimes war was necessary, but it was always devastating and terrible in its effects, and it could not be associated with glory as in the old military ethic of the *noblesse d'épée*. Indeed, the man who had been raised to be a warrior, far from being a hero, was like a dog, who is necessary to defend a house, but must be kept chained up for fear that it does not turn on its own masters and devour them. The military ethic pursued for its own sake was a 'false value': actions were not glorious because they were difficult, but because they were 'useful and virtuous'. The duel, that mark of nobility, was 'a false point of honour', motivated by private quarrels and a desire for personal vengeance. But to speak to 'ferocious duellists' of virtue and 'natural equity' would be of little point, for this would be 'to speak a language which they did not even understand'.[24] In these terms the values of noble 'military' virtue were overturned and a new code set in their place. True heroism, true manly courage, lay in virtue, not in honour.

The idea of noble virtue as justice was also subjected to scrutiny, although it was not attacked in the way that military values were. Toussaint agreed that justice was one of the most important virtues, but wondered if the magistrates were always the best people to administer it since the administration of justice in France fell far short of the ideal that it should be 'free, prompt and without partiality'. 'Of all the professions, that of the magistrate is, I believe, the most important for society: but I know of no other office for which less proof of competence is required.' In order to have integrity in his public life a magistrate ought to be virtuous in his private life. To illustrate this point Toussaint presented scathing portraits of the inadequacies of two corrupt magistrates. One was a young magistrate who had an aversion to long legal works, preferring to lead a frivolous life, devoted to the pleasures of the flesh. The other was an elderly magistrate, whose age and infirmities preserved him from the seductive wiles of women, so that he was not corrupt in that sense; but he slept soundly during the pleading of the barristers before giving his opinion of the case at length; and his corrupt notion of his own 'virtue' meant he felt insulted by the offer of only mediocre bribes.[25]

One of the 1748 editions of *Les Mœurs* was published together with the *Pensées philosophiques*, suggesting that Diderot and Toussaint were collaborators in a joint project to promote the idea of social virtue. But the *philosophes* were not the only source of Toussaint's notions of social morality. In the attack on corruption and suspicion of excessive wealth there were echoes of older classical-republican concepts of public service. Toussaint was a lawyer by profession and his unflattering portraits of magistrates who fell far short of the civic ideal may have been drawn from personal observation. There was also a glimpse of Jansenist scorn for the trappings and false values of the world. Toussaint had earlier in his life been exposed to the moral austerity of Jansenism. He came from an impoverished Jansenist family, and had once composed a hymn in praise of Deacon Pâris, the figure at the centre of the miraculous cult at Saint-Médard. Although the activities of the Jansenist *convulsionnaires* appear to have eventually repelled Toussaint, he retained affinities with Jansenism all his life. Like Rousseau, Toussaint kept some religious convictions and was not really at ease amongst the circle of the *philosophes*; but also, like Rousseau, he had a gift for popularising their ideas in a way which proved more acceptable than outright discussions of atheism in works such as the *Pensées philosophiques*. Toussaint set out purposefully to write a book which would reach the minds of many people. As an early critic commented, Toussaint had acted astutely in not defining what he meant by deism, and in concentrating on agreeable feelings: 'By this means he had the secret of making himself acceptable to everyone.'[26]

Les Mœurs was too radical to be condoned by the most orthodox Catholics, but plenty of people had no qualms in reading it. The book was published 'without privilege', that is, without having been sanctioned by the censors. It was a calculated risk. The success of *Les Mœurs* was, ironically, increased in some quarters by its condemnation in May 1748 by the *parlement* of Paris. An extraordinary number of attacks appeared against Toussaint's book. What provoked outrage was not so much the idea of natural virtue in itself (many orthodox Catholics found this a conducive idea), but the explicit way in which these moral values were detached from revealed religion. Another factor may well have been its less than complimentary portrait of the magistrature. Similarly, his satirical portraits of certain recognisable figures in public life (including Madame de Pompadour), who were far from being models of virtue, may well have played a part in drawing down official wrath on his head. Toussaint himself gained the unfortunate distinction of being the first *philosophe* to be forced into exile as a result of his book (Voltaire had left for England voluntarily) and numerous 'refutations' of the work appeared. The lawyer Barbier described the stir which *Les Mœurs* had made and which he attributed in large part to its condemnation:

> At last I have obtained a copy of the book *Les Mœurs*, which has become very rare and very expensive because of the order suppressing it on the 6th May 1748. It should be noted as well that without that condemnation few people would have bothered to obtain this book, whereas now there is no one, man or woman, in certain sections of

society, who takes pride in having a certain kind of discerning spirit, who has not desired to see it. They all ask each other, have you read *Les Mœurs*? A single copy will pass rapidly through fifty hands. Good taste and curiosity mean that people are always avid to obtain forbidden things.[27]

Having read the book with great interest and attention to its arguments, which he summarised in detail, Barbier warned against anyone else reading it. Although the book was filled with 'the finest sentiments about virtue and probity', he said, it was 'very dangerous, and could not be acceptable in any country'. But such warnings of the political subversiveness implicit in the language of virtue only served to enhance its attractions. It went through eighteen editions between 1748 and 1777, eight of which came out in 1748.[28] Similar works began to appear, launching a vogue for natural virtue which continued until the outbreak of the Revolution.

Political virtue in Montesquieu's *De l'Esprit des lois*

Although Montesquieu was well aware of the concept of natural social virtue which was firing the enthusiasms of the younger generation of *philosophes*, it was not a central feature in his own work.[29] His own ideas had developed significantly since his earlier writings. It was in his culminating study, *De l'Esprit des lois*, that he was to make his greatest contribution to the politics of virtue through the broadening in scope and application of the classical-republican concept of civic virtue. In this work Montesquieu identified three forms of political authority: republics, which he further sub-divided into democracies (where the people as a body constituted the sovereign power), and aristocracies (where 'certain families' had sovereignty); monarchies (where a monarch had sovereign power, but ruled according to laws and in consultation with established institutions such as the law courts and the Church); and despotisms (where the monarch took no account of any other authority than that of his own will). Each of these forms of government was maintained by means of a different principle which served as the basis for its authority. 'Virtue' was the principle of republics; 'honour' that of monarchies; and 'terror' (*la crainte*) that of despotisms.[30]

Montesquieu defined virtue after the classical formula as 'the love of the laws and of the *patrie*', a love which necessitated 'a continual preference for the public good over one's own good'. The twin obligations of 'love of equality' and 'love of frugality' were also at the heart of civic virtue.[31] Montesquieu made rather contradictory claims as to whether this form of virtue was a 'moral' virtue. In his 'Foreword' to the 1757 edition of *De l'Esprit des lois* he insisted that it was a political and not a moral concept:

> that which I call *virtue* in a republic is love of the *patrie*, that is to say, love of equality. It is by no means a moral virtue, nor a Christian virtue, it is *political* virtue. . . . I have had new ideas; it has been necessary to find new words for them, or to give different meanings to familiar words.[32]

This 'Foreword' was, however, written specifically in order to counter allegations that he had claimed in the first edition of his work that people were not virtuous (i.e. were immoral) in a monarchy – and therefore that the French were immoral. So it was partly in order to defend himself that he stated here that by republican 'virtue' he meant something quite different from morality.[33] Elsewhere in the text, however, he made it clear that he considered political virtue to be a higher form of morality than private virtue because it entailed putting the good of others before oneself, even before the good of those people to whom one was attached by personal links, such as family and friends:

> I speak here of political virtue, which is moral virtue in the sense that it directs itself towards the general good, very little of particular moral virtues, and not at all of that form of virtue which relates to revealed truths.[34]

This was in accordance with the notion of virtue inherited from the classical authors. Indeed, of all the subsequent interpreters of classical republicanism, only Machiavelli had dared to claim that morality and politics could be seen as distinct from one another. Montesquieu agreed with Machiavelli that political virtue was different from Christian virtue, but disagreed sharply with Machiavelli's contention that political virtue need not be moral. On the contrary, for Montesquieu, political virtue was, quite simply, the highest form of morality. His view differed, however, from Shaftesbury's account of virtue as a natural human quality. For Montesquieu, the practice of virtue was an agonising rather than a joyous process, which entailed the denial of 'natural' feelings: 'Political virtue is an abnegation of self, which is always a very painful thing.'[35] The highest forms of virtue demanded an almost inhuman level of denial of natural emotions, in which the public good superseded private emotions and family ties – as when Junius Brutus had ordered the execution of his own sons, or Marcus Brutus had killed the man reputed to be his natural father.

The peoples of antiquity, he said, lived mostly under the superior, democratic form of republican government which had such virtue as its principle. As such they were superior to any other people that now walked the earth: 'they did such deeds as we no longer see today, and which amaze our little souls'.[36] The republic was an exalted ideal, but one which rested on a form of virtue which, according to the classical concept, was inevitably subject to decline. Thus, Montesquieu's conception of the democratic republic was that of a political form that had outlived its historical moment: it was a lingering vision of a golden bygone age. It was the political system which was most worthy of mankind, but one which was doomed to eventual failure. Montesquieu's primary purpose in depicting the 'republic of virtue' in *De l'Esprit des lois* was not in order to call for its renewal, but to use it to practical effect, as a model of how politics ought to be, against which he could delineate the weaknesses of the actual political system. His account of the inevitable decline of the political ideal served to illustrate his far more pressing political concern, which was to show how easily monarchy might lapse into despotism.

In a monarchy, by contrast, it was for the king to be virtuous, but it was correspondingly more difficult for 'the people' to be so. Instead of virtue they turned to honour, which was based upon public acclaim. Of monarchy, he wrote: 'There one does not judge the actions of men as good, but as beautiful; not as just, but as exalted; not as reasonable, but as extraordinary.' Honour was sustained by means of those very social distinctions: hierarchy, privilege and the maintenance of social rank, which were anathema to civic virtue. Under monarchy the relative values of 'that which is called the honest man' replaced the absolute values of virtue: 'This bizarre notion of honour of the honest man means that he only has the virtues he wants to have, and in the manner that he wants them.'[37] The pursuit of self-interest substituted for the selflessness of virtue, in a manner that recalled Mandeville's concept of 'private vices, public benefits' rather than the altruistic visions of Shaftesbury or Fénelon: 'Each man furthers the public good, in the belief that he is pursuing only his own interests.'[38] Thus his critics were not so far off the mark in reading Montesquieu as having said that the French political system was immoral – in a sense he was saying that – but this did not mean that he thought that the French monarchy was an *ineffective* political system, or that he wished to undermine it: 'One speaks here of what is, and not of what ought to be.'[39] He judged monarchy in terms not of its integrity, but of its efficacy.

Like Toussaint, but for different reasons, Montesquieu made a clear distinction between 'virtue' and 'honour', two words which had previously been closely linked. Whereas other defenders of the nobility, such as Boulainvilliers, had identified particular 'noble' forms of virtue, Montesquieu did not attempt to define a specifically 'noble' virtue, instead he linked nobility far more closely with honour. Only in the aristocratic form of the republic (where a 'corps' of nobles exercised sovereign power) did nobles specifically embody virtue. But he did not depict their virtue as different in kind from civic virtue, stipulating only that it should be more moderate in character. An aristocracy, he said, could be a good form of government, as it constituted a moderate and stable compromise between the strains of democracy and the corrupting effects of monarchy. But it functioned best when the nobles were close to the people and democracy, and less well when it resembled monarchy. The worst form of aristocracy was that which had diverged so far from equality that the people were in effect the 'slaves' of the nobles.[40]

One category of nobles, however, was described by Montesquieu as being the antithesis of virtue: they were the court nobility. Montesquieu depicted their antics in vivid contrast to those of the great majority of the nobility. Most courtiers, he observed with visible contempt, were distinguished only by their ambition, arrogance, idleness, greed, treachery, deviousness, their 'contempt for the duties of the citizen', 'fear of kingly virtue' and, above all, their readiness to pour 'perpetual ridicule on virtue'.[41]

Despite his distaste for the court nobility, Montesquieu was the great defender of the rights and privileges of the nobility in general, particularly of the judicial nobility from which he came. The last part of *De l'Esprit des lois* contained a justification of the entire system of feudal laws and of privileged institutions such as *parlements* and Church. He claimed that the privileged status of the nobility was essential in order for them to act as a bastion against possible growth in monarchical 'despotism'.[42] In many ways this argument recalled Boulainvilliers's *thèse nobiliaire*. But whereas Boulainvilliers had given the nobility a distinct role in society as a regenerative moral force, based on their possession of a form of 'noble virtue' peculiar to themselves, Montesquieu did not distinguish a specific 'noble' form of virtue. There was nothing to prevent nobles from acting virtuously in Montesquieu's framework of ideals, but it was not a quality which was exclusive to themselves in terms of birth, blood, service or valour. It was a quality to be shared with other, non-noble 'citizens'. Moreover, the 'love of equality' and 'love of frugality' which were said to be intrinsic to civic virtue made it appear an unlikely attribute to be associated with the nobility.

Montesquieu did not depict nobles – except courtiers – as being opposed to virtue. But he did ally the noble ethic much more closely with the attributes of honour. He thus provided the rhetorical ammunition for rejuggling language and concepts, so that honour, nobility, and political corruption were separated onto one side of a linguistic divide, with virtue, citizenship, and political integrity on the other. It was far from being a rigid distinction, however: many nobles, particularly the judicial nobility, interpreted the distinction as being between court nobles and the rest of society (under which notional category could come all other nobles, including themselves, as well as the people). Thus, in their periodic disputes with the monarchy, noble magistrates would be able to see themselves displaying civic virtue, on behalf of the 'people' and against the 'corruption' of the court. But for other readers of Montesquieu, the distinction seems to have lain, not between court and non-court nobles, but between nobles and non-nobles. This ambiguity remained a source of tension and contradiction in the language, whilst its dynamics would also be played out in political situations, for example, during the Maupeou coup.

It has been said of Montesquieu with some justice that whatever his many merits as a theorist, internal consistency was not one of them. One of the most fundamental contradictions in his work was that between his praise for the egalitarian ideal of civic virtue and his defence of a powerful privileged nobility. Both these ideas wielded immense influence, although not necessarily on the same readers. Montesquieu had articulated a mode of thought and a moral code against which to judge political systems. By stripping virtue of any lingering exclusive associations with nobility, he helped shape political virtue into a more overtly egalitarian and radical discourse. Whilst he himself had no desire to push his criticisms of the French system to their logical conclusion, he had provided a conceptual framework which enabled others to do so. His ideas were to have a considerable impact on the concept of political virtue for the rest of the eighteenth century.[43] People accepted both his argument that the republic of virtue constituted the political ideal, and his conclusion that it was impracticable. Most commentators, including Rousseau, accepted Montesquieu's premise that France could not be a republic because they agreed with his definition of what a 'republic' was, and with his definition of political virtue.[44] Montesquieu's ideas continued to be used as a conceptual framework even after the setting up of the first French Republic, and by those who rejected his moderate conclusions.

New ideas of social virtue and *bienfaisance* in the 1740s

Although Diderot, Toussaint and Montesquieu each had a marked influence on the concept of political virtue, they were themselves part of a wider ferment of ideas which was intensifying in the 1740s. The ideas of civic virtue and of natural virtue, with their different intellectual roots but with many points of communion between them, provided a framework for rethinking the relationship between the individual and society, and the role of morality in political thought. Both these concepts could be incorporated into the argument that the highest form of virtue was political. But there were important differences between them. Civic virtue was no less terrible than it was pure, existing on so high a plane of moral abstraction that it was scarcely possible to breathe there. Even Montesquieu, who saw the ancient republic as the political ideal, confirmed that the idea of putting the 'public good' even before that of those people to whom one was closest could appear 'atrocious' rather than virtuous. Moreover, accounts of the 'ancient peoples' who had lived according to the dictates of civic virtue appeared to emphasise quite repellent aspects of their societies. For many eighteenth-century thinkers the Spartans in particular, but also to some extent the Romans, had been unacceptably belligerent, barbaric and brutal. Their principles of equality only extended to those men who came within the narrow definition of the *patrie*. Their women were relegated to being second-class citizens whose civic function was to produce children – though admittedly many eighteenth-century men did not consider this to be a problem. Far more troubling for most of them was the idea that other peoples, outside the *patrie*, could legitimately be killed or enslaved. The debate on the merits and demerits of the ancients was one to which eighteenth-century writers constantly returned.

Whilst classical republicanism offered the most overtly political language of virtue, it was by no means the only route to the idea of virtuous citizenship. The idea of natural virtue also had political dimensions. For example, writers who were repelled by the harsh political and social organisation of the Spartans might turn instead to the societies of 'noble savages' far from Europe's Old World legacy of Christianity or classicism. The belief that so-called primitive peoples had qualities long since lost by 'corrupted' and decadent Europeans had begun to take hold within a relatively short period after the discovery of the New World. One of the first works to suggest this had been Montaigne's account of the South American cannibals in 1580. By the mid-eighteenth century the argument that primitive peoples were more virtuous than Europeans was playing a polemical role as it fed into controversies on the derivation of human nature, and the political and social organisation of European societies.

For other writers the path to political virtue lay through inner awareness or sensibility. A succession of authors developed the sensationalist arguments derived from Locke, and taken up by Shaftesbury and others. One of these was the marquis de Vauvenargues, who had given up a military career in order to become a 'man of letters', quarrelling with his family in the process. Shyness and long sickness seem to have kept him lonely and isolated from the milieu of the *philosophes*, except for Voltaire who greatly encouraged him. He died young, in 1747, but not before having explored a number of the ideas that would later reach their zenith with the cult of sensibility. For Vauvenargues, the highest form of virtue was political or public virtue: 'The preference for the general interest over one's personal interest is the only definition which is worthy of virtue, and which has the right to fix our ideas about it; by contrast, the mercenary sacrifice of the public happiness to one's own self-interest is the eternal mark of vice.'[45] The basis of such virtue was 'sentiment', which one felt in one's heart, and which stemmed from God. Some years before Rousseau did so, Vauvenargues rejected the world of the salon as essentially false because it turned people from virtue. Of La Rochefoucauld's *Maxims*, that bible of the ethics of the salon, Vauvenargues wrote:

> Whatever his intentions may have been, the effect to me appears to have been pernicious; his book, which is full of delicate invectives against hypocrisy, even now turns men away from virtue, by persuading them that there is no true virtue.[46]

The *philosophe* and novelist Duclos agreed that our knowledge of the world and of virtue stemmed from sensibility or heightened awareness. In the *Considérations sur les mœurs de ce siècle* (1750), he stated that 'sensibility prepares the ground for the virtuous man'.[47] He claimed that, rather than reason, the best judge of morality was 'the internal sentiment which we call the conscience'.[48] The essence of virtue, however, lay not only in the perception of what was morally good, but in acting to promote the good of others. He contrasted 'probity', or moral uprightness, with 'virtue' which stemmed from 'sensibility'. Probity consisted in obedience to the laws and to the moral codes of society. A man of probity could do nothing and yet remain within the boundaries set out by laws. The man of virtue provided a striking contrast: 'Probity consists almost in inertia: but virtue is active'; it was not enough for him to feel sympathy with the plight of his neighbour: he would do whatever he could to help them. Virtue was 'a sentiment, an inclination towards good, a love of humanity'.[49] Although it stemmed from feelings of sympathy for others, it still required an effort over oneself, over one's natural inertia and self-interest, to achieve it:

> *Do not do to others that which you would not want them to do to you,* the exact and precise observation of this maxim makes for probity. *Do those things for other people which you would want to be done for you,* that makes for virtue. Its nature, its distinctive character stems from making an effort to put the well-being of others before your own self.[50]

Honour, on the other hand, was different from either probity or virtue. It emphasised self and social eminence: 'The man of honour thinks and feels as a noble. It is not the laws that shape his conduct; nor is it reflection, still less imitation, that guides him: he thinks, he speaks and acts with a kind of haughtiness, and appears to be a law unto himself.'[51]

Duclos's concern to define virtue in terms of action indicates one of the most politicising factors in the new understanding of virtue. No longer contemplative, as was the seventeenth-century ideal, the new concept of morality envisaged humanity as a fellowship, in which each member recognised their dependency on the others. Virtue was seen as a moral obligation to put right social ills. This brought it into intimate contact with another very important concept which had recently come into common parlance.

This was the idea of *bienfaisance*, which meant the act of doing good to others. Its literal English translation is 'beneficence' but that word was only rarely used in the English language, whereas the French developed a virtual cult of *bienfaisance*.[52] A more familiar English equivalent was 'philanthropy', although this term did not really take hold until the end of the eighteenth century. Shaftesbury himself had consistently used the term 'benevolence' to signify the natural goodwill which each individual feels towards their fellows. But the French term *bienfaisance* was more forceful than 'benevolence' since it put its emphasis on action rather than on sympathy alone. *Bienfaisance* appears to have been a relatively new word to come into common usage in the eighteenth century, probably adapted from *'bienfaits'* which meant 'good deeds', or 'kindnesses'.

It had first come to prominence earlier in the century through the writings of the abbé de Saint-Pierre.[53] He used it to denote an active sense of fellow-feeling which was expressed in the form of tangible generosity towards the less fortunate. *Bienfaisance* emphasised love of man, whereas traditional notions of charity had emphasised love of God.

The person who was *bienfaisant*, like the possessor of natural virtue, was explicitly contrasted with the seventeenth-century ideal of the *honnête homme*. The *honnête homme* dispensed charity to the poor, but he did so because it was his duty to love his neighbour and because the Church required it of him for his own salvation. In that sense his charity was a selfish and calculating act, designed to procure God's indulgence for his soul, rather than a selfless act of generosity towards his neighbour. Indeed, the *honnête homme* was advised to be wary of excessive generosity which might endanger the souls of the poor, who were believed to be morally weak and prone to corruption, and whose lives, anyway, could not be tangibly improved: they are always with us. On the other hand, *bienfaisance* implied sympathy for the 'unfortunate' (*les malheureux*) or indigent, who were not presented as social or moral inferiors, but as equals and fellow citizens, brought low by exterior misfortune. It was a revolutionary idea, which required a new vocabulary. In the 'Avertissement' to *Un Projet pour perfectionner l'Education*, the abbé de Saint-Pierre had explained that in coining this word he was consciously bringing about a new vocabulary in order to expound and justify a new set of ideas. The words 'love' and 'charity towards one's neighbour' do not, he said, have the same connotations as *bienfaisance*:

In this work I have used the term *bienfaisance*, which I believe to be either a new word or a renewed one, and I am using it for reasons which I explained in a discourse on the perfectioning of languages, namely that new words are formed when they are needed, either to make one's meaning clearer, or to indicate certain changes in our sentiments that other words cannot express with the same clarity or the same precision. We have no word in our language to express precisely the meaning of the action of the *bienfaisant* man, the action of doing good, to give pleasure to others, to work for the benefit of other men.[54]

Bienfaisance, or the desire to do good, came to be seen as a virtue, linked directly to sensibility. It was believed to stem from the happiness which doing good gave to the giver. It was an emotional rather than a calculated response to the spectacle of the misery of others, and as such was believed to be surer, and more genuine than the tradition of alms-giving to the poor. But the status of *bienfaisance* in the hierarchy of virtues was open to some debate. Duclos, for example, whilst he stressed the importance of acting virtuously, added that the true extent of some-one's virtue could only be known if one also knew what their material circumstances were. Since it was much harder to be poor and virtuous, there was greater merit in a poor person being virtuous than a wealthy person. 'A poor unfortunate... beset by need... humiliated by want', who resists 'the greatest temptations' was, for Duclos, more worthy of admiration than 'a prosperous man' who freely does good for the unfor-tunate. Both of them merited praise, but it was the 'poor unfortunate' who showed 'virtue'.[55] It was a point to which writers would frequently return.

The idea that sensibility was a guide to virtue had taken root in the writings of Duclos, Vauvenargues and others, well before the eloquence of Rousseau burst onto the horizon. Virtue could be sensed by 'the heart', which could prove a surer guide even than 'reason'. The feelings or passions, providing that they were uncorrupted by artificial social values, were depicted as good qualities. Women were often depicted as being closer to virtue than men, for their sensibility was argued by many to be less likely to be led astray by the sexual impulses which under-mined the virtue of men. Echoing Shaftesbury, virtue came to be seen as a characteristic which sprang from natural sociability and fellow-feeling. Natural virtue was, therefore, more than a matter of individual morality, it was also fundamentally a social quality, and dictated the means whereby society might be better organised. In thinking socially, the devotees of natural virtue were already very close to thinking politically if, by 'political', was meant ways in which society might be made to function better for the benefit of its members.[56] The *philosophes* did not have the argument for virtue all their own way, however, nor did the significance of the link between virtue and politics go altogether un-noticed or unchallenged. The legitimacy of a politics of virtue rested on the transparency of that virtue. If that was in doubt then the entire argu-ment would be in danger of collapse. As one hostile critic wrote: 'As it is common enough to confuse... misdeeds and bad faith, with politics. So also politics is often indistinguishable from the spirit of libertinism and debauchery.... There is no vice which does not ape one of the virtues.'[57]

The emphasis on virtue as abnegation of self was not the only alternative available. The writings of Mandeville (whose *Fable of the Bees* was translated into French in 1740) were influential with some of the *philosophes*, most notably Voltaire. Mandeville had inverted the arguments of Shaftesbury, and taken a diametrically-opposed view of human nature. He argued that human nature was self-interested, but that this did not matter, since private vices (or the pursuit of self-interest) could lead to public virtues. Although he couched his arguments in terms of vice and virtue, it is clear that for him the realities of politics or of economic growth cannot be explained in terms of morality; the vocabulary of virtue was ultimately an irrelevance. Nevertheless, the social consequences which Mandeville predicted were not so different from those of Shaftesbury. Whether people acted virtuously from altruistic motives, or inadvertently, in the course of the pursuit of their own interests, society as a whole would be the beneficiary.[58]

Mandeville's ideas had many precedents: similar ideas had reached France through the work of Jansenists such as père Nicole, for whom 'self-love' (*l'amour-propre*) served the public good in spite of itself. But Mandeville's pragmatic approach never achieved the kind of purchase in French thought that it had in Britain. Many commentators found his cynicism unacceptable, deploring the way in which it seemed to provide an insidious justification for vice. Vauvenargues put the contrasting point of view that if people acted virtuously out of self-love, this was because such actions gave them happiness. Arguing that the desire for virtue was an innate sense, he claimed that such happiness was a true, not a fictitious, sensation. God himself had ensured that his creation would act virtuously by implanting in the human heart those feelings of happiness which stemmed from doing good.[59]

The idea of natural virtue also proved acceptable to some members of the clergy, particularly some who took an interest in problems of social morality but who rejected classical republican ideas for their paganism. As far back as Thomas Aquinas a theological interest had existed in natural law in the sense of the natural moral order of the universe and belief in the natural goodness of man inspired by reason. To a number of Catholic theologians (outside the more austere theological traditions of Jansenism) the idea of innate virtue proved both appealing and not incompatible with the tenets of orthodox faith. By 1752 the idea of natural virtue had gained some ascendancy amongst certain members of the Sorbonne, one of whose members, the Irish abbé Hooke, published a treatise on 'Natural and Revealed Religion' in which he argued that virtue was a natural phenomenon, perceived through the senses, whose message is transmitted through the conscience:

> There is a certain sense of right and wrong placed by nature in the minds of men.... We know by conscience that this moral sense is in us, and it would be vain to try to demonstrate it by argument; it is analogous to the intuitive perception of truth which is the basis of all knowledge, or to the sense of taste by which we distinguish foods.... This sense is so natural, so constant and uniform, that it can be stifled by no prejudices and extinguished by no passions; its sacred judgement can be corrupted by no bribes; it lives in the most wicked men, to whom virtue is so pleasing that they involuntarily admire their betters.[60]

The American historian R. R. Palmer gave an intriguing account of this work, although his description of it as being 'warm with the pathetic eloquence of Rousseau' is possibly misleading, since it hardly seems likely that Rousseau (whose only major work at that point had been *Discours sur les sciences et les arts*) could have been a significant influence on Hooke. Rather the abbé drew on a pre-existing body of philosophic ideas which also influenced Rousseau. It was far from unusual for clerics to use a very similar language to that of the *philosophes* to argue that there was a natural form of virtue which could be discovered by reason, or perceived through nature. The difference was that of intention: the *philosophes* were trying to show that revealed religion was unnecessary, the clerics to reinforce the authority of revealed religion by showing that reason and nature concurred with it, that the natural order visible in nature was a confirmation of the moral order articulated by the Church. The fact that Hooke's arguments, made at the Sorbonne, the institution responsible for regulating censorship, appear to have been considered acceptable, suggests that these ideas had already gained a significant foothold at the heart of the *ancien régime*. There were, however, tacit codes as to how far such ideas could go, or to how far they could be *seen* to go.

Hooke's book was composed in Latin, for the purpose of training the priesthood: its circle of influence was understood to be a narrow one, its destined readership not one which would be expected to be in danger of corruption from the implications of natural virtue. It was a different matter, however, when Hooke became implicated in the scandal of the Prades Affair. This was the occasion when it became known that the abbé Prades, a friend of Diderot's, had somehow had a thesis which was clearly inspired, if not written, by the *Encyclopédistes*, passed at the Sorbonne in November 1751. Prades's panel of examiners had been presided over by Hooke, who found himself dismissed from his chair of theology. Although subsequently reinstated, he never regained the confidence of the archbishop of Paris, Christophe de Beaumont, a man emphatically opposed to *philosophic* principles.

Virtue in the new novels of sensibility

It was not only in the hallowed halls of the Sorbonne that such ideas were mooted. A far more general appeal than that of rather dry Latin works on theology was exerted by the novels of sensibility with their ceaseless explorations of the rewards and vicissitudes of virtue. Such novels gripped readers through their attention to human psychology and the analysis of feelings and motivation. Although the vogue for such novels did not reach its peak until after the mid-eighteenth century, early examples had been appearing since the 1690s. During the 1730s and 1740s the theme of sensibility and of virtue was treated in a succession of novels by Marivaux, Duclos, Crébillon *fils*, and Prévost.[61] The novel form was frequently attacked for its frivolity and incitement to immorality. These attacks culminated with the scathing condemnation of the novel form given in 1755 in the *Entretien sur les romans* by the abbé Jacquin, who argued that novels confused vice and virtue and endorsed libertinism. Authors responded to such attacks by defending their works on the grounds that they educated their readership in good conduct.[62] Notwithstanding, the lessons they gave were often morally ambiguous, especially in the pre-Richardson era. In *Manon Lescaut* (1731), for example, Prévost's claim in his preface to the book that it would teach virtue was not necessarily to be taken at face value. The story itself, of des Grieux's headlong pursuit of Manon and her headlong pursuit of luxury, hardly offered edifying models of virtue. Des Grieux engages in gambling, deception and even murder, whilst Manon's feelings for him do not prevent her from taking wealthy lovers. Manon's death in the wilds of America and des Grieux's despair could be seen as a cautionary tale, but the two characters achieve a kind of grandeur in their obsession with passion and each other which gives depth of characterisation, but render the 'moral lesson' decidedly ambiguous. Ironically, their worldly vice and self-centredness meet with reasonable success, and it is only when, as des Grieux says, they 'began to return to virtue' by seeking to marry and thus to obtain God's pardon, that disaster strikes them.

In other early French 'sensibility' novels, virtue was an important theme, but it was one quality amongst others, and not necessarily the strongest. In Marivaux's *La Vie de Marianne* (1731–41) the heroine's vicissitudes are those of virtue. Marianne is originally of good birth, but has lost her social status, thus making her a prey for would-be corrupters. Her trials are handled with a humour and a lightness of touch often lacking in later full-blooded 'sensibility' literature. Although there is no doubt of her fundamental moral integrity, her virtue is not of the austere type. As a woman who must make her way in polite society through her own resources she is not averse to applying a little judicious coquetry, and she becomes adept at 'reading' the codes of high society and moulding her own behaviour in accordance with social expectations in order to make herself acceptable. Marianne's path to success did not prove easy, for her lover, Valville, proved unfaithful. But we presume that virtue was to triumph in the end, since Marianne recounts the tale when she is in middle age, by which time she has become a countess and consequently a social success. Marivaux, however, had lost interest and left her in mid-trauma – from which she was only rescued many years later when Madame Riccoboni wrote an ending to the story.

Many novels were composed of a curious mixture of 'sensibility' and 'libertinism'. The portraits of vice were not necessarily incompatible with the teaching of morality. What better way, it was said, could there be of showing the subtle traps laid by the morally corrupt than by unfolding the true sentiments and motives of the libertine? The letter form in the novel provided the means whereby the reader could 'see' into the mind of both the libertine and the virtuous woman whom he sought to make his victim, and were thus precursors of those notorious libertines, Lovelace and Valmont. Crébillon *fils* wrote many 'libertine' novels which dealt with the psychology of love affairs, of which *Les Egarements du cœur et de l'esprit* (1736) came closest to being a novel of 'sensibility'. The avowed intention was to guide readers towards the right moral path by showing the dreadful consequences of following the route of libertinism. But this tactic did not necessarily succeed in the way it was supposed to do. The morals of these tales were frequently ambiguous: the danger was, as ever, that vice would appear more seductive than virtue, which, if not handled very carefully by the author, could easily appear dull, if not hypocritical. Crébillon himself was not above enjoying the effect of his own reputation as something of a libertine, even though he took the moral lessons of his novels very seriously, and appears in fact to have led a life of fairly regular morality.

The preface of *Les Egarements* set out the form which Crébillon intended to give to the novel. It was to have three stages: the seduction of the ingenuous young hero by an experienced older woman; his subsequent lapse into dissipation and social hypocrisy; and his ultimate reform into virtue, brought about by an 'estimable woman'. Despite these worthy intentions, Crébillon never got further than the first stage, and never wrote his moral ending.[63] Perhaps he found writing about vice easier and more pleasurable than writing about virtue.

Duclos in his early life had the reputation of being a libertine. He was the son of a wealthy hat manufacturer from Dinan. His widowed mother had sent him to Paris for his education, where he seems to have spent an inordinate amount of time engaged in debauchery learned from the nobles' sons with whom he mixed, and squandering the money his mother had set aside for him to study for the solid bourgeois occupation of advocate. Yet, as he grew older and was drawn into the circle of the *philosophes*, virtue became a veritable 'obsession' with him. His novels combined a jaded and cynical libertinism typical of the Regency period with a restless search for something more meaningful in life. In *Confessions du comte de* *** (1742), Madame de Selve, is a woman of virtue who finally reforms the errant comte, who sickens of the monotony of dissipation and learns from her the value of true sensibility and virtue. It is notable that Madame de Selve's status as a woman of virtue is not challenged by Duclos, even though she and the comte have been lovers. The woman of virtue was usually chaste, but this was not invariably the case, especially in the earlier French novels, although the English were inclined to take a far less flexible view.

But the full torrent of sensibility broke over France with the translation of the novels of Richardson. *Pamela; or Virtue Rewarded* (1740–1), *Clarissa* (1747–8, and translated by Prévost as *Clarissa Harlowe* in 1751) and *Sir Charles Grandison* (1753–4) generated an immense vogue for literary explorations of sensibility and virtue.[64] Richardson exploited the potential of the novel as a way of working out the implications of Locke, Shaftesbury and Hutcheson, whose *An Enquiry into the Origin of Our Ideas of Beauty and Virtue* (1725) tightened the links between virtue and benevolence and was translated into French in 1749. In the works of Richardson, the novels of sensibility assumed their classic form, which served as a model for many others. In these models the link between sensibility and virtue was made explicit. Virtue was personified in the form of a young woman, Pamela or Clarissa, or, and notably less successfully, in a man, Sir Charles Grandison. Typically, the virtuous heroine was of lower class and status or reduced circumstances, without the protection of male relatives, and was pitted against vice, which generally came in the form of men of high status and power, often nobles, almost invariably wealthy. In novels, the power of the man of vice was not equal to that of the woman of virtue. Pamela herself was of course the epitome of virtue rewarded. But Richardson felt uneasy at the simplistic – and highly unlikely – conclusion to Pamela's sufferings, and *Clarissa* presented the darker side of virtue. Clarissa also triumphs finally over the vice of her social superior, but her 'victory' is achieved at the cost of her life, which is the only way in which she can 'vindicate' her virtue following her rape by Lovelace. This was not 'virtue rewarded' but 'virtue as sacrifice'. It is the virtuous woman who, Christ-like, pays and atones for the sins of all, forgiving those who have done most to harm her and by her death, the ultimate sacrifice, transfigures the lives of those people who had known her. The concept of virtue put forward in such novels was not without inherent ambiguities: the inner purity of the heroines might well be open to doubt. Sceptical readers might well imagine that Clarissa's and Pamela's secret responses to the sexual invitations made to them by the men who desired them were otherwise than those they avowed in the seemingly transparent texts. The possibility that the language of virtuous sensibility was open to hypocritical exploitation was perfectly apparent to contemporaries such as Fielding, who showed that *Pamela* lent itself readily to satire. But ultimate uncertainty about the authenticity of virtue did not negate its value, but served to give the rhetoric added dimensions. Such novels invited readers to engage in a constant process of self-questioning and examination, as they sought to establish the true feelings, not only of fictional characters, but of themselves.

But what, one might ask, could such novels have to do with politics? They were not about political ideas in any straightforward sense: they were first and foremost stories of individuals in which the normal real-life outcome of an encounter between a privileged male and a lower-status female without male protection was reversed. But they did proffer a particular kind of vision of society. From Pamela, Clarissa and their many successors, readers could absorb the idea that virtue was not the prerogative of the aristocratic and wealthy. People of lower status, even well-read servants of the same class as Pamela, might think of themselves as morally equal to the most privileged orders. Such novels helped to impart a sense of pride and self-worth to readers who were, or felt themselves to be, social outsiders (as Richardson had been) as they sympathised with the sufferings of the virtuous and weak. But again, it would be difficult to see the social effect of novels of sensibility in explicitly class terms, as a 'victory' for the bourgeoisie. Many of the most avid readers of such stories were themselves from the aristocratic classes. The literature of sensibility involved a suspension of disbelief, but this did not mean that society's rules genuinely changed: far from it. It would be most unlikely that the wealthy readers of *Pamela* would actually have welcomed a servant girl, be she ever so virtuous, into the family.

Richardson's novels inspired several generations of French writers. Some writers would draw only on the 'virtue as suffering' theme, and produced their own versions of the somewhat salacious idea of the virtuous woman under sexual threat from the plotting libertine. For others, the positive moral doctrine assumed greater importance. Diderot's *Eloge de Richardson* (written in 1761 after Richardson's death, although Diderot had long been familiar with his work) enthused over the moral impact of Richardson, which, he said, was intensified by its emotion, which acted almost like a conductor of the electrical current of virtue, imprinting its image on the mind of the reader. He too was not immune to the suppressed sexual undercurrents eddying through Richardson's novels, and the added *frisson* which these gave to the overt moral purpose.[65] But for Diderot the growing self-awareness expressed through the literature of sensibility contributed to the notion of the moral autonomy and integrity of individuals, who were entitled to make moral decisions by referring to their own consciences rather than to the precepts of others.

By the late 1740s all the major elements of the political vocabulary of virtue which were to be at the disposal of the revolutionary generation had already been formulated. Montesquieu, Toussaint and Diderot had led the way in establishing a new preeminence for the rhetoric of virtue. They used ideas taken and adapted from such sources as classical antiquity, natural law theory and the theorists of the English Enlightenment to formulate arguments that put virtue at the centre of the moral basis of political and social relations. Montesquieu gave new dimensions to the classical republican idea that, in the highest form of political organisation, those who engaged in politics should be led by virtue. He was also partly responsible for the increasing distinction that was made between the concepts of 'honour' and 'virtue'.

Equally important was the discourse of natural and sociable virtue, which was brought to the French reading public in the first instance by the efforts of Diderot and of Toussaint. Shaftesbury had put forward the idea that true happiness came in helping others; an idea that was to be further refined by, amongst others, the abbé de Saint-Pierre and Duclos into the identification of 'virtue' with *bienfaisance*. The idea that ordinary people are capable of virtuous sentiments and actions, even more so than the 'great' since they are less liable to the corruption of wealth and status, was to have an extraordinary impact on the polemical power of the concept of virtue during the second half of the eighteenth century. It spilled over into popular literature of the day, thereby reaching a wider audience, including perhaps many readers who preferred novels to dry political treatises. Like Montesquieu's concept of virtue, the discourse of natural virtue also differentiated between virtue and honour. This new discourse was not political in the sense that the classical republican version of civic virtue was political. It was concerned far more broadly with the question of individual human relations in a social context. But it had significant political ramifications in that the virtue attributed to ordinary people gave a voice to those who hitherto had been voiceless. Virtue gave people the right to have opinions on matters of public concern, and to participate in the public good. The language of virtue made people into rhetorical citizens long before the Revolution gave them the actual political rights as citizens.

3
Virtue and Radical Political Theory: Rousseau and Mably

> *from then on I became virtuous, or at least intoxicated with virtue.*
> *This intoxication had begun in my head, but it had passed into my*
> *heart. . . . I did not play act at all; I became in effect what I appeared*
> *to be. . . . That is the origin of my sudden eloquence; the origin of this*
> *truly celestial fire that devoured me and inspired my first books.*
>
> J.-J. Rousseau, describing his conversion to virtue,
> *Confessions*, Book IX

It was in the heady speculative atmosphere of the late 1740s that Rousseau began to formulate the ideas which would lead to his acquiring his reputation as the most profound and articulate spokesman for virtue of the eighteenth century. Far more is known about Rousseau's extraordinary contribution to the rise of virtue than that of any other writer. Important though he undoubtedly was in this respect, he may have been given rather more credit than he deserved for the originality of his concept. In order to understand what virtue meant to Rousseau his ideas must be situated in the context of those wider ways of thinking about politics and society which influenced him. So close has been the identification between Rousseau and virtue that it is not uncommon to see political virtue referred to in historical studies as 'Rousseau's' concept of virtue, as though the idea began and ended with himself – a misconception which Rousseau himself did much to encourage. Blum, for example, in her study on *Rousseau and the Republic of Virtue*, claimed that it was Rousseau himself who 'forged the vocabulary of this new virtue' which replaced the earlier idea of virtue held by Louis XIV.[1] But the process involved was rather more complex than this would suggest. Rousseau seized upon a vocabulary which had already been forged in many different fires. In his writings he brought together pre-existing concepts of virtue, juxtaposing them to create new angles, reformulating them, and giving them his own distinctive slant. His original contributions must be acknowledged, but so too must the existence of an entire vocabulary of interconnected ideas about virtue which formed a common currency of intellectual thought pre-dating Rousseau's writings.

We need, therefore, to establish the parameters of Rousseau's specific contribution to the politics of virtue. The precise extent to which Rousseau was influenced by other thinkers is difficult to ascertain, partly because of the autodidactic nature of his education, but also because he himself was somewhat selective in admitting to his intellectual debts. In formulating his concept of virtue Rousseau drew on a number of well-established ideas: on the traditions of classical republicanism (one of his earliest and most vivid influences was Plutarch's *Lives*); on Montesquieu's refashioning of civic virtue as the basis of the ideal form of government; on natural law theory and ideas on the basis of sovereignty; on the growing literature of sensibility; on Jansenist theologians and their characteristic suspicion of virtue as disguised 'self-love'; as well as lingering echoes of the Calvinism of his native Geneva. All this, of course, as well as his debt to his close friends and associates of the later 1740s and early 1750s, those who gathered around the project of the *Encyclopédie*, including Diderot and Toussaint, whose attempts to popularise the idea of an innate and secular concept of virtue we have already considered.[2] So close was the friendship and cooperation between Diderot and Rousseau during the early years of their association that it is difficult to be sure who exactly was influencing whom. Certainly Diderot encouraged Rousseau to be outspoken about ideas which they shared – such as aspects of the *Discours sur l'inégalité* – but it seems also that Rousseau at that time positively enjoyed the controversy he provoked and was prepared to go further than Diderot considered either sensible or prudent.[3]

Rousseau drew freely on this network of ideas and language in order to construct a political perspective which had virtue at its heart.[4] His own contribution was particularly vital in three ways. First, he made explicit the politically radical and egalitarian implications of virtue. Secondly, by his self-conscious mode of life, modelled on what he believed to be virtuous principles, he did much to encourage the development of a cult of virtue. Thirdly, he brought together ideas about virtue from disparate sources and bound them together in his own uniquely personal vision. He, more than anyone else, brought together the discourses of civic virtue and of sensibility so that they converged in a common stream.

His more literary works, *La Nouvelle Héloïse*, and the semi-fictional treatise on education, *Emile*, were as inspiring on the subject of virtue as were his political treatises – and much more widely read. It was his *Confessions* which were to inspire a cult, a positive passion, for virtue and truth amongst his many readers. These works were engaging on an emotional as well as a philosophical level; many people read them who perhaps would not have been attracted to more abstract political treatises, and from their reading came to identify with Rousseau. It was from Rousseau that they knew virtue.

The nature of Rousseau's influence on his contemporaries and the subsequent generation is incalculable. The intensity with which he expressed this personal vision was both powerful and problematic. Few of his contemporaries were quite so inconsistent as Rousseau, especially on the subject of women. But for most of his readers this did not much matter: they were carried along on the waves of his prose, and though they might reject some of his specific ideas they identified with his aims as a whole. Even though he himself grew increasingly paranoid and at times almost unbalanced, not one of his contemporaries was able to strike up a more personal and intense rapport with his readers. It was his very single-mindedness, that blazing heat in which he wrote, which made the writer in him so expressive of much of what his contemporaries also felt, and which he articulated for them. He was prepared to communicate with his readers, to 'bare his soul' as it were, in a way that no one else could, or was prepared to do. His autobiography as he composed it in the *Confessions*, with all its shameful and pathetic revelations, became also the record of a life vindicated, a life made worth living, by virtue. His readers felt that he spoke for them, articulated what they had felt about themselves and their relationship to the world: they too had had failures in life and had fallen short of being what they wanted to be and to do, but they too could be transfigured by virtue.

This powerful eloquence gives rise to a singular difficulty when assessing the political influence of Rousseau. His enormous popularity was due largely to his most personal works, to *Emile* and to *La Nouvelle Héloïse*, rather than to his overtly political writings. Many scholars have commented on the fact that the *Contrat social* was not widely read until the Revolution.[5] This does not mean that he had no political influence, for Rousseau's readers could learn his political ideas from his other writings. His was not a 'revolutionary' politics: Rousseau himself was no advocate of violent revolution. His visions of a better society were not intended for France, but for small countries where republics already existed. Prior to the Revolution, the impact of his political ideas operated mostly on a diffuse and vague level. His readers could, if they wished, ignore the radical and egalitarian side of Rousseau, and many did so. What they took up from Rousseau was the importance of conscience as a guide to virtue; the self-worth of the individual; the potential of education for the fashioning of the virtuous citizen. They turned to Montesquieu, even to Mably, to derive the formulas for a specific politics of virtue. As we have seen, even Robespierre, who owed so much on the level of emotional identification to Rousseau, fell back on Montesquieu's classic framework when describing the political role of virtue in revolutionary government.

It is this rapport between himself and his readership which makes the personal side of Rousseau, present in all his writings, but especially in the self-revelatory *Confessions*, so important to an understanding of the impact of his concept of virtue. The language of virtue had an intense and personal meaning for Rousseau. He encouraged emotional identification with virtue, and saw the common man as closer to virtue than the rich, who had become more alienated from their true selves by the false values of wealth and social status. For Rousseau virtue represented a reconciliation with his inmost self, his 'true nature'.[6] Virtue was more than a system of politics, it was a means of fusion with other minds, a fusion which is expressed in the lyrical descriptions of the community at Clarens in *La Nouvelle Héloïse*, and in the country retreat described in *Emile*. Here was the counterpart to the seemingly rather remote Spartan utopia of the *Contrat social*. In Rousseau's mind both utopias (natural rural idyll and classical republic) served a similar purpose, to express the yearning to belong, to be part of a community in which one could be truly oneself.[7] Paradoxically, the physically timid Rousseau who in his own life abhorred both violence and collective discipline idealised the military virtue of the Spartans, and was attracted by the ideal of community and of a moral order. The virtuous community was one where a man might feel whole once more, where he might truly live in harmony both with his inner self and with his fellows. It was the idealised counterpart to the real world of the adult with its disappointments and failing inspirations. Since his youth, Rousseau confided, he had felt 'half dead'.[8] The path of virtue was the route by means of which he attempted to regain that childhood sense of life, purpose and oneness with the world; and as he successively lost his actual friends the 'companions' in his mind assumed yet greater importance for him. He was not the first to yearn for a community of minds guided only by virtue, but no one else was so single-minded about it, so stubborn and so articulate.

Much has been written about Rousseau's complex relationship with the Enlightenment – both with its overall values and with individual *philosophes*. Certainly Rousseau came to see the Enlightenment ultimately as inimical to virtue, but this was not so much because his theoretical conception of virtue differed markedly from that of his contemporaries as because he was so famously to choose to live his life in accordance with these principles: a piece of self-righteousness (and strongly implied criticism of themselves) which his erstwhile friends would never forgive. For most people the distinction between the literary flights of the rhetoric of virtue and the way in which life was actually lived was unspoken but clearly understood. Other writers might enthuse over *Pamela*, but they did not live openly with a woman of the servant class as Rousseau did, although certainly the real-life Thérèse was no educated, cultivated Pamela, and Rousseau's reasons for living with her were far from being based on theoretical principles alone. Rousseau's contemporaries and friends might deplore the idea of patronage and venality as inimical to virtue, but it formed part of the very structure by which they earned their living and secured their careers. Only Rousseau would turn down an invitation to meet the king and decline to receive a pension from him; the former out of timidity and embarrassment, as he later said, the latter out of the desire to preserve his independence. Diderot was appalled: he was a practical man, and tried to tell Rousseau that one had, after all, to live and to support one's family. Whatever Rousseau was, he certainly was not practical. It may well have been of Rousseau's obstinacy that Diderot was thinking some years later when in *Le Neveu de Rameau* he had the opportunist and unscrupulous nephew declare: 'We praise virtue, but we hate it, we flee from it, because it freezes you like ice, and in this world what is needed is warm feet.'[9] Rousseau would take a quite different path, at first by developing his criticism of current social and political values, and later, by his attempts to construct a new set of moral precepts by which people might live.

Rousseau's *Discourses*

The definitive nature of the break which Rousseau eventually made with his fellow *philosophes* has tended to obscure the extent of the common ground they had once shared. Diderot and Rousseau in particular had far more in common on the subject of virtue than Rousseau later liked to avow. It was on the road to Vincennes to visit Diderot languishing in his imprisonment, that Rousseau experienced the revelation which was to change his life. He 'saw another universe and became another man', sending him into a fever for 'truth, liberty and virtue' which, he declared, for several years affected him 'as powerfully perhaps as it has ever worked in the heart of any man'.[10] It was Diderot then who encouraged him to publish his ideas and gave him confidence.

The first product of that inspiration was the *Discours sur les sciences et les arts*, which was a curious mixture of familiar themes and startling conclusions. Although Rousseau studiously avoided speaking of God in this text, his opposition to progress in the arts and sciences as inimical to human society recalled in many ways the arguments of the Church fathers against commerce and progress and the ways in which they fragmented communities and set people against each other in competition. His argument was based on the defence of two ideals: humanity as an integrated community, and virtue, by which he meant devotion to that community. These two ideals had been debased by apparent progress in society, which had broken up the human community, setting individuals adrift, with no fixed centre to themselves, no virtue. Virtue had been ousted by false values, by duplicity under the guise of 'politeness'. Modern society was obsessed with appearances, and only imitated virtue: 'We no longer dare appear to be what we really are.'[11] Virtue here signified inner integrity and a unity of self. 'Luxury' (*le luxe*) was the great destroyer of human integrity for it corrupted those who possessed it, made them greedy and divided them from their true selves, 'what will become of virtue, when people want to get rich whatever the consequences? The politicians of the ancient world spoke ceaselessly of morals and of virtue; ours speak only of commerce and money.'[12] In contrast to modern society, Rousseau invoked the rhetoric of both civic and natural virtue. His idealised accounts of the virtues of the ancients with their integrated communities were modelled closely on Plutarch's account of the Spartans as well as on Tacitus' depiction of the German tribes. But he concluded with the argument that virtue was natural and could be perceived through the senses. Its principles were 'engraved in every heart' and in order to understand its laws people had only to 'examine their innermost selves and listen to the voice of their conscience when the passions are silenced'.[13]

The discovery that he had won a prize for this first *Discours* sparked off a further revelation for Rousseau. He decided, as he later wrote, to act on his principles and to live 'free and virtuous'.[14] By the time he wrote the *Discours sur l'origine et les fondements de l'inégalité parmi les hommes* (written in 1754 for the contest of the Academy of Dijon and published the following year) he had developed a much more intense political critique and decided to go to the heart of the question of why inequality existed in modern society, knowing that this was not at all the sort of text that the Academy expected. He decided to account for how the modern system of social values had arisen, by comparing 'man in the state of nature' with 'man in civil society'. Whilst he wrote within the tradition of natural law theory, he was also critical of many aspects of it. He now took up a different position on virtue from that in the *Discours sur les sciences et les arts*. Virtue no longer flowed naturally from the senses, engraved on every heart. Man in a state of nature was not virtuous; he was neither good nor bad. He simply was: he was content to exist and needed nothing beyond the fact of his existence. He was at one with himself, possessing 'love of self', which Rousseau called *amour de soi* to distinguish it from 'self-love' (*l'amour-propre*). He characterised *amour de soi* as a natural valuing of self and desire to preserve oneself. Man in a state of nature avoided his fellows, and lived a solitary life, except for brief moments when men and women came together in order to reproduce. Families therefore did not exist, and so there was no basis for society to develop and no need for social feelings. Consequently natural mankind did not possess fellow-feeling, only a weak sentiment of 'compassion' (*la pitié*). This compassion was the only natural virtue. From this innate quality would stem the social virtues that would come into being with the establishment of civil society. This argument constituted a rejection of many of the basic precepts of natural law theory, which presented man as innately sociable, and especially of Shaftesbury's concept of virtue as a natural and sociable quality. Rousseau's 'natural man' was neither sociable nor virtuous, content to exist only with himself, with no ties or connections.

Society had developed as a result of human greed. Slowly human beings learned language and began to live together as families, and then as larger social groups. From this early social basis came consciousness of difference and subsequent competition. But it was 'iron and corn' which finally brought about the enclosure of land, the acquisition of property, competition, wars and the onset of institutionalised social inequality. The process was one of loss: loss of equality, but above all, loss of self. 'Natural' man had fragmented. He developed civil society in order to defend his property, but in the process he lost himself. In place of *amour de soi* he developed an artificial form of 'self-love' (*l'amour-propre*) which could find its value only in the eyes of others, in appearances. This emphasis on *l'amour-propre* as a quality which undermined the moral health of mankind was much influenced by Jansenist ideas.[15]

For Rousseau, therefore, virtue was not to be found in a state of nature. It was not natural to be virtuous, for virtue was essentially a set of moral values which formed a basis of rules for living in a community. Virtue was intrinsically social and therefore also political in the broad sense that it formed a code for conducting relations between people. Rousseau did not suggest that it was possible to return to a state of nature – although some of his detractors, such as Voltaire, would maliciously attribute to him the idea that people could go 'back to nature'. For Rousseau acknowledged that, for good or ill, civil society could not be uninvented. The only way, therefore, for humanity to live in a better manner together was to devise a political system based on the civil quality of virtue. It would be based on the primitive quality of natural 'compassion' expanded into social virtue.

Rousseau's egalitarian conception of virtue was based on his identification of virtue with natural qualities rather than with 'civility' and 'politeness'. He did not consider that virtue was an attribute to be found in equal measure throughout all members and classes of society. In so far as compassion (natural virtue) existed it was to be found more amongst the lower classes because they were 'closer to nature' than the respectable sections of society. In an image which he later admitted had been devised by Diderot (for the two were still close collaborators at this point), Rousseau described the man of philosophy who stands by and lets someone be murdered in the street below him. His reason tells the philosopher, 'let them die if they want to, I am safe'. By contrast, it is 'the mob' and the 'market-women' who intervene to stop the 'respectable people' (*honnêtes gens*) from cutting each other's throats.[16] Elsewhere, Rousseau's beliefs about the virtues of the poor were sometimes more ambivalent. Usually, in his vocabulary, the virtuous people were the hard-working and honest peasants and artisans, but the most abjectly poor and indigent might be too degraded by their circumstances to be capable of active virtue.[17] In Rousseau's political framework, 'the people' would stand conceptually at the centre and did so on the basis of their greater degree of virtue than that found in the so-called superior classes.

Rousseau and the vicissitudes of virtuous citizenship

The problem for Rousseau was how one could, in the artificial context of society, make both people and politics moral. He thought that this could be achieved only if people were prepared to act according to the 'general will'. Rousseau's conception of virtue was at the heart of his political ideas and was essential to his understanding of the general will. This concept, as Rousseau understood it, echoes in some respects Shaftesbury's notion that true happiness for the individual came from conforming to the 'general interest' of the species, as well as earlier Jansenist political and religious theory.[18] This concept of 'the general interest' based on virtue was a theme of Rousseau's article on 'political economy' for the *Encyclopédie* in 1755, where he defined the 'general will' as the principle of virtue brought into politics: 'Do you want the general will to be accomplished? You must ensure that all the particular wills conform with it; and since virtue is nothing more than this conformity of particular wills with the general, in other words, you establish the reign of virtue.'[19] He added: 'The *patrie* cannot be sustained without liberty, nor liberty without virtue, nor virtue without citizens. You will have everything if you make citizens.'[20] For the 'general will' to be the *general* will, which was a different thing from 'the will of the majority', it must be founded on virtuous citizenship. Where there were no citizens, that is, where people were not willing to put the interests of the community before their own interests, there could be no general will.

In the *Contrat social*, Rousseau went on to work out his system for an ideal form of politics. What mattered to Rousseau was not so much the form of government: it could be a monarchy as well as a republic. Indeed, like many others, his vision of what constituted a republic was based on the classical ideal of the city state, in which direct democracy was a feasible option, and he assumed that France was too large to be an effective republic as he understood the term. What mattered to him was that the political structure was organised on a moral basis, and that the people, the repository of virtue, remained the sovereign body. As has been often remarked, the utopia of the *Contrat social* is a curious mixture of Sparta and the ideal of a fulfilled community, united by authentic feeling. No man had 'natural' authority over another. People came together in civil society in order to defend themselves and preserve their right to liberty and equality by artificial means, through a legal framework. In the *Contrat social* he went beyond traditional natural law theory by claiming not only that sovereignty or 'the body politic' was 'popular' (that is, comprised of the individuals who lived in society), but also that such popular sovereignty was inalienable.[21] The people made a contract to live together in civil society, whereby they formed a sovereign body.[22] This sovereign body was also known as a republic or body politic; its members collectively were termed 'the people', whilst as individuals they were 'citizens'. Although it was the right of the sovereign to take a democratic form of government this was comparatively rare, for a democratic government was felt to be 'too perfect' for men to sustain easily.[23] It was much more common and, in larger countries, more practical for the people to delegate their executive authority to another form of government, whether a monarchy or an aristocracy, to administer the laws and conduct the business of the state. This government, whatever its form, remained an agent of the sovereign, for the sovereignty of the people was inalienable. A government that usurped that power became illegitimate and illegal and the people had the right to bring it down. The goal of government was to preserve as much liberty and equality as was compatible with the rights of others. Thus, the executive authority given to the government could be revoked if the executive power usurped the people's sovereignty and failed to rule according to the 'general will' (that is, the will of the people), which was based on virtue.[24] Rousseau's political edifice thus depended on virtue, which was to sustain the 'general will'.

So much has been said of this work, and of the problems of defining and implementing the 'general will', that it seems almost impossible to reconstitute the impression made by the book when it first appeared. Some political commentators since Rousseau have claimed to see in the *Contrat social* a blueprint for 'totalitarianism', seeing the 'general will' as a formula that could easily be manipulated by unscrupulous politicians who would then dictate what was effectively their own will, in the name of the people. But this is to misunderstand Rousseau's purpose and the context in which he wrote. For him the 'general will' was based on virtue; that is, it was moral, and endorsed by the citizens for the greater good of all. If it was not based on selfless virtue, then it was no longer the general will at all, but a perversion of it. The general will could *only* work if the people had political virtue and the political decisions that they made were genuinely a collective decision made in the public interest. Without political virtue exerted by all the citizens, the 'general will' would be a minority rule and no more than a euphemism for tyranny. For Rousseau, 'anyone who seeks to understand politics and morality separately will never understand anything of either'.[25]

It has often been said that Rousseau's *Contrat Social* illustrates the pitfalls inherent in attempting to mould societies on moral lines. Certainly there were paradoxes here, and dangers of 'stifling liberty in the name of liberty', as Rousseau's contemporaries themselves recognised; but the *Contrat social* was not intended as a blueprint for actual government, Rousseau's concern here was the political ideal, not the practice. The *Contrat social* was a piece of speculation on how the ideal society might be fashioned. It would be moulded on virtue, with no thought to how people might actually have to be managed, and to the problems of effective government. But the assumptions on which the *Contrat social* was based; the centrality of morality in politics; the twin ideals of equality and liberty; the theories of a social contract and of a 'general will', were in themselves not particularly unusual for the political thought of his time. In place of an autocratic form of government, based on absolute monarchy, Rousseau set out the idea of a government in which sovereignty was still absolute, but was based on the people's rights.

Emile was the counterpart to the *Contrat social* in that it dealt with individual rather than collective virtue. As Rousseau said, 'Society must be studied in the individual and the individual in society.'[26] Whereas the *Contrat social* set out to trace a theoretical basis of the ideal form of civil government presupposing that the citizens were already virtuous, in *Emile* Rousseau sought to show how, by the right education, one might create the individual man of virtue. But if the two works need to be understood in relation to one another, the fact that each of them existed negated the possibility of the other ever being more than an abstraction. The social contract could not be forged, nor the 'general will' adhered to, unless the citizens were already virtuous. But Emile cannot be made virtuous within civil society, because it is corrupt. He must be educated outside society, 'close to nature', and only when false values have been expunged from him, so that he is both natural and open to reason, can he be taught virtue. Like the 'chicken and egg' story, a politics of virtue could not be formed unless the individual citizens were already virtuous, but they could not be made virtuous precisely because civil society was corrupt. Together these two models of society and the individual were paradoxical evidence of the elusiveness of a politics of virtue.

According to Rousseau, the process of education was vital in order to cultivate virtue: virtue was not natural but learned. *Emile* was written to show how an education for virtue might be encompassed. In writing it, Rousseau drew on a tradition of educational writing which had the aim of instilling virtue. It was a tradition which stretched back to *Télémaque*. Indeed the connection with *Télémaque* was made explicit by the fact that Fénelon's book is the favourite reading of Sophie, the heroine of *Emile*. And it is no coincidence that she takes Emile at first to be the embodiment of the classical hero with whose image she is in love, because she finds the idea of the virtuous hero overwhelmingly attractive.[27]

The years immediately after the publication of *Emile* in 1762 would also see a growing concern about education for virtuous citizenship in the context of the expulsion of the Jesuits, the principal teaching order, and the consequent need to reconsider the methods and principles of education. *Emile* would therefore have an influence on the beginnings of a renewed debate on education. Its impact was inspirational and wide-ranging. But it was not intended as a feasible framework for some form of state education – indeed, as a blueprint for education it was altogether impracticable. Rather it was a philosophical treatise on the nature and potential of the individual. Readers learnt from it much about the politics of virtue, but this was a politics of virtue conceived for the individual rather than for society as a whole. There were fewer political abstractions in *Emile* (except for the summary of the *Contrat social* which was included in the last section of the work) but there was much about the integrity and value of the virtuous citizen. Most importantly, *Emile* emphasised the message that the poor were as virtuous as the rich. 'All men are equal,' in the eyes of Emile.[28] The 'people' are depicted as rough, and not immediately attractive, but the true observer must learn to look beneath surface appearances to distinguish true virtue. The 'fashionable world' only appears attractive because it has learnt to disguise itself so successfully, with all the trappings of social inequality, conspicuous wealth, artificial rank and status. Emile must learn to 'act in such a way that he is not a member of any class', he must transcend social class and see people as they really are.[29]

The book appears on the face of it to be a defence of the idea of natural virtue; but Rousseau's understanding of virtue was far more subtle. When he actually defines what he means by virtue and the place it must occupy in Emile's education, Rousseau is quite specific. His argument is that Emile, by having been raised close to nature, has not had his natural sentiments quashed and is altogether without the false quality of *amour-propre*. He can learn private morality, but it is only in civil society that Emile can become truly virtuous. Throughout his youth, Emile is kept out of civil society; he learns only the virtues which relate to himself and needs only to go into civil society to learn social virtues.[30] Civil society had this advantage over a state of nature, that here one could learn virtue.[31] Virtue, for Rousseau, remains here, as in the *Discourse on Inequality*, a quality which can only be acquired through civil society.

The account of nature in *Emile* is both contradictory and complex. As has frequently been pointed out, there is much that is far from natural about the way in which Emile is educated. This is particularly apparent in the many instances in which the young Emile is manipulated and deceived by his mentor, who, despite his disclaimers, actually leaves little to genuine nature but constantly intervenes in Emile's upbringing and fashions the child in accordance with his own aims by being constantly present to determine Emile's growing personality. The mentor is also prepared to deceive his pupil on a fundamental basis, as when he leads Emile, all-unknowing, to meet and fall in love with Sophie who has been selected for him as a suitable bride. Emile, now no longer a child, and on the verge of becoming an unruly and headstrong adolescent, is still to be controlled, but now through the medium of his growing sexual emotions. Rousseau's concept of what is 'natural' also differs markedly between the sexes: a distinction which many commentators have remarked upon then and since.[32]

Rousseau differed from Shaftesbury in his denial that virtue was 'natural'. For Rousseau, virtue was an intrinsically social phenomenon which could only be attained in civil society and with a great effort. Nor did virtue bring about happiness as far as Rousseau was concerned: it was only in heaven that virtue would be recompensed and happiness attained.[33] Rousseau, in the vein of Jansenist writers of the seventeenth century, thought that virtue was incompatible with the passions.[34] True virtue meant self-mastery and self-denial, rather than the delicious sensation of succumbing to the emotions. Thus, Emile's education is only completed when, at the end of the book, he learns from his tutor that he must leave his affianced wife and the prospect of a rural idyll shared with her; he must master himself, and venture out into civil society in order to understand what it is to be virtuous:

> there is no happiness without courage, no virtue without a struggle. The word *virtue* comes from the word *strength*, and strength is the foundation of all virtue. Virtue belongs to a being who is weak in nature, and strong in will, it is only in this that the merit of a just man consists; and although we call God good, we do not call him virtuous, because he has no need for effort in order to do good. In order to explain to you this word which has been so profaned, I have waited until you are ready to hear me. Whilst it costs one nothing to be virtuous, one has little need to understand it. This need arises when the passions are wakened....
>
> In bringing you up in all the simplicity of nature...I have made you good rather than virtuous. But he who has nothing but goodness to rely on is only good so long as it gives him pleasure...the man who is only good is only good for himself.

What then is the virtuous man? It is he who knows how to vanquish his own affections; because then he follows his reason, his conscience; he does his duty. . ³⁵

Virtue differed from 'goodness' therefore in that it was a positive quality, involving commitment, and action that benefited others. Nor was virtue necessarily pleasurable. It was a recognition of one's social duty – and duty generally necessitated the denial of natural desires. Diderot in his later works was to stress a similar theme of virtue as a mastery of self and of the emotions.[36] But where Diderot took inspiration in this respect from the traditions of stoicism, Rousseau's ideas were closer to the Christian, particularly Jansenist and Calvinist, theme of distrust of the passions.

So strongly did Rousseau believe that virtue was a matter of complete self-mastery and self-denial of the pleasurable that, like Diderot, as he grew older he came to doubt the possibility of virtue. He even came to doubt the existence of his own virtue, a belief which had sustained him over many years. He was to concede that his own propensity, which was to prefer not to act at all, rather than to follow the line of duty when this conflicted with pleasure, made him incapable of being truly virtuous, 'for there is no virtue in following your inclinations and indulging your taste for doing good just when you feel like it; virtue consists in subordinating your inclinations to the call of duty, and of that I have been less capable than any man living'.[37]

Rousseau's own uncertainties and pessimism did not prevent his name being frequently associated with the idea that virtue was natural, easy to achieve, and led to happiness. Rousseau has often been misunderstood in this respect, both by subsequent commentators and by his admirers and devotees amongst his contemporaries, who often failed to give due weight to the complexity of Rousseau's idea of virtue.[38] Ironically, he was sometimes credited with assumptions about virtue which he had specifically rejected. With yet greater irony, the assumption that virtue was natural, easy and pleasurable was in many respects to exert a wider influence during the 1770s and 1780s than Rousseau's more demanding idea of virtue as the mastery of self and of the passions.

Mably's revolutionary rhetoric

Virtue was also central to the political formulations of the abbé Gabriel Bonnot de Mably (1709–85). Mably is a paradoxical figure. In some ways his radicalism exceeded that of Rousseau – he is often credited with being an ideological precursor of socialist and communist ideas, largely because some of his writings displayed a theoretical hostility to the idea of private property. But, in marked contrast to Rousseau, Mably led a life which, outwardly at least, was relatively tranquil and uneventful. Although he had been educated by Jesuits and took minor religious orders, he gradually moved away from the Church and into the fringes of Enlightenment circles. As the elder brother of Condillac he was acquainted with many of the group around the *Encyclopédie* but he was not a contributor. He defended his privacy and steadfastly refused all public distinctions. He never had either the fame or the notoriety that Rousseau was to achieve – nor did he desire them. He was in his way a respected thinker, and the radicalism of his writings is at odds with the conventional part of his life. His influence on political thought was slower to make itself felt than was that of Rousseau, although his *Entretien de Phocion sur le rapport de la morale avec la politique* was a work of explicitly political theory much respected by certain polemicists, particularly those who moved in *parlementaire* circles. Some of his most radical writings did not appear in print until the French Revolution had already broken out.

From about 1787 onwards Mably's ideas were to find their way into pre-revolutionary and then revolutionary debates via political pamphlets by men of such diverse views as Target, Barnave and Mousnier. But his conception of the relationship between citizenship and morality was to strike its most resounding chord with the more radical revolutionaries of the period of the Republic. A curious story is told of how, at the height of the Jacobin government, one of its most extreme members, Saint-Just, rushed one day into the Committee of Public Safety clutching a copy of Mably's works. He had just read Mably's account of the role of religion in social cohesion, and thought that here was a means whereby the revolutionaries might regenerate society on moral lines.[39] The parallels between Mably's ideas and the Jacobin 'republic of virtue' were striking. Interestingly, this does not seem to suggest that Mably's ideas in any sense *caused* the radicalism of the Year II; rather his writings appeared to offer solutions to problems that revolutionaries were already confronting. His approach mirrored their own in certain ways: both were seeking answers to the problem of how to make virtuous citizens.[40]

Mably's approach to virtue offers some points of comparison with Rousseau's position. Both men used classical-republican conceptions of politics in order to legitimate the notion of democratic participatory politics. They shared the belief that civic equality based on virtue provided the necessary authority for the ideal form of politics. In contrast to Locke and classical natural law theory, neither Mably nor Rousseau thought that property constituted an absolute right, although Mably was prepared to go much further in this respect than Rousseau. This hostility was not based on some anachronistic form of early socialist theory but was due to their belief that excessive property and attachment to property was detrimental to political virtue.

Despite this shared political ground there were significant divergences between the two men's ideas. Mably was much more firmly located within the classical-republican framework of ideas and preoccupations, whereas Rousseau's concerns were wider: for him the themes of social virtue and of sensibility had come to assume as least as much importance as the classical authors. Nevertheless, there were other influences on Mably's political thinking, notably the natural-law theorists. In addition, he was well read in the tradition of republican 'commonwealth' political theory in Britain. His political ideas were also affected by contemporary political debates in France, most notably the successive Jansenist controversies such as the 'billets de confession' struggle of the 1750s.

Despite the extremely democratic nature of Mably's political theory he had no wish to change or subvert society, and he appears to have been alarmed at Rousseau's readiness to openly challenge received notions of politics and religion. This tension came to a head in 1765 when Rousseau heard a rumour that Mably had criticised his *Letters from the Mountain*. Rousseau, feeling betrayed and incredulous, wrote to Mably expressing disbelief in the story, but Mably made no attempt to deny what he had done. He was uneasy at the way Rousseau seemed to be prepared to confront social conventions head on. He did have some sympathy for Rousseau and compared him to the martyred Socrates, but pointed out that Socrates had not attempted to revenge himself on the Athenians by arousing sedition amongst them.[41]

It is hard to be certain how far Mably and Rousseau directly influenced each other's ideas, although it is probable that Rousseau had more impact on Mably than *vice versa*. They were certainly on visiting terms with each other from as early as 1741 and were well-acquainted during their formative years.[42] Mably in his later works had the benefit of Rousseau's major writings and these probably constituted a significant influence. But it is notable that his political treatise *Des Droits et des devoirs du citoyen* was written in 1758, some years before *Emile*, or the *Contrat social*. Although conclusive evidence of direct influence is hard to ascertain, they appear to have pooled some ideas, particularly on the question of the government of Poland. They certainly shared a deep enthusiasm for the classical-republican past. On certain specific political problems, however, such as communal property, and the question of how far a legislator was justified in tampering with the status quo, there was much that divided them. In later years, Mably wrote that he had loved Rousseau and wanted to lose no opportunity to do him justice, but that Rousseau had had the misfortune to become paranoid and deranged, for which he ought to be pitied.[43]

Mably, like Rousseau, owed much of his underlying conception of the nature of politics to Montesquieu, although he too was not an uncritical admirer of the Bordeaux *parlementaire*. Mably's early debt to Montesquieu was at its most emphatic throughout the former's *Observations sur les Romains* (1751), where he referred to Montesquieu as one of the greatest geniuses the French nation had produced. They shared a belief in the rhetoric of political virtue. Where they differed was in the question of its relevance to the political system of contemporary France. Mably had begun his writing career as a defender of absolutist monarchy, but by 1758 he had moved away from this position towards a politically radical egalitarianism that was quite distinct from the pragmatism of Montesquieu.[44] In *Des Droits et des devoirs du citoyen*, Mably was outspoken in his oninion of Montesquieu, condemning him as too superficial and hasty in his judgements. He went further than this, declaring that 'the fundamental ideas of his system are false'. Mably considered that Montesquieu was too willing to accept the political 'status quo' as unchangeable, and that he had built his justification of monarchical government on false premises. Mably disagreed with the contention that the existing French constitution and fundamental laws were sufficient to curb the excesses of monarchical despotism. But even here Mably acknowledged that it was Montesquieu, and his exposition of civic virtue and classical-republican tradition, who had made it acceptable to oppose arbitrary power and had accustomed his readers to the idea of liberty.[45]

The fact that *Des Droits et des devoirs du citoyen* appears to have been written as early as 1758, although it was not published until early 1789, indicates two significant points. The first is that it is doubtful that this text of Mably's, even in manuscript form, exerted any influence on political ideas before the Revolution. And the second point, still more curious, is that this early date shows us the radicalism of the political vocabulary available to Mably thirty years before the Revolution – a vocabulary which we have tended to assume was not invented until the late 1780s. In a key article, Keith Baker points out that Mably in this work elaborates what constitutes almost a 'script' for the French Revolution, which in its predictions almost uncannily echoes some of the events and debates which were actually to take place.[46]

Des Droits et des devoirs offered a sustained discussion of citizenship and the necessary conditions for political liberty, taking as its focus a comparison between French and English forms of politics. The work was structured as a series of fictional dialogues which take place between the (French) author and an English *milord*, Lord Stanhope, as they walk together in the gardens of the palace of Marly. Stanhope is a 'Commonwealth' man, that is, he represents the republican legacy in English ideas and draws on the tradition expounded by theorists such as Toland, Sydney and Bolingbroke, for all of whom, political virtue was central to the protection of political liberty. These ideas are used to give authority to a discussion which is intensely subversive of the French monarchical system. With the exception of Locke, few English political theorists are praised by name. It is probable, however, that Mably also had in mind a number of English writers in the classical-republican tradition whose work was translated into French during the 1740s and 1750s, including Shaftesbury, Hutcheson, Bolingbroke and Sydney. In terms of French influences, the Jansenist struggle over the 'billets de confession' had politicised many people who had previously been unaware of such issues. Inspired by those events, Mably has his French speaker express the hope that the *parlementaires*, the only group with sufficient political power, would be the instigators of a political revolution. It is notable, however, that he had little confidence in their virtue. He believed that they would act out of corporatism and self-interest rather than genuinely in the public interest. He hoped that they would bring about a revolution in spite of themselves rather than with the intention of so doing, and he envisaged a situation in which the *parlementaires* would find themselves driven into calling for the summoning of the Estates General, an action which Mably believed would have results far beyond what the *parlementaires* themselves would have desired.

Thus, the two men discuss the prospects of a political revolution taking place in France which would overturn 'despotism' and give the French a proper constitution. It is assumed that for their political and constitutional model the French should look to the English political system. In the course of the work Milord Stanhope puts the case against corruption, venality, and hereditary privilege, convincing his listener and, it is also intended, the readers, of the justice of his case. The difficulty for Mably was that within the accepted French political system there was no legitimate means of conceiving of politics as anything other than the will of the monarch. He therefore had sought authority for his argument that the political constitution of France might be changed through the rhetoric of classical republicanism. Morality is at the heart of Stanhope's conception of the political principle. Milord argues that 'cet instinct morale' precedes civil society, that nature has given mankind pleasure in acts of *bienfaisance* and that it is from this basic drive towards morality that mankind derives its ability to frame laws and secure justice.[47] The current political order is not legitimate but a despotism, and he argues for civic responsibility towards the political process based on the moral integrity of citizens. A revolution may be necessary in order to recover liberty. In Letter VI, Stanhope outlines the form which such a revolution may take. He envisages that the Paris *parlement* may extend the opposition to the court, which it had adopted on behalf of the Jansenists into a wholesale resistance to absolute monarchy. Its formal opposition, and most importantly, its justification of such a position, should be made public by the publication of remonstrances. The *parlement* cannot itself represent the nation but it can give the nation its liberty by demanding the reassembly of the Estates General. Public pressure will mount as, inspired by the remonstrances, ordinary people will realise that they too may legitimately play a role in political decisions: 'Your humblest little Bourgeois will suddenly find themselves regarded as citizens.'[48] Stanhope anticipates that the king and his ministers would be obliged to submit to the force of such public opinion and give France the Estates General and a proper constitution.[49] Once liberty is established, it must be rigorously defended. Liberty is dependent upon virtue. Any necessary measures may be taken to defend the revolution for liberty provided that one is motivated only by political virtue and has the public interest at heart. Milord goes so far as to state (in an old argument rewritten) that in defence of liberty 'a virtuous citizen' may with justice engage in civil war, provided that it is in order to save the nation from despotism, just as a gangrenous limb must be severed in order to save the rest of the body from its poison.[50] Once a republic has been established, the best way to defend it is not by punishing faults, but by positively encouraging the necessary virtues.[51]

From morality to politics

Mably's most influential political work during his lifetime was the *Entretien de Phocion sur le rapport de la morale avec la politique* (1763). It was a study of political virtue as the basis of government. In it he set out in greater depth the ideas which provided the foundations for his radical and revolutionary theories. Here he took up the classical-republican theme once more, his conception of virtue again was close to Montesquieu's, but it was harnessed to a political vision undiluted by Montesquieu's concessions to expediency and pragmatic readiness to compromise. Mably addressed himself solely to 'what should be'. The work took the form of a series of conversations between an Athenian patriot and a soldier, Phocion and Aristias, on the science of politics, and how this might be used to reform the ancient republic of Athens. The first rule of politics was to obey the natural laws. Politics must be subject to reason. The aim of politics was to guide people towards virtue, which was invariably conducive to happiness. People could not be coerced into the love of the *patrie*, which could only come about through the cultivation of other virtues such as temperance, love of work, and respect for the gods. It was a plant that could not grow in foreign soil; the ground must first be prepared.[52] 'Love of the *patrie*' was an essential virtue but Mably was not parochial. There was, he said, a greater virtue than this, which was 'love of humanity'. Phocion envisaged a time when the world would no longer be divided into individual nations; a time when everyone would desire the happiness of all their fellows.[53] Wealth and 'luxury' were inimical to virtue and would lead inexorably to the dissolution of the republic.[54] In order to fashion virtuous citizens, capable of active political participation, it was necessary to cultivate devotion to the Supreme Being.[55]

Unlike *Des Droits et des devoirs*, the *Entretiens de Phocion* enjoyed great success in Mably's lifetime. Mably's readers readily understood that this was not just meant to be an abstract historical treatise on history – it was as much about the social injustices of the *ancien régime* as it was about the ancient Greeks. Mably's vision of a republic of virtue helped to shape the political mind-set of many radical polemicists in the quarter-century before the Revolution. One of the most notable of these was Guillaume-Joseph Saige, of whose ideas Baker has made a close study. Saige modelled his *Catéchisme du citoyen* (1775) upon Mably's text, adapting Mably's framework to fit the context of contemporary political struggles between monarchy and the *parlements*.[56]

In conclusion, then, the ideas of Rousseau and Mably illustrate the extent to which political arguments of extreme radicalism (in the context of an absolute monarchy) were possible in the period of the 1750s and early 1760s. These arguments derived much of their force and focus from the rhetoric of political virtue. Rousseau undoubtedly played a crucial role in appropriating such a rhetoric, but he was by no means responsible for its invention and it was possible to develop radical arguments on the basis of traditional (primarily classical republican) concepts of virtue independently of Rousseau, as Mably did in his works of the 1750s such as *Des Droits et des devoirs du citoyen*. Both Mably and Rousseau show the importance of the classical-republican tradition in their political theories. British theorists were an important influence here, but it is notable that both Mably and Rousseau brought out the explosive potential for radicalism and political egalitarianism present in the discourse of virtue. This is particularly visible in their treatment of the question of the desirability of luxury and commerce, towards which both displayed considerable hostility, in contrast to the greater propensity amongst British theorists to see luxury, commerce and the generation of consumer goods as benign and conducive to public virtue. Classical republicanism, important though it was, was not the only discourse within which the rhetoric of political virtue flourished. Rousseau's work had a more popular appeal than Mably's in part because of the way in which he linked his political ideas to the themes of sensibility and social virtue. In the work of Mably and Rousseau it is possible to see the extremes to which the rhetoric of political virtue could be taken, established from a long tradition of political writing that reached back to the classical authors but which, at least in Rousseau's writing, had since undergone a notable transfiguration.

4
Making the Man of Virtue, 1755–70

> *one is noble only through virtues, one is a commoner only through vices.*
>
> Prévost, *Suite de l'Histoire du Chevalier Des Grieux et de Manon Lescaut* (1762)

Hitherto we have concentrated on the development of a variety of theoretical positions on political virtue. Now we shall turn to ways in which the rhetoric of virtue was appropriated and used in specific polemical contexts. Between about 1755 and 1770, the literature of virtue seems to have tightened its hold over educated mentalities. To a certain extent dates for concepts must be somewhat arbitrary but 1770 was the 'cut-off' date that Mornet gave for the 'victory' of the *philosophes'* ideological challenge. It was also the year which witnessed the commencement of the political struggle known as the 'Maupeou coup'. By the beginning of this period the essential features of the rhetoric of virtue were already well established: it evoked a set of political and social resonances drawn from a shared linguistic landscape of the mind. Now this rhetoric began to reach a broader audience amongst the educated classes as it was incorporated into specific debates and contexts, such as the new project of the *Encyclopédie*, the prize contests of the *Académie Française*, in the theatre, and in educational projects. Used polemically in these contexts, the rhetoric of political virtue began to command wider recognition as an authoritative language in which to discuss matters of social and political import.

Whilst the rhetoric of political virtue tended to invoke the ideal of equality, it was not confined to any particular doctrine or political belief; rather it was, and continued to be, part of a much wider body of ideas from which people could draw at will. These ideas could be enlisted by different writers, or groups of writers, who used the rhetoric without necessarily having the same political and social agendas.

By the early 1750s the outlines of the 'man of virtue' had taken shape as an ideal of social and political conduct. As a political model its influence would increase throughout the rest of the century and into the revolutionary period. He was a composite of qualities derived from older ideas of classical republicanism and newer concepts of natural virtue. There was space for considerable variation within the model, but the main outlines were clear enough. Integrity was his most essential quality. He was independent, open, and 'incorruptible', both in public and in private life. He was a citizen, devoted to his *patrie*, and to his fellow citizens. This devotion was not necessarily incompatible with his loyalty to the monarchy, but it was based on the assumption that the monarch also served the best interests of the *patrie*. Where this common purpose was seen to break down, a conflict of loyalties would ensue. Political theorists attempted to resolve this potential tension by giving great attention to the question of sovereignty. The 'man of virtue' was, like the hero of Mackenzie's novel, a 'man of feeling' (*sensibilité*). His natural impulses were good but, unlike the 'woman of virtue', he was generally depicted as being able to 'master' his emotions when necessary. He took his familial obligations with the utmost seriousness, and was an exemplary father, son and husband. This was in marked contrast with the figure of the 'aristocratic' libertine, whose relationships were characterised by calculated cynicism, exploitation and betrayal. The model of the virtuous man contrasted with the 'man of honour', whose self-esteem derived from his social appearance and prestige.

There were, however, points of tension, and potential conflict within this idealised model revolved around several areas. One such was the relationship of the man of virtue with political authority, and how much respect was due from the virtuous citizen to the law of the land in which he lived. The 'man of virtue' was sometimes shown as respecting the rule of law, the Church, the authority of the king, and sometimes not; for actual laws were made by men, and men, if they were not virtuous, might err. Tensions also clustered around the distinction between public and private virtue and the potential incompatibility between the virtuous 'family man' and the upright citizen.

The relationship between the idealised model of 'the man of virtue' and social class in the *ancien régime* is not a subject which can be easily or definitively resolved. The issue of class here is problematic but needs addressing. There are two aspects of this question which we need to pursue. The first is, was there a specific class or classes who spoke the language of virtue? The second point we may address is, were there characteristics of the discourse itself which were class-specific? The rhetoric of civic virtue largely replaced the concept of noble virtue, but this does not necessarily mean that the new conception of political virtue can be characterised as a 'bourgeois discourse' and this is a phrase which we should be very careful about using. The idea of a 'bourgeois discourse' might be interpreted in two quite distinct ways. The first possibility is that it was members of the bourgeois who were the primary speakers of the discourse of political virtue. The second possible interpretation is that, whilst members of the bourgeois classes spoke the language of virtue, so did members of the nobility, who could thus 'buy in' to the discourse; but that, nevertheless, it was a discourse which tended to benefit the bourgeois classes rather than the nobility. Both these possibilities merit consideration, although neither can entirely explain the complex reasons why people seized upon the discourse of virtue to express political opinions.

It must be said that it is always dangerous to adopt a reductionist view of something as complex as a concept or discourse. Perhaps we should, therefore, give some consideration to a third possibility. It may be that the discourse of virtue appealed both to nobles and to the bourgeoisie, but for different reasons. It was in the interests of the bourgeoisie to adopt a code which placed value upon them as men and as citizens. But it was also in the interests of a certain section of the higher nobility, preoccupied as they were with internecine warfare, to enlist the rhetoric of virtue (and its subtext, the condemnation of vice and corruption) in order to undermine the moral authority of rival sections of the nobility. In certain circumstances a noble might use this 'bourgeois rhetoric' against another noble. For example, court nobles who were out of favour with the monarch were often not above using the rhetoric of vice and virtue to obtain the discomfiture of their more successful rivals.

In order to understand how a noble might successfully employ a 'bourgeois discourse', we need to examine the ways in which the discourse of political virtue itself was bound up with the matter of class. Several aspects of the rhetoric of virtue were opposed to the noble 'lifestyle' or at least to the popular conception of how nobles lived. First, there was the emphasis on virtue as a product of 'sincere' natural feeling. The court and the Parisian milieu of 'the great' were believed to stifle virtue under layers of artifice. So the virtuous life was best lived far from the centres of corruption, in the country and close to nature. Secondly, there was the belief that adherents of virtue should be moderate in their consumption of material goods and the pleasures of life. This theme of 'anti-luxury' lent itself to a hostile assessment of the nobility, and especially of noblewomen, who were depicted as especially prone to lavish expenditure on dress, trinkets and frivolities. Thirdly, there was the idea of the man of virtue serving and benefiting the community. This notion was posited against the concept of the nobility as a parasitic social group who performed no useful function. Seen in these terms, the discourse of virtue could serve as the antithesis of a nobility which was increasingly characterised as frivolous, artificial, decadent, luxurious, spendthrift and lacking a social function.

But not all nobles by any means were seen as (or saw themselves as) implicated in such a disparaging assessment. The hostile evaluation of nobility was directed primarily against the highest nobles, those who spent their time at court. The vast majority of nobles were not necessarily impugned by it and certainly they did not see this critique as applying to themselves. Following the precedents set by Boulainvilliers and by Montesquieu, nobles outside the glittering ranks of the Versailles courtiers could be as scathing about courtly 'vice' as were bourgeois commentators. The judicial nobility in particular, distinguished itself from the courtier class, and continued to pride itself on its social functions. The old concept of judicial noble virtue was retained amongst the linguistic repertoire of the *parlements*, although this judicial virtue would co-exist on terms of increasing unease with the rise of more egalitarian interpretations of virtue, an unease which would come to the fore in the context of the political struggle of 1770–4.

The concept of virtue was egalitarian in a way that the nineteenth-century language of class-consciousness could not be, for it was an ideal that transcended class boundaries. Despite his opposition to noble values the virtuous man was not necessarily bourgeois. He was aware that privilege and status were social conventions; that they were gifts of providence which it was his duty not to abuse, they were not grounds for cultivating inordinate pride. It is not hard to perceive why a disregard for the status derived from birth and privilege would appeal to those who were outside the ranks of the nobility. What appears particularly significant is that so many nobles (though by no means all) were also attracted to the model, and liked to think of themselves as men of merit, who did not owe their social position to rank alone. Outside the court, there were some in the ranks of the nobility who were eager for political reform, and agreed with the association of the court with 'vice'.[1] Many of the *philosophes* as well as minor 'men of letters' who prized virtue were themselves nobles, a fact which makes it difficult to claim in any simple sense that this was a 'bourgeois' discourse. Chaussi-nand-Nogaret, who has argued the case for an 'enlightened' French nobility, has gone so far as to give 1760 as a precise date at which it adopted 'bourgeois' values of virtue. From then on, he says, there was no distinction between noble and bourgeois conceptions of virtue.[2] Certainly, there are many signs that a growing sense of uncertainty about the ethical basis of their privileged status was developing by this time amongst many nobles. But it would be rash to take too literally the extravagant claims made by individual nobles about their love of virtue and the simple life and their dislike of the rigid formality, hierarchy and institutionalised inequality which provided the basis for their own social preeminence. As the language of virtue began to enjoy a cult status amongst the educated classes, so widely-read nobles also wished to indulge in the rhetoric of virtue and to speak of their sincere attachment to it. In practice, relatively few nobles were quite ready to abandon the notion of status based on birth, and very few saw a need to actually renounce the accompanying wealth and privileges.

A number of the *philosophes* campaigned to turn public opinion against the idea that exalted birth was in any way synonymous with virtue.[3] Elsewhere, the moral status of the nobility continued to be a pressing issue, both for those who sought to challenge its preeminence and for those who defended it, but found themselves obliged to resort to changing grounds as a basis for their claims. This was the difficulty confronted in the abbé Coyer's *La Noblesse commerçante* (1756), a work which sparked off a controversial debate in the late 1750s, the ramifications of which were still being felt at the outbreak of the Revolution. Coyer's principal concern was to extend the economic and social role of the nobility. He argued against the traditional prohibition (defended in *L'Esprit des lois*) which forbade nobles to soil their hands – and lose their honour – by engaging in retail trade, even whilst he sought to preserve the nobility's privileged social position within the structure of the *ancien régime*. But for Coyer as for other eighteenth-century commentators the economic role of the nobility could not be treated in isolation from the issue of their moral role, a position which necessitated a rethinking of the legitimation and justification of nobility. He sought, therefore, to redefine noble honour as moral integrity and industry, but it remained unclear in what way nobles might lay an exclusive claim to the possession of such qualities.

Honour and virtue in the nobility were also reevaluated in Champdevaux's *L'Honneur considéré en lui-même et relativement au duel* (1752). This took the form partly of a fierce attack on the practice of duelling and the noble code of honour which sustained it, but it also incorporated a more general attempt to reevaluate the nature of the nobility and its social role. The traditional noble code of honour was subjected to critical scrutiny. Champdevaux made a distinction between 'true' and 'false' honour: identifying 'true honour' with 'moral virtues', whilst 'false honour' (which corresponded to Montesquieu's general definition of honour) was based on 'self-love' and false appearances. Champdevaux's concept of 'true honour' thus bore a close resemblance to Montesquieu's notion of political virtue. 'True honour', according to Champdevaux's framework, was not confined to the nobility and those of exalted birth. Each 'estate' in life had its own honour, or virtue.[4] 'Plebeian virtue' existed as well as noble.[5] Only at the court were 'virtue' and 'true honour' unknown. Courtiers prided themselves on their 'honour' but by this they meant only the false form of honour.[6] The duel was to be condemned on the grounds that it, too, was based on the 'false' concept of honour. The duellist prefers 'vice accompanied by public esteem to virtue and the derision of others'.[7] Champdevaux took the line of the *philosophes*, who regularly condemned the practice of duelling as a relic of the nobility's older 'virtuous' function as fighters for king and country, now debased into picking private quarrels. The campaign against duelling was also supported by the monarchy, frustrated by the assumption of pugnacious nobles that their codes stood outside state law. Duelling undermined the political authority of the state. Champdevaux attacked duelling as contrary to 'sound politics'.[8] Champdevaux's account of how the nobility could recover their political and social role was based on the premises and language of civic virtue. Nobles should be educated in the principles of true honour and moral virtue, and taught the duties of citizenship. Their primary function was to serve their *patrie*, but Champdevaux interpreted their patriotic duties in accordance with the traditional military function of the noble class. More specifically, therefore, he argued the case for the reform of the *Ecole militaire*, the military training ground for young nobles.[9]

To those outside the privileged ranks of the nobility, however, the appeal of the 'man of virtue' had a more personal meaning. The nobleman, after all, could always fall back on alternative bases for his social and political authority. The bourgeois man did not have such a choice of models open to him, unless he too could join the nobility. He might copy the manners of the noble; he might, if he was rich enough and sufficiently well-connected, purchase an ennobling office. Nevertheless, a man who aspired to join the ranks of the nobility must brave the attendant risks in the course of his precarious climb up to the desired new status. In particular he was vulnerable to social ridicule. The 'bour-geois gentleman' (*gentilhomme*) who pretended to be what he was not and unknowingly displayed his ignorance of the codes of the nobility was a recognised comic figure of long-standing. By contrast, the 'man of virtue' provided an empowering and dignified model for the aspirant bourgeois, for his social and political importance rested solely on his own merit. To that extent, it may fairly be said there was a particular (but not exclusive) affinity between the bourgeoisie and the discourse of virtue.

Matters were further complicated by the growing link, not only between virtue and a rising and assertive bourgeoisie, but also between virtue and the 'common man' or 'common woman'. This connection between the lower orders and virtue derived from the belief that virtue was most easily to be found 'close to nature' rather than in 'civilised society'. This was the most potentially radical concept of political virtue: much of the revolutionaries' language would be based on it. In 1750 such a link was as yet rarely made. Since the lower orders, the peasants and artisans who made up the vast majority of French society, were themselves in no position to write in defence of their own virtue, they were at the mercy of the educated classes for the manner in which they were portrayed. For most commentators, the lower orders were, as Vol-taire put it, the ignorant and brutish 'rabble'. Under the pens of Rous-seau, Mably and like-minded figures, the unflattering image of the rabble began to be transfigured into the much more positive concept of 'the people'. The idea of the virtuous common people in turn would lend itself to the formation of egalitarian political theory based on the concept of popular sovereignty.

The *Encyclopédie*

The possible repercussions of social tensions in the appropriation of the rhetoric of political virtue were not readily apparent by 1755. But already the theoretical position of such a rhetoric as an appropriate model for social and political behaviour was well established. It remain-ed for the implications of the ideology of virtue to be further developed, and for the model to be disseminated. Here the generation of younger *philosophes*, who contributed to the *Encyclopédie* after it commenced publication from 1751, played a leading part. These *philosophes* were not revolutionaries before the event but they were, in their different ways, eager for social and political reform. 'Reform' might mean a range of things, from 'popular sovereignty' to 'enlightened absolutism'. But there was general agreement that the French system of government was prone to many abuses, and that the secular sway of the Church constituted an oppressive weight upon humanity.

Lacking political power themselves, the *philosophes* could only hope to bring about change through the impact of their writing, particularly its effect on those people of power and influence on whose goodwill the 'men of letters' largely depended. Any reforms would have to be preceded by a profound change in the way people conceptualised society, and the possibilities for change within it. The success of the *philosophes* in devising alternative ways of conceptualising the basis of social and political authority depended in part on the extent to which they could generate a new linguistic framework. The vocabulary of virtue offered a means by which alternative social moral values could be articulated. It provided an acceptable alternative to the traditional doctrines of Church and State. The *philosophes* recognised the part played by language itself, with its shifts and ambiguities, in subtly influencing the ways in which people thought. They compiled their own dictionaries, partly in order to arrive at a fuller understanding of truth by giving words clearer and more precise definitions, but also as a deliberate tactic to make language work polemically. This latter aim entailed deliberately shifting (rather than simply clarifying) the meaning of words by giving them subtly altered meanings and by placing them in new contexts. A favourite tactic was to juxtapose different sets of words and to forge links between them, thus setting up a discourse of related words, each of which could then be used to invoke and reinforce the others.[10]

The leading role in this linguistic mission was taken by the compilers of the *Encyclopédie*. A chief object of the *Encyclopédie* was to reach a more mainstream, wealthy and privileged audience (including many pillars of *ancien régime* respectability) than was possible with clandestine works.[11] Its chief editor, Diderot, used his article on the term 'encyclopaedia' to disclose the methods whereby he and the other collaborators on the *Encyclopédie* used language to promote new ideas. He wrote that the aim of an encyclopaedia was 'to juxtapose ideas, to contrast principles; to attack, shake up, and secretly reverse the ridiculous opinions one would dare not insult directly'; for example, 'a national prejudice' (presumably Christianity) could be undermined even whilst treating it with apparent respect. The avowed aim was to change 'the ordinary way of thinking' and to teach virtue and happiness, 'that we may not die without having deserved well of the human race'.[12] The essential object was not simply to undermine the received sources of moral authority and reduce people to cynicism and disbelief, but to replace the old beliefs with a new justification for morality, one based on virtue and faith in humanity. Without its lessons in virtue, Diderot declared, the project of the *Encyclopédie* was without point.

The irony was that, like most Enlightenment texts, these lessons in virtue were available only to the sort of people who could afford the books themselves. As Darnton showed, the price of the *Encyclopédie* tended to make it prohibitively expensive, except to the actual administrators of the regime which was criticised; its officials and office holders, the higher clergy, and of course a sizeable section of the nobility. If a wider public were to be educated in the new ideas, other means would have to be adopted in order to reach them.

The article on 'virtue' in the *Encyclopédie* came out in 1763, that is, after Diderot had been driven underground by its condemnation and had compiled the last volumes in difficult circumstances. This article, written by a Genevan pastor, Romilly *fils*, was not innovative in its meaning. Rather, its purpose was to summarise and reinforce the terms on which virtue was now to be understood. Its definition was said to be simple:

> Sentiment is a surer way of recognising virtue than being led astray by philosophising over its nature.... Sentiment recognises itself only through sentiment; do you want to know what humanity is? Close your books and look upon people who are suffering. Reader, whoever you may be, if you have ever tasted the appeal of virtue, look inside yourself for a moment, its definition is in your heart.[13]

Here sentiment replaced reason a as means of recognising virtue. Virtue was far more than a narcissistic contemplation of one's own self-worth – it was essentially a sociable quality. It formed the common bond of humanity which brought together the reader and those less fortunate. Virtue was inimical to (self-) 'interest', and it was 'equally essential for politics and for morality'. Virtue was not the prerogative of an intellectual or affluent elite. In lines which recalled the passage from the *Discours sur l'inégalité* which Rousseau had admitted he owed to Diderot, Romilly claimed that virtue was said to be found more often amongst the poor and uneducated. The *philosophes* themselves could be corrupted by the very sophistication of their ideas, which might obscure or denigrate basic moral laws, whereas: 'the common man is often in this respect more advanced than the philosophers; his moral instinct is purer and less distorted'.[14]

The 'vulgar' populace might possess a greater degree of natural morality than the educated classes but, according to the *Encyclopédie*'s article on 'the people', they were looked down upon by the more affluent. Once, the category of 'the people' had included all those who were not 'the great' or 'the nobles', but now the bourgeoisie disdained to be thought of as members of 'the people', and they expended all their efforts to climb out of this despised category. Only 'hard manual labourers' (*ouvriers*) and 'peasants' (*laboureurs*) were still numbered amongst 'the people'. They had been reduced to extreme poverty by the greed of the wealthy – a point which was reinforced by the implications of cross-referencing the article on 'the people' with one on 'indigence'. But the people had natural affections, married, cared for each other and for their children. Moreover, they were the most numerous and most necessary part of 'the nation'.[15] This idea contained echoes of La Bruyère and of Fénelon, but it would also resurface as a basis for some of the more radical political theory of the Revolution.

The *philosophes* and the promotion of *bienfaisance*

It was no longer enough to *feel* virtuous; one ought also *to act* virtuously: from the language of sensibility flowed the language of *bienfaisance*. Although the formal recognition of this term lagged behind its acceptance into common use (for example, it was only included in the *Dictionnaire de l'Académie* in 1762), by the 1750s it had become a key social term. The rise of the term *bienfaisance* was attributable to the deliberate strategy of the *philosophes*, who scattered liberally the words *bienfaisance*, virtue, happiness and *patrie* in their writings, linking these concepts in the minds of their readers.[16] In 1764, Voltaire in his article on 'virtue' in the *Dictionnaire philosophique* made this link explicit: 'What is virtue? It is doing good (*bienfaisance*) to your neighbour.' He identified the cardinal and Christian virtues (which had formed the basis of the old dictionary definitions of virtue) as guides to one's *private* conduct, rather than indications of one's virtue. True virtue was public: 'The prudent man does good for himself, the virtuous man does good for others.'[17]

The status of *bienfaisance* as a *secular* virtue was an ambiguous matter. It had, as we have seen, been presented as being a quality independent of the jurisdiction of the Church. The Christian concept of 'charity' was contrasted unfavourably with *bienfaisance*. Charity, said its disparagers, was a puny thing compared with *bienfaisance*: a matter of doling out measured quantities of alms, more for the good of one's own soul than for the benefit of others. *Bienfaisance* was something more: it entailed giving a part of one's own self to one's fellows. Through *bienfaisance* was forged a direct link between citizens, that is, between the 'philanthropists' (*bienfaiteurs*) and the 'unfortunate' (*les malheureux*).

Despite these secular overtones, it was an idea that recalled one of the most fundamental tenets of Christianity: Christ's most essential commandment, 'to love one's neighbour as oneself'. To some observers, the ideas of 'social virtue' and of *bienfaisance* were appealing precisely because they appeared to offer a return to the essential truth of Christianity, a truth often obscured by the worldliness and wealth of the Church as an institution. This idea was not without political implications, for had not the primitive Church been characterised by its equality, so that it formed almost a republic of citizens? Such a terrestrial republic reflected the perfect republic of Heaven, where all were equal in the love of God, united in their virtue.

Paradoxically, therefore, social virtue and *bienfaisance* offered alternative and contrasting strategies that might serve to undermine the power of Christianity, or by contrast, to revitalise it. This point is central to an understanding of the way in which the appeal of 'social virtue' far transcended the ranks of deists and atheists. 'Social virtue' also struck up particular resonances with *richerism*, that brand of Jansenism which expressed the desire for a return to the egalitarianism of the primitive Church. Richerism took a hold on many parish priests who rejected the wealth and hierarchy of the higher echelons of the Church, and from whose ranks emerged many strong supporters of the 'Third Estate' in the last years of the *ancien régime*.[18]

The idea that virtue could be judged entirely by its effects gave rise to doubt over people's motives. If doing good was pleasurable the question arose of whether it really constituted a virtue. At the heart of the philosophy of virtue lay the problem of motivation. Then there was the added dimension of social class. It was the rich who were in the best position to do good because they could afford it without themselves suffering deprivation. The merit of a virtuous act from a rich man was arguably less than that of a poor one. In addition, the praise and admiration said to be heaped upon the *bienfaiteur* might provide more sinister motives for an action than those of pure disinterested virtue. Thence arose the idea of the good act done in secret as the truly virtuous act. But this also might be liable to misuse. The idea that people could fake and exploit virtue and *bienfaisance* was very troubling. It was more than a question of abstract philosophy, but a dilemma over which the *philosophes* anguished in their own lives as well as their public writings. They wished to reassure themselves that they were men of virtue, through their feelings, or through altruism. The difficulty was that the only virtuous act which was certain not to have ulterior motives was the one that never came to be known at all – like the widow's mite, known only to God. Duclos managed this feat successfully: the extent of his *bienfaisance* was not discovered until his death, when it was found that he had considerably depleted his own fortune by helping the unfortunate.

For Diderot the situation was more problematic. He liked to think of himself as a *bienfaiteur* to whom all and sundry applied for help. But he found it hard to maintain the requisite silence. He could not resist the pleasure of letting people know and publicly acting the part of the 'virtuous *philosophe*', particularly when, following his break with Rousseau, he could show himself to be, and feel himself to be, the 'better man' of the two. Rousseau, as we have seen, was more content to feel virtuous than to 'prove' himself with actions. In their quarrel with each other, the most cutting wound that either could inflict, worse even than the many personal betrayals, was the public accusation that the other lacked virtue. Diderot was deeply hurt by Rousseau's comment in the *Lettre à d'Alembert* that it was impossible to be virtuous without religion; Rousseau for his part decided that the lines in *Le Fils Naturel* 'only the bad man lives alone' must have been meant for him.[19]

Promotion of virtue within the *Académie Française*

The campaign to promote virtue as a social and political value which had found an initial voice through the *Encyclopédie*, began to intensify in other areas. Inspired initially by the *philosophes*, these ideas began to take hold and to disseminate through new publics. A particularly effective method of teaching virtue was considered to be that of the eulogy, a traditional forum for teaching the value of good behaviour by example, which now began to take on a more secular form. As with the concept of *bienfaisance*, the *philosophes* recognised that eulogising virtuous behaviour did not necessarily make people more virtuous. But it did, according to Duclos, encourage people to emulate virtuous behaviour with the social benefits which then entailed: 'one should not examine too closely the principles behind actions, when their effect is to benefit society'. Beginning with the unpromising motives of desire for glory and prestige inspired by *amour-propre*, would eventually develop, it was to be hoped, genuine virtue, contracted from the 'habit' of doing good.[20]

A chance to put this theory into practice appeared in 1755, when Duclos was elected 'permanent secretary' of the *Académie Française*. In principle the *Académie Française* was a haven of equality in which the only criteria for membership were intelligence and merit, and social distinctions were suspended. The concept of civic virtue was central to this egalitarianism: a virtue which transcended social boundaries. In practice this form of equality was confined mostly to rhetoric: it was the equality of an intellectual elite, and was understood to have no wider political implications outside the confines of the *Académie* itself.[21] The academicians were proud of their status, of their corporate identity, and were determined to preserve and extend their autonomy and independence. The situation was complicated by the involvement of many of the academicians in struggles and political intrigues at court. The contrast between egalitarian rhetoric and self-interested practice exasperated 'outsiders' such as Mercier. In his utopian novel *L'2440*, he depicted the *Académie Française* of the future as being truly impartial, promoting virtue and merit, and laughing over an account of the antics of their eighteenth-century predecessors.

Unlike d'Alembert (whose membership of the *Académie Française* dated from 1754), Duclos himself was only a marginal member of the *philosophes'* social group, but he was sympathetic to many of their ideas, and he was also determined that the *Académie* should assert its independent status at the head of the growing 'Republic of Letters'. Diderot, on the other hand, to his secret chagrin was never a member. He was too radical even for Duclos to be seen to support him, let alone for the more conventional academicians. Between them, Duclos and d'Alembert initiated changes within the *Académie*, though not without a considerable degree of opposition, both from the court and from within the *Académie* itself from the ranks of the so-called *dévots*, the 'devout' faction at court, headed by the queen and the dauphin. Duclos's position was helped by the fact that he enjoyed the support of the rival faction, that of Madame de Pompadour and the duc de Choiseul. Reform of the *Académie Française* could only be initiated slowly, taking care not to ruffle too many *dévot* feathers within the ranks of the academicians. It was not until 1770 that the *philosophes* became a majority of the forty 'immortals', and even then, the 'battle' for control of the *Académie* was only beginning.[22] The desire of the academicians to organise their own prize contests without outside interference or censorship was a matter of corporate autonomy. But the escalation of the three-cornered fight between the *Académie Française*, the Sorbonne and the court, and the interest of the outside public, would result in the effective politicisation of the conflict.

The *Académie* had a long-established tradition of teaching morality through the strategic use of rhetoric, by means of prizes offered for eulogies on a religious or moral subject, with many references to the scriptures. The transformation in 1759 of the 'prizes for eloquence' offered by the *Académie*, from religious and individual subjects into more secular 'eulogies of great men', did much to bring the concept of civic virtue to a wider reading public. The new eulogies still used rhetoric for persuasive moral lessons, but they focused on public acts rather than individual morality. The heroes' private virtues would still be shown, but the emphasis was to be on how these sustained and reinforced public virtues. Again, the idea for this project was far from new. According to d'Alembert the inspiration for it had come from the abbé de Saint-Pierre's suggestion that the *Académie* itself should draw up a history of the lives of great men who had been 'the *bienfaiteurs* of their *patrie*' and use the opportunity to give examples of 'civic morality' on the lines of Plutarch's *Lives*.[23] By making the discussion of secular virtues the subject of open contests the academicians thereby encouraged members of the reading public from outside their own ranks to take part in the conceptualisation of the virtuous men of the *patrie*.

The projected heroes of virtue; the 'great men', were drawn mostly from the ranks of military 'defenders of the *patrie*', ministers or 'servants of the *patrie*', great literary figures who were 'citizens of the Republic of Letters', and kings or 'guardians of the *patrie*'. There was a strong emphasis on history as the proper forum for learning 'citizenship'.[24] Present and past were refracted by means of each other, and each took on new colours accordingly. The past was refashioned, using virtue as an instrument of moral legitimacy; so that, for example, Fénelon was chosen as the subject of the 1771 contest, with the implication that it was he, rather than Louis XIV or Bossuet, who had been the spokesman for virtue and the public good in the dispute which had ended with Fénelon's disgrace and banishment.[25] The interpretation of the past also affected the present. Parallels were implied, and understood by the audience, between past and present heroes. The vicissitudes and opposition suffered by a hero of the past, emanating from political opponents less virtuous than himself, could by extension give an indication of the kind of behaviour the academicians considered was to be expected of ministers and officials. These parallels were delivered on a general level, however, rather than as endorsements or criticisms of particular individuals, which would have been a very dangerous game to play. The primary wish of the academicians, after all, was to establish their independent status, not to become openly enmeshed in factional court politics.

The most successful writer of the *Académie*'s eulogists was Thomas, who finally entered it as a member in 1767.[26] He was a man of plebeian birth, whose reputation was founded, not on originality or profundity, but on his understanding of what was required in the eulogy form and his facility in penning them. There was a note of earnest sincerity in his eulogies of civic virtue which appealed to both the academicians and the wider public. In his portraits of virtuous great men people could see an image of themselves as they would wish to be. Although he specialised in the depiction of virtuous heroes, he seems to have been torn between delight and anxiety: his eulogies brought him into the limelight as a focus for displeasure from the censors, with the latter sentiment invariably prevailing when the danger escalated. Thomas always backed down when it came to the crunch. But he skilfully played up the role of eulogies of virtue in forming public opinion and defining the boundaries of acceptable behaviour amongst the powerful, describing the influence of the eulogies in grandiloquent terms:

> In the last half century there has been a kind of revolution amongst us: glory is better understood; men are better judges, talents are better distinguished from successes; useful qualities are distinguished from those which are glittering but dangerous; those people who have genius but lack virtue will not be pardoned; on occasions respect will be granted to those who have virtue without social grandeur; finally, rank is seen through, so that the man is respected for himself. Thus, little by little, an idea of elevation or rather of justice has formed in people's minds. Noble beings, when contrasted with the vile beings that exist on every social level, are accorded their rightful place. Then the eulogy is founded on true merit. Even those people who are capable of corrupt and cowardly actions are restrained by the force of opinion; and the fear of public shame saves them at least from degradation.[27]

Thomas's own eulogies were skilful examples of his avowed purpose. His eulogy of d'Aguesseau in 1760 extolled the ideal of the virtuous magistrature who fulfilled the important public function of the administration of justice. The *noblesse de robe* were thus compared favourably to longer-established nobles, who could pride themselves only on the length of their pedigrees, whilst serving no useful function for the public good. The only justification for nobility was merit: 'If the distinction of birth is not a complete illusion, if it is based on some kind of reality, it is because it means that one's ancestors were virtuous: because to inherit dignities is worthless, if they are not accompanied by merit.'[28]

Sully in 1763 provided an opportunity to define the model of the virtuous minister who defended the best interests of the state against corruption, factionalism and despotism. Sully was a particularly effective choice as the model minister since the premature death of Henri IV meant that Sully's virtue did not have to be considered as a form of opposition to the moral authority of a ruling monarch, which would have placed the *Académie* in some difficulties (a difficulty which came more to the fore with the choice in 1771 of Fénelon as a hero). Sully could be depicted as the lone defender of the public good against the factionalism and corruption of the court, a man unjustly forced into exile. He exemplified 'the dignity of virtue itself, over which men, courts and kings cannot prevail'.[29] The eulogy of Sully was much admired. Grimm wrote that 'it is perhaps the first academic discourse which has had so great and widespread an effect'.[30] But there was indignation in other quarters, for Thomas used the legitimising framework of the proper conduct of the virtuous minister to make many highly critical comments about the financial administration of the *ancien régime*, attacking the much-hated salt tax and the custom of making forced use of peasants to repair the roads. He also made many references to the oppression of the peasants by 'the rich'. There were complaints about this offending eulogy, and some tax farmers protested to the king. According to Brunel, whose study of this subject is still the most thorough work available, Thomas was forgiven for his use of language which already evokes what Brunel terms 'the tone of revolutionary eloquence', partly because the *Académie* protected him, partly for his own patent lack of dangerous political ambitions.[31] In the course of a few years, therefore, the *Académie Française* had made significant steps in establishing accepted codes of political conduct, based on the moral legitimation of the model of the 'virtuous hero'; and it had shown that such a model might, in particular circumstances, be used to endorse specific criticism of government policies.

Virtuous citizens in the *drame bourgeois*

The rhetoric of virtue began to permeate other cultural forms. The theatre was seen as an ideal medium through which to convey the values of secular virtue, and provides us with an interesting example of how the politicisation of virtue fared within that context. As a cultural form the theatre was more accessible – and more lively – than the *Encyclopédie* or the prize essays for the *Académie Française*. A new theatrical genre, the *drame bourgeois*, came into being, whose avowed purpose

was to teach the moral philosophy of virtue. Although, literally translated, this meant 'bourgeois drama', the phrase 'citizens' drama' may
better convey the sense intended. Once again, it was the tireless Diderot
who took a major role in inventing this new method of teaching virtue.
He was not the first person to write dramas which dealt with domestic
virtue, but he was the first to provide a theoretical framework and
justification for the new form, a justification which was founded on its
moral purpose. In place of traditional theatrical subjects, such as classical mythology and lives of 'the great', the *drame bourgeois* would focus
on ordinary people and show how they contributed much that was of
value to the community and family amongst which they lived.[32] The
precepts of the *drame bourgeois* could easily be related to people's own
lives, and give them a new sense of their own self-worth. Diderot contributed two plays, *Le Fils naturel* (1757) and *Le Père de famille* (1758), and
two major theoretical works on the subject, the *Entretiens sur Le Fils
naturel* (1757) and *De la Poésie dramatique*.

The *Entretiens* take the form of purported conversations between
Diderot and Dorval, the chief character of *Le Fils naturel*. The play itself
had a complicated plot, in which Dorval, secretly in love with Rosalie,
who is the fiancée of his dearest friend, Clairville, makes the virtuous
gesture of sacrificing his own desires for the sake of his friend, despite
having discovered that Rosalie returns his love. The characters are only
saved from this false situation by the singularly awkward contrivance of
having Rosalie's father, newly arrived from the Indies, turn out also to be
Dorval's 'natural' father, so that Rosalie is Dorval's own half-sister. Thus,
there is no longer any danger that Dorval and Rosalie's love would recur
to endanger their respective marriages to other people, an outcome
which would have disrupted the 'virtue rewarded' ending. The plot
certainly creaked alarmingly, but the ideas which it presented had
much deeper implications, and in the *Entretiens*, Diderot elaborated on
the moral doctrine of which the play itself was so flawed a realisation. In
these 'conversations', Diderot treats Dorval and the other characters as
real people. It is Dorval himself who is said to have written the play,
which is said to be a 'true account' of events in Dorval's life. In the
course of the 'conversations' it is Dorval who describes and justifies the
new form of theatre, and explains to Diderot the importance of a new
moral theatre, while Diderot puts forward questions and mild objections
to the proposal, with which Dorval deals in a manner which Diderot
finds entirely convincing.

Naturally, Diderot's critics did not find the arguments put forward by
this literary ploy nearly as convincing as he did. Dorval himself was a

new type of hero, darkly pre-romantic, with an air of melancholy, except when he was 'transfigured' by speaking of virtue.[33] As we have seen, Rousseau thought that the melancholy and austere Dorval was intended to represent himself. But the question of who, if anyone, Dorval was meant to represent remains unresolved. For Diderot clearly admired his character, and if there was something of Diderot's erstwhile friend in Dorval, this clearly was not a straightforward satirical portrait. One could also consider the case for Dorval having in some sense represented Diderot's own better virtuous self: the man of virtue that Diderot yearned to be. When Diderot depicted himself as attempting later to 'recreate' Dorval's play he described his feelings as an immense sense of loss and inadequacy: 'It is in vain that I try to revive within myself the impression that the sight of Dorval's character and presence made upon me. I cannot recover it; I no longer see Dorval; I no longer hear him. I am alone, amongst the dust of books and in my dreary study...and the lines I write are weak, sad, and cold.'[34]

Dorval/Diderot says that the new genre should deal with people from different social backgrounds (*conditions*). The way in which a person's background or occupation affects their life is said to be of greater significance than their individual character. Despite the title *drame bourgeois*, the characters to be portrayed were not confined in any narrow sense to the ranks of the bourgeoisie. The term was used here fairly loosely to indicate those who worked for their living, that is, who performed a useful social role. Diderot/Dorval declared that all kinds of professions should be portrayed on stage: 'the man of letters, the *philosophe*, the tradesman, the judge, the lawyer, the politician, the citizen, the magistrate, the financier, the great lord, the intendant'. Equally important was the whole network of family connections: 'the father of the family, the husband, the sister, the brothers'.[35] These characters, placed in naturalistic situations, would demonstrate the need for conduct to be guided by the principles of virtue, which they would show through the problems with which they were confronted in their occupations, and family ties. It was the purpose of theatre 'to inspire in men the love of virtue, the horror of vice'.[36] Virtue was here defined as 'the desire for moral order'. The theatre, said Dorval/Diderot, should reflect 'the spirit of the age', by which he meant people's growing interest as citizens in matters of public concern: 'If morality purifies itself, if prejudices are weakened, if people's minds incline themselves towards a general *bienfaisance*, if the taste for beneficial deeds spreads, if the people interest themselves in the workings of public administration, it is necessary for all this to be shown, even in a comedy.'[37] Such civic virtue was grounded in domestic virtue: the *Entretiens* ends with Diderot having supper with his own characters, amongst whom he is accepted as 'one of the family', and they put into practice this fusion of domestic and political values, of the happy family and virtuous citizens, by their animated conversation on 'government, religion, politics, literature, philosophy'.[38]

Sadly for the plays themselves, plots and characterisation were sacrificed to the moral vision, as Diderot's anti-*philosophe* critics such as Palissot and Fréron were not slow to point out. There was a considerable delay before they were performed in Paris: *Le Fils naturel* did not receive its first Paris performance until 1771; *Le Père de famille* received its Paris premiere in 1761. This was partly because of their many weaknesses as dramatic forms, but also because the plays constituted an overt attempt to win over public opinion, and members of the *Comédie Française* did not wish to lend themselves to what amounted to a political contest. Diderot, despondent, was reduced to filling in the names of the actors from the *Comédie Française* whom he had hoped would play each part. On the other hand, the plays attracted much attention and were widely read, and were fairly frequently performed outside Paris. *Le Fils naturel* went through four editions in 1757 (its year of publication) and twenty-five French editions by 1800. Diderot's ideas had a significant impact, both on the development of a more realistic, naturalistic French theatre, and on the ideological development of the theatre as a school for virtue.[39]

One of the most successful examples of the *drame bourgeois* was Sedaine's *Le Philosophe sans le savoir* (1765), which, as Diderot recognised with delight, was a considerably more effective version of the kind of drama of virtue in ordinary life which he had himself attempted. Its immense success in the theatre, which the *philosophe* party did its best to encourage by placing its own claque in the theatre, ensured the brief ascendancy of the cult of moral theatre.[40] The plot concerned a noble turned merchant (the *philosophe* of the title), whose son becomes involved in a duel which arises as a result of his opponent having uttered some derisory comments about merchants. The father discloses to his son that he is of noble birth, a fact which the father admits he had kept back before, for fear that 'pride in a great name would weaken your virtue'.[41] In the original version the father permits his son to fulfil this engagement of 'honour', even whilst he himself condemns the code of the duel as being against 'reason, nature and the laws'. It is, he says, symptomatic of the false code of values whereby 'each individual thinks his own person counts for everything, and his *patrie* and his family for nothing'.[42] The duel was the antithesis of political virtue. Some modern commentators have found inconsistency in Sedaine having made what appears to them to be a 'glorification of an enlightened bourgeoisie' emanate from a man who is himself a noble by birth, and who has also in his youth fought a duel.[43] But the moral theme of the play is more complex than the idea of virtue as the exclusive attribute of a particular class. Sedaine's concept of virtue is an egalitarian quality which transcends the confines of social and class boundaries, but he suggests that the social and cultural code of the nobility may suppress their natural inclinations toward virtue. The noble ethic retains its powerful hold, even for the father who recognises it as fallacious. His first-hand knowledge of the noble ethic makes his condemnation of it more effective than if the same arguments had emanated from a representative of the commercial bourgeoisie, whose criticism could be seen as the ignorance or resentment of the 'outsider' who is socially excluded from the 'superior' caste.

In Sedaine's original version the father accepts that 'honour', futile though it is, must be satisfied. He permits his son to risk death in order to remain an 'honnête homme'.[44] In the event the two opponents are reconciled, and despite a dramatic moment when the father receives erroneous information of his son's death, which he receives with exemplary fortitude, all ends happily with the vindication of virtue over honour. Nevertheless, in what seems to have been a political move against the *philosophes*, the censors obliged Sedaine to tone down the effect, by having the father forbid his son to fight, so that the son leaves by stealth to fight his opponent.[45] This 'emasculation' of his virtuous hero was greatly resented by Sedaine, who, in the note with which he accompanied the censored editions of the play, compared his hero to Junius Brutus who endorsed the execution of his sons.[46] He included the omitted scenes as an appendix, so that 'the public' might judge the rights of the case.

The attack on the code of the duel at the centre of *Le Philosophe sans le savoir* was no mere rhetorical or sentimental literary device. The duel remained a focus for preserving masculine and noble status in France (with a brief interruption during the period of the Revolution) until the First World War finally curtailed the authority of aristocratic codes. For example, the father of Jacques-Louis David, the future painter and violent revolutionary, died in a duel when his son was only nine, possibly as a consequence of his trying to 'rise above' his bourgeois background. The young David was later taken into the household of Sedaine, who was, for many years, almost a surrogate father to him. It may be more than a coincidence that many years later, and in quite changed political circumstances, David would make such telling account of the subject of the patriotic virtue of Brutus in his painting *The Lictors Returning to Brutus the Bodies of his Sons*.[47]

From these origins the *drame bourgeois* went through many subsequent modifications, and grew more outspoken in its criticism of the noble code of values on the basis of the new politics. Desertion from the army provided a particularly popular theme for dramatic interpretation, offering opportunities to reassess the relative value of traditional elitist notions of noble masculine honour and the egalitarian idea of the virtuous common man. Two of the most effective dramas on this subject were Sedaine's *Le Déserteur* (1769) and Mercier's *Le Déserteur* (1771). Sedaine's play was a fairly light-hearted affair, with much romantic comedy, but Mercier's version was a much more political work. At a time when memories of the disasters of the Seven Years War were still vivid, and when the penalty for desertion was death (though it was rarely carried out, the principle remained in force), these plays were not mere sentimental dramas, but also hard-hitting social criticisms of the military ethic, which was dominated by the noble officer class; a defence of the rights of the 'ordinary man' against the officer class.[48] Mercier intensified the political vision of the *drame bourgeois*: he persistently took the side of the oppressed and weak against the wealthy and privileged. Although his hero was but a common soldier he was 'a virtuous man', 'touching, sincere', who had been provoked after five years of systematic victimisation into striking his commanding officer, a hard and inflexible man. In the original version Mercier arranged for the soldier to be hanged by the military authorities; but the censors made him save his hero with a last-minute reprieve. The play was reasonably successful, and won for Mercier a pension of 800 livres from Marie-Antoinette, then the dauphine. The efforts of Sedaine and Mercier may well have contributed to the change in official (as well as public) opinion which led to an ordinance of December 1775 which mitigated the circumstances in which the death penalty might be exacted, confining it to deserters in wartime who took up arms against their own *patrie*.[49]

The role of education to forge virtue

The best way to 'make' people virtuous was to catch them young. The right education was the key to the attainment of political virtue. But the question of whether such an education was appropriate for the vast bulk of the populace remained intensely problematic. The common people, that is, the poorer and landless peasants and the urban poor, were fated to work hard relentlessly all their lives, simply in order to eke out a living on the edge of subsistence. Would such people benefit from education for citizenship, or would this make them dissatisfied with their lot in life, and make them less effective workers without fashioning them into active citizens? Most of the *philosophes* agreed that a basic education (preferably not at the hands of the Church) in appropriate and useful subjects to encourage hard work and honesty was all that the peasantry required. Education for active citizenship might do them more harm than good. It was acceptable for peasants to be taught patriotism, but of a kind appropriate to their social station. The peasantry would serve the *patrie* best by working to feed it, or by enlisting in the army to fight for it.[50]

Active or more intellectual patriotic citizenship was generally held to be the prerogative of the leisured classes, those who could afford a secondary education for their boys. The need to develop a system of education able to mould boys into patriotic citizens at the secondary level of the *collèges* became a subject of much debate, particularly after the expulsion of the Jesuits.[51] Education in France was in the hands of the Church, specifically the teaching orders, amongst whom the Jesuits had been by far the most significant with 111 *collèges* in 1762. But the closure of the Jesuit-run *collèges* in 1762 opened up a space within which not only might the purpose of education be rethought, but also the question of who should be responsible for overseeing it.[52] The State found itself obliged to intervene, and actively encouraged the writing of treatises on the secularisation and reform of education. Such treatises dwelt with enthusiasm on the idea of educating the French into civic virtue. This was not a new argument: for example we have already seen how Champdevaux, in calling for the reform of 'honour' from a private to a civic quality, had argued that young nobles should be given a civic education to teach them social responsibility. But by the early 1760s such arguments were being extended into calls for a much wider reform of education; emphasising the need for a more secular education, in which the State recognised its responsibilities, and whose purpose was the formation of virtuous citizens. When, a generation later, the French revolutionaries embarked on their project of creating a 'new man of virtue' through education, their principles and rhetoric bore a close resemblance to those invoked by projects for educational reform in the 1760s.[53]

A curious alliance had formed between philosophic sympathisers and Jansenists in order to obtain a secular education which would instil social and civic virtues. One of the most far-reaching and radical of such treatises was the *Essai d'éducation nationale* (1763), written by La Chalotais, the controversial attorney-general of the *parlement* of Brittany. La Chalotais had taken a notable role in the battle against the Jesuits, and he now called for the general reform of *collège* education on the model of a secularised 'civil education'. He reinforced the legitimacy of his argument by invoking the authority of 'the nation', which was, it seemed to him, convinced of the necessity of a 'general reform'. Reforms in education and the laws could transform a people, he said, citing the example of the Spartans. Education was too important to be left in the hands of those clerics who might not have the interests of the *patrie* at heart. He was at pains to point out that a more secular education did not mean a less moral education. But the dictates of revealed religion were a matter for the Church and separate from the business of the educator, who would instil general 'public morals', and the civic virtues of an education for the public. Virtue derived from 'reason' and 'nature' and predated revealed religion. His plan for 'a civil education' proposed the teaching of secular morality as a preparation for good citizenship: 'the teaching of Morality is the responsibility of the State, and has always belonged to it: this responsibility predates the recognition of its existence, and consequently it is not dependent on Revelation'.[54]

If we consider the influences on La Chalotais's concept of an education in virtue we can see how very complex was the mesh of ideas from which people might draw for the notion of political virtue at this time. He was a foremost defender of the *parlements* (indeed it was he who played the leading role in the *parlementaire* conflict with the monarchy of 1766, known as the Brittany Affair). But even within the milieu of the *parlements* there were different rhetorics for opposition. The most important and effective of these was that of Jansenist *parlementaires* and their supporters. Jansenism itself had established two divergent rhetorical paths at this time. The first of these was strictly theological and, in the tradition of Pascal, Nicole and Esprit, looked on secular virtue with intense suspicion. But the second, following the direction of more political and constitutional concerns, and this strand of Jansenism, following the precedent set by Duguet, was permeated by the rhetoric of civic virtue. It was this latter 'political' Jansenism which had the most effect on magistrates in the *parlements*: the appeal of its language of virtue extended far beyond the circles of those who were believing Jansenists themselves. This form of constitutional and political Jansenism is evident in La Chalotais, although there seems to be no conclusive evidence that he was one himself.

Indeed, he was also subject to a very different set of influences. The Jesuits accused him of being a *philosophe*; and he was clearly much influenced by Montesquieu; and Duclos (who came from the same region as himself) was a friend. The existence of a close link between La Chalotais and Enlightenment projects for reform is suggested by his having published, together with his own treatise, another work on educational reform, an anonymous treatise *De l'Education publique*, written in late 1762. La Chalotais was reticent about the authorship of this treatise, but it is widely believed that Diderot had a considerable hand in writing it. It was a thorough-going call for the setting up of a form of 'public education', whose principle was 'to include people from every level of society, to mould virtue and patriotism in all subjects, and foster in them the appropriate skills'.[55] It was by no means pure Diderot, in that it retained a substantial commitment to formal religious education. This complex mingling of ideas shows how hard it is to identify the rhetoric of civic virtue, when it appears at this generalised level, as specifically Jansenist or *philosophe*. What they have in common is a willingness to employ the rhetoric of civic virtue.

The links and divisions between Jansenism and Enlightenment thought are difficult for us to reconstitute. In many ways their ideas were opposed, but what brought them together, at least in temporary allegiance, was some common aims, the secularisation of education, less power for the Church, and a language of legitimate opposition in which both groups freely drew on the language of political virtue.

Virtue is easy: virtue as self-interest?

Outside the employment of the rhetoric of virtue in these strategic battles, the concept of virtue was continuously undergoing theoretical development. Such theoretical positions varied greatly in sophistication. Since the publication of *Les Moeurs*, a whole series of 'conduct' works and books of moral precepts for how to live had been turned out by the printing presses: works such as Beausobre's *Essai sur le bonheur*; Dragonetti's *Traité des vertus* (translated from the Italian); and Castilhon's *Traité de l'Influence de la Vertu et du Vice sur le Bonheur et le Malheur*. Such works reiterated on a simplified level the ideas put forward by Shaftesbury, namely that virtue was natural, easy to achieve, was rewarded, and led inexorably to happiness. Their arguments were often not very convincing: Beausobre declared that in order to be perfectly happy, one would need both to be very enlightened and to possess 'all the virtues', and that many men come reasonably close to achieving such a model of perfection; whilst Dragonetti affirmed that virtue would be rewarded, but he was unable to bring a more convincing argument to support this idea than the fact that any other outcome was unthinkable, for that would 'benefit the scoundrels and result in the loss of virtuous men'.[56]

Whether virtue was regarded as an innate moral sense, or as resulting from enlightened self-interest as Helvétius argued, the tendency was to believe that virtue was easy, and therefore to negate it as a moral problem. Either people were naturally virtuous, or they could be persuaded to act virtuously by means of education or legislation. Both these evaluations of virtue were based on similarly optimistic views of its possibility, efficacy, and the benefits it bestowed on society.[57] But what such populist writings sometimes lacked in terms of sophisticated analysis, or consistent argument, they made up for, as far as much of their audience was concerned, by their sheer enthusiasm, but mostly because they said what people would like to hear: that life has a purpose, that we live in a mutually supportive society, that happiness is possible, that good people will be rewarded and that bad actions will be punished. Many such works appeared together in a collection known as *Le Temple du Bonheur* (1769). Here Castilhon combined natural virtue with classical republicanism, but it was a classical republicanism made soft and smiling. His favourite from the classics was Plutarch, whom he worked hard to popularise, complaining, with scant evidence, that his hero had been neglected since the Renaissance. Castilhon contrasted Plutarch's idea of virtue favourably with Seneca's concept of virtue as self-mastery:

> the candour of Plutarch who, without sophistry, leads me effortlessly towards virtue, by roads more certain [than those of Seneca]. Wise by choice, virtuous by sentiment, he teaches me a gentle morality, which is easy to practice, and is all the more appealing because it is of benefit to society... and his *bienfaisant* hand leads me to virtue.[58]

One way in which the meaning of virtue provoked particular contention was when it was bound up with the debate on luxury. In Britain the idea that luxury had a softening and civilising effect which led to a greater degree of virtue had a considerable impact. Mandeville's *Fable of the Bees* was a pioneer work in this respect. According to Mandeville, individual hard work and industry, although motivated by private self-interest, had the general consequence of public benefits in the form of civilisation and luxury. This argument was taken up and received its most sophisticated exposition from the Scottish Enlightenment thinkers, Smith and Hume.[59] The French, however, proved on the whole to be far more resistant to this notion. Mandeville, Hutcheson, Hume and Smith were well received in France by certain thinkers, including Voltaire and, to some extent, Montesquieu, and particularly the physiocrats, but they never enjoyed the same degree of popular appeal among the wider reading public as did the proponents of civic and natural virtue. Both Mably and Rousseau were vehemently opposed to the idea of 'luxury', which they saw as profoundly corruptive of civic virtue. Significantly, perhaps, when this subject was debated in these controversies, the term 'luxury' (*le luxe*) was used more often than 'commerce'.[60] Luxury was already a familiar term in both classical-republican and Christian discourses, where it was used in a hostile sense to indicate a superfluity of wealth and the consequent moral corruption of humanity. Both these traditions of thought were opposed to the idea of necessary luxury. The civic virtue of the classical republican tradition, particularly the Spartan version, was profoundly inimical to the form of virtue derived from luxury and self-interest.

Difficult as it is to generalise on this subject, the majority of French theorists seem to have accepted the premises evoked by the classical republican and Christian identification of wealth with corruption. Even Helvétius, whose utilitarian concept of virtue was closer to that of Mandeville than to Shaftesbury, was suspicious of the effect of 'riches' on public virtue:

> The love of riches does not necessarily. . . lead to the love of virtue. The commercial countries need to be more productive of good merchants than of good citizens, of wealthy bankers than of heroes.
>
> It is not therefore in the terrain of luxury and riches but in the soil of poverty that the sublime virtues grow. . . . The virtue that is content with little is the only kind that is safe from corruption.[61]

Helvétius himself, being one of the hated 'tax farmers', whose life-style was certainly far from Spartan, presumably had little first-hand experience as to whether virtue was really engendered by poverty. But his argument was typical of the attitude of many of his contemporaries. Few commentators appear to have seen the irony in maintaining that a 'sublime' level of virtue constituted the true political ideal, although such a level of virtue depended on an implicit rejection of that very 'corruption' by means of which the *ancien régime* actually functioned.

For Diderot, the rather facile optimism of *Le Temple du Bonheur* contributed to his growing sense that he himself had been misguided in

putting forward similar arguments, and he wrote a critique of the simplistic connections between virtue and happiness made by its authors;
ideas which he had himself so forcefully defended.[62] Virtue did not lead
to happiness. Diderot was not the kind of man to abandon his commitment to the moral ethic on which he had based his life. But he recognised that if one was to act virtuously it must be for other reasons. He
did not, however, adopt the kinds of mechanistic and utilitarian views
of virtue which had appeared in Helvétius', *De L'Esprit* (1758), and wrote
a refutation of Helvétius' argument that virtue might be brought about
by legislation, an idea which seemed to Diderot to leave no space for
questions of individual morality. To the end of his life he remained
obsessed by the idea of virtue as secular morality, and the conviction
that a *philosophe*, though the enemy of religion, must be a man of virtue.
In his last years he grew both more pessimistic and more politically
radical. In his *Essai sur les règnes de Claude et de Néron* he defended virtue
once more: this time as a matter of individual stoical self-mastery, rather
than of happiness, sociability and *bienfaisance*. He wanted to write a
work which would demonstrate that virtue could provide an effective
moral, political and social system, that virtue would be rewarded and
vice punished, but admitted that he was too afraid that he would not be
able to prove it. The price of failure would, he recognised, be the loss of
his integrity, which for him constituted his sense of self.[63] He seems to
have settled, as best he could, for trying to be a reasonably virtuous man
in his own life, and when introducing his young daughter Angélique to
a simple form of ethics, he fell back on the old arguments for why one
should act virtuously, because 'there is no virtue which is not doubly
rewarded, by the pleasure of acting well and that of gaining the good
will of others'.[64]

When we examine these overtly political concepts of virtue it
becomes apparent that it is not always easy to distinguish the respective
impacts which civic and natural virtue had in shaping these ideas: it
may even be misleading to attempt too hard to separate them. Although
natural and civic virtue had different origins and distinctive sets of
associations, they were brought together not only by the word they
had in common, but also by the way in which they were indicative of
a shared social perspective, through the notion that private and public
virtue were related, and by the idea that the individual citizen should
consider the public interest over private interest. The equality of citizens, the primacy of the citizen as a basis for political authority, the
importance of devotion to the *patrie*, were all ideas which were common
to both civic and natural virtue. Often there was a blurring of the

distinction between these two discourses, a blurring which may some-times have been brought about deliberately by the author concerned, for by this mingling of meaning, both discourses reinforced each other and each acquired new layers and intensities of meaning.

Many commentators had found the civic virtue of the ancients in itself an austere, remote and even repellent quality, epitomised by those women of Sparta who rejoiced over their dead sons who died for the *patrie*. The impulse towards *bienfaisance*, love of one's neighbour, the power of sensibility, were often more attractive than the self-denying virtues of the Spartans or Romans. Natural virtue complemented and humanised civic virtue, and helped to make it more acceptable by stressing its familial qualities and the acceptability of the passions. Civic virtue, for its part, imparted to natural virtue a rhetorical political tradition and the recognised authority of the classical authors.

Both discourses of virtue were closely linked to the term *patrie*. According to the concept of natural virtue, patriotism was the highest form of morality because it was the highest form of love. As Beausobre wrote: 'This love of the patrie...is a virtue because the love of men is itself a virtue.'[65] The abbé Coyer in his influential essay on patriotism brought out this emotional aspect. He visualised *la patrie* as a commu-nity united by feeling, which paralleled the family unit: 'the word *patrie* which comes from the word *pater*, invokes a father and his children'. He contrasted the *patrie* with 'the realm', 'the state' and 'France'. The virtues of the Greeks and Romans were such that these people were attached to their *patrie* by their emotions. He went further, asserting that it was 'the people' who were the most virtuous, and therefore the most important, part of the *patrie* or the nation: 'The people were formerly the most useful, the most virtuous: and consequently the most respectable part of the nation. They comprised the cultivators, the artisans, the merchants, the financiers, the men of letters, and the men of law.' But now only 'the cultivators, servants and artisans' were still numbered amongst 'the people' and pursued useful virtues: the rest of society had preferred to pursue the false values of 'glory'.[66] It was this link between 'natural virtue' and 'the people' which provided the basis for the most fervently egalitarian discourses of political virtue.

5
The Virtuous King:
a Rhetoric Transformed

The universal monarchy,
Is nothing other than the empire of the virtues.
> 'The People of Lorraine to King Stanislas',
> *Mémoires secrets* (1763)

In the second half of the eighteenth century a 'desacralisation' of
the French monarchy is said to have taken place, whereby the king
gradually lost much of his semi-divine status in the eyes of his
subjects. Emphasis was placed on his human attributes rather than
his sacred ones. This decline of the sanctified status of the crown is
also said to have affected its political authority.[1] 'Desacralisation'
itself is a nebulous term. One way of addressing this issue is to ask
who might have contributed to a desacralisation of the monarchy
and why. Outside the court the *philosophes* took a lead in questioning
the sacred character of monarchical authority. From a different perspective, Robert Darnton has uncovered the role of the clandestine
press in writing scurrilous attacks on the monarchy. One of the most
renowned of these publications was the *Mémoires secrets* and the
many works which emerged from the same circle of writers, which
included several active supporters of the *parlements*.[2] This kind of literature dated back at least as far as the *Mazarinades* of the Fronde in the
mid-seventeenth century. But it was now better organised, more vehement and more widely circulated than ever before, peaking in the early
1770s and again from the mid-1780s.[3] Other historians, most notably
Dale Van Kley, have argued with conviction that the challenges of
Jansenists and *parlementaire* supporters to the sacred character of royal
authority from the 1750s or even earlier amounted to a form of desacralisation.[4]

129

Ironically, there is little doubt that the individual who did most to demystify the monarchy between 1745 and 1774 was Louis XV himself. In the early years of his reign his youth meant that he had been generally well regarded by his people despite increasing indications of weaknesses inappropriate in a monarch. Such public anguish was shown and so many Masses said on his behalf when he fell dangerously ill at Metz in 1744 that when he recovered he was given the soubriquet of Louis the Well-Beloved (*bien-aimé*). It was meant to signal his willingness to renew his commitment to his office, but once he recovered his health he took up once again the life of a man rather less than virtuous. His popularity underwent a steep decline.[5] This was partly the result of circumstances for which he himself bore only a limited responsibility. The disasters of the Seven Years War, and the politico-religious crises of the 1750s and early 1770s, were to a large extent beyond the control of Louis, who was a timid man, inclined to rely on the advice of his ministers. Nevertheless, it was inevitable that he would be subjected to some opprobrium for these calamities. In the matter of personal conduct he bore considerably more responsibility: the tales that were told of his immorality were lavishly and enthusiastically embroidered in the telling, but were not without some basis in truth. Hardly anyone in France was unaware that Louis had a reputation for dissipation, rather than virtue. But it was not Louis's sexual promiscuity in itself that attracted such condemnation: the double standards which exempted masculine virtue from the obligation of chastity applied to kings as much as to commoners. What aroused indignation in Louis's subjects was the widespread belief, emanating originally from court and *parlementaire* circles and nurtured by the clandestine press, that the king let his mistresses dominate political policy, particularly the appointment of ministers. The king's private 'vices' were thus at the heart of the perception of monarchical government as a corrupt and 'unvirtuous' public politics.

Rumours at the expense of the monarch and his family were a constant feature of court life, co-existing alongside the elaborately deferential public rhetoric of the courtiers. Discontented courtiers, whose factions were 'out' of royal favour, were the usual source of some of the most outrageous stories, which circulated through society by word of mouth and in printed form despite strenuous efforts at censorship. Such defamatory attacks were as old as the institution of monarchy itself. But they grew more challenging from the mid-eighteenth century with the growth of 'public opinion', whether this is defined as a notional legitimation of political opposition or as a literal growth in a reading public interested in, and ready to pronounce upon, public affairs – including the virtues and duties of kingship.

But some of the most fundamental criticisms of the monarchy in the second half of the eighteenth century originated from people whose intention was not to undermine the monarchy, but to reform or even to regenerate it. They encouraged the formation of a new ideal of kingly virtue which would have profound implications for the way in which royal authority was viewed and its role justified. Changes in the strategic use of the concept of kingly virtue may have done as much, or more, to undermine the idea of a sanctified monarchy and to destabilise monarchical authority as did the scurrilous accounts of kingly vice that emanated from 'Grub Street'.

As we have seen, there was an accepted discourse of kingly virtue in the seventeenth and early eighteenth centuries, but this had been a carefully limited concept, which served to endorse the authority of the monarch as the source of justice, whilst retaining traditional Christian scepticism about the extent and power of human virtue, including the royal variety. From about the mid-century, however, a change began to take place in the rhetoric of kingly virtue. To a new generation, the ideas of Fénelon (which had been derided in his lifetime) on the importance of virtuous monarchy began to appear more compelling than those of his contemporary and one-time opponent Bossuet. A king who depended only on his divine status had only to exist and to keep his throne: his right to rule did not depend on his personal qualities but on the divine source of his authority. His relationship with his people was traditionally depicted as paternal: like a father, a king should concern himself with his subjects' welfare, whilst they in turn owed him filial loyalty. His authority did not rest on his paternalism. But when apologists for the monarchy began to speak of the king's virtues, his compassion for his people, his *bienfaisance* on their behalf, as being fundamental to his kingship they also opened up the possibility of the question: but what if the king is not virtuous? As expectations of the king on moral grounds increased, so did the possibility, almost the inevitability, of his being seen to fall short of the model.

Discussions on the virtue of the king are interesting precisely because they tended to undermine the authority of the monarchy from within, from the ranks of those who supported the principle of monarchy. The language of virtue was a singularly appropriate linguistic vehicle to carry a critique of the functions of the monarchy. It was already situated within the sphere of accepted commentary on the monarchy and it already served to invoke the authority of moral legitimacy.

Sermons on the duties of kingship; panegyrics, whether of living royalty or of long-dead kings; funeral eulogies of members of the royal family; and even works by members of the royal family themselves, invoked the discourse of virtue to refashion the ideal of kingship. These texts emanated from people who held positions of considerable authority within the hierarchy of the *ancien régime*, particularly members of the higher clergy. Their social position makes their adoption of the language of virtue in many ways more surprising, and implicitly more challenging, than the polemical writings of 'outsiders'.

The rise of *bienfaisant* monarchy

Between 1745 and 1789, in the place of the older kingly virtues of glory and justice a new concept began to grow, that of the *'bienfaisant* king'. Relatively little account has been taken of this phrase by historians, but it was central to the shift in public perceptions of the role of the monarchy. There had been earlier references to the good deeds (*bienfaits*) of kings, and to their potential capacity to create happiness amongst their people. Duguet, for example, had referred to the need for princes to be *'bienfaisant* and liberal' but he had seen these as qualities which princes needed in moderation. It was not until after the mid-century that this idea came to wider prominence.[6] Natural sociable virtue was used to redefine the role of kingship. Kings, by means of their authority, power and wealth, were in a uniquely advantageous position to give vent to their natural virtuous impulses by spreading happiness amongst their people. It was the duty of a king, his whole *raison d'être*, to make his people happy.[7] Whereas older notions of kingly virtue had stressed qualities specific to kingship, *bienfaisance* was a virtue which all men (and women) could possess. The notion of the *bienfaisant* king stressed the humanity of the king: his virtues were no different in kind from those of other men. The *bienfaisant* king was seen as approachable and humane rather than exalted and remote. The image of Louis XV as 'the beloved king' had long since become a somewhat embarrassing irony.[8] By contrast, the ideal of the *bienfaisant* king would offer a much more active model. But as a model of behaviour, it would ultimately prove even more difficult for Louis XV's successor to live up to.

The *Oeuvres du Philosophe bienfaisant* by the exiled king of Poland, Stanislas Leczinski, made much of the idea of the virtuous monarch. Stanislas had been forced to abdicate from the Polish throne but had been allowed to keep his royal title and was given the duchy of Lorraine for his lifetime as a form of compensation. He enjoyed a somewhat paradoxical reputation both for keen piety and as a patron of the 'republic of letters'. The idea of *bienfaisance* was compatible with optimistic tendencies in both Christianity and moral philosophy: whilst *bienfaisance* had been popularised by the *philosophes*, it also represented Christ's commandment to 'love one's neighbour'. Significantly perhaps, Stanislas found Rousseau's more pessimistic view of human nature and society unacceptable and he published a critique of Rousseau's *Discours sur les sciences et les arts*.[9] *Bienfaisant* monarchs, he wrote, are, like all 'great men', motivated by their natural virtue. The virtue of kings did not lie in conducting wars for their own 'glory', but in making people happy:

> Thus all the heroes, thus all the great men, whoever they might be, cannot themselves enjoy a truer happiness than that which they procure for the rest of humanity. Their virtue consists, not in ravaging provinces, laying waste to towns, or cutting the throats of the unfortunate, but in rendering their *patrie* and their fellow citizens happy.[10]

Lorraine was of small account in European terms and Stanislas held it only with the support of his son-in-law, Louis XV. But as a king effectively without a kingdom, Stanislas could afford to indulge himself in the role of the virtuous *bienfaisant* monarch, without the burden of maintaining his authority. This was no doubt an irritation to Louis XV, for the utopian image of a Polish republic with an accountable monarchy was far removed from the realities of governing the ungrateful and recalcitrant French. The model of the *roi bienfaisant* was a small but persistent thorn in the royal side, a reminder of what a king ought to be.[11] Ironically, of course, Stanislas himself was effectively a pensioner of Louis's, dependent on him. Notwithstanding, Stanislas's book found favour with the French press: Madame de Maisonneuve, editor of the *Journal des Dames*, quoted the passage given above approvingly and praised Stanislas, who 'makes virtue cherished on the throne'; whilst the *Mémoires secrets* called the book the work of 'a citizen'.[12]

On Stanislas's death in February 1766, his status as a model of virtuous monarchy was confirmed in his funeral eulogy by Boisgelin, then bishop of Lavaur, delivered in the presence of the royal family, including the new dauphin, the future Louis XVI. Boisgelin described *bienfaisance* as the most important virtue which religion teaches to sovereigns, 'a virtue which dispels the prejudices which surround the high birth of princes, and which makes it an easier and simpler task for princes to fulfil the obligations required of them'.[13] It was for the poor amongst the people, he continued, to judge this virtue of kings:

> It is by no means amongst the palaces and tranquil hearths of the rich that the reputation of kings is forged.... This imposing reputation emanates from the heart of the poor man: the simple homes in the towns, the cottages in the hamlets, here dwell the voices that bear witness to the true reputation of kings. Go, visit the dwelling places of poverty; study the sentiments that are forthrightly expressed in uncouth language: it is the poor man who, by his complaints or by his acknowledgement, dictates to history its judgement of kings for all time.[14]

Two months before the death of Stanislas, had come that of the older dauphin, the father of the future Louis XVI. Like Stanislas, this prince had a reputation for piety, although he had certainly not shared his grandfather's philosophic sympathies. In the various eulogies dedicated to his memory he was also depicted as someone who would have been a *bienfaisant* and virtuous monarch – had he lived. The dauphin's disapproval of his father's libertine propensities was well known. In contrast to Louis XV, the clerical eulogists felt able also to discuss the dauphin's private virtues as a husband and father, although they struggled a little to reconcile their account of his virtues with the way in which he had pointedly ignored his second wife when they married. It was well-known that the dauphin had retained a poignant devotion to his first wife, the Spanish infanta who had died in childbirth, and for a long time had shown little affection for his second wife, Marie-Josèphe, the rather stolid, but fertile and devoted Saxon princess who had dutifully provided him with so many royal offspring.[15] The name 'Louis le Bienfaisant' had been reserved for him, in a deliberate evocation of his Polish grandfather rather than his French father.[16] After his death, as we shall see, attempts were also made to bestow this soubriquet on his son, Louis XVI.

Ironically, the reality of the old dauphin's life – one of obscurity, inactivity, piety, and self-indulgence, invisible to his people behind the walls of Versailles – was a stark contrast to the ideal of the active and sociable *bienfaisant* king. The eulogists of the dauphin, perfectly aware of the gap between the ideal of kingship which they wanted to portray and the basic raw material with which they were obliged to deal, conceded that his virtues were only potential ones. This did not impede their speculations, however. Quite the contrary, the absence of concrete evidence provided more space in which to construct the model of a virtuous king. For example, the most extended and political of the eulogies, that of Thomas, that inveterate eulogist and minor *philosophe*, was a deliberate work of construction which bore scant relation to the reality. Thomas depicted the dauphin as a model of virtue, a citizen of a moral republic, deeply egalitarian, who maintained the privileges of rank only with reluctance, because it was his allotted task to rule.[17] According to Thomas, had he lived he would have been:

> very far from adopting that senseless style of politics habitual to some tyrants who whilst believing that it might perhaps be advisable to praise virtue in public, nevertheless take good care to keep it well away from their thrones.... Oh people, by what monsters have you all too often been governed![18]

The implied parallels with the civic education given to *Emile* would have horrified the dauphin. According to Thomas the dauphin spurned the luxury and pride of the court and desired to visit the poor in their 'cottages' – for it was there that the 'nation' was to be found:

> the nation is by no means in palaces; it is in the furrows of the countryside, under the soil of the farm worker, in the home of the artisan, beneath the obscure roofs of the poor.[19]

The dauphin invited 'virtue' to share his throne: 'it is vile without you', and declared that together they would 'show the earth a new league, a league of all the virtuous men in order to make the happiness of a nation'. Thomas ended by having the dauphin remind his young son that chance, not merit, had placed them both in line to the throne, and that it would be his son's duty to be virtuous for he belonged to the '*patrie*'.[20]

Thomas's eulogy was not admired in every quarter. To the *philosophes* there was nothing especially new or radical in its political ideas and there was much to be deplored in the way it fawned to a man who had been their declared enemy. Never, according to Diderot, had the art of writing been so ignominiously 'prostituted'. The orator's art, he said, was that of truth, or at least of appearing truthful.[21] The rhetoric of virtue, it seems, was of no value if it was not used with sincerity. Cynics thought that Thomas had written his eulogy in order to achieve his election to the *Académie française*, and indeed he finally secured this position shortly afterwards in January 1767.[22] The *Mémoires secrets* found the style of the eulogy dull and commented that it gave the ironic impression of being 'an extended satire on the king's conduct'.[23] Nevertheless, the eulogy provides a notable example of how the language of patriotic virtue had worked its way into the heart of the *ancien régime*.

It appears that the monarchy and their closest adherents were anxious to regenerate the public image of the monarchy, which had suffered through the somewhat tawdry reputation of Louis XV. To a certain extent this led to a rethinking of the nature of monarchy. The old dauphin, Louis Ferdinand, had been eager to cultivate more virtue at court, of the conventionally pious kind. He thought it of vital importance that a king should give the lead to his courtiers in this respect. With his mother, Queen Marie Leczinska, he led the devout [*dévot*] party at court. Occasionally they secretly encouraged clerics who were prepared to speak out boldly against Louis's morals, in the hope of reclaiming the king from the embraces of vice. But here again, the notion of public opinion as the legitimate judge of the vices and virtues of kings, together with the growing tendency to print such sermons, were complicating factors. Indeed, as Kaiser has observed, by making the king's sins with Madame de Pompadour more publicly known, the devout party inadvertently helped to further damage the image of the monarchy.[24]

The dauphin's moral disapproval had little impact on his father, but did exercise a greater influence on his son, the duc de Berry, the future Louis XVI. The dauphin had given this son the names Louis-Auguste, after the Christian names of Saint Louis himself, a burden of responsibility which the boy felt obliged to live up to throughout his life. When the death of his elder brothers made Louis-Auguste heir, his father took a more active role in his education, attempting to instil into him piety and Christian virtues. After the old dauphin himself had died, the son was informed by his governor, the duc de la Vauguyon, that he must meditate on his father's virtues every day and seek to emulate them.[25] These virtues went beyond personal piety: they also entailed those qualities necessary for a king to successfully rule the nation. De la Vauguyon set the new dauphin (then only twelve) the task of writing out precepts from *Télémaque* as a schoolboy exercise. A king should choose his courtiers for their virtues, promote virtue amongst his subjects, avoid 'luxury', rule with 'an absolute authority, but guided by the rules of justice'; and a king, wrote the little Louis-Auguste, must be 'the model of virtue'.[26] So Fénelon, who was once exiled by Louis XIV, prohibited from teaching the duc de Bourgogne, and his book banned, now returned in triumph to instruct Louis XIV's descendant kingly virtue! The little Louis-Auguste printed up these precepts on his private printing press at Versailles to show how well he had understood his lesson. It is said that he presented the first copy to Louis XV, who understood its implications rather better than his twelve-year-old grandson, and remarked drily, 'Monsieur le Dauphin, you have finished your work; you had better break up the type.'[27]

Virtue in the pulpit: clerical criticism of Louis XV

The tradition of clerics using the sanction of the pulpit to criticise the king's vices, established by the great orators such as Massillon and Bourdaloue, continued into the eighteenth century, but in the period between the 1760s and Louis XV's death in 1774 they became exceptionally outspoken and showed changes both in style and language. They no longer confined themselves to the king's private shortcomings, but began to broach the subject of how private vices in a king had public consequences. Amongst the most influential of the clerics interested in natural virtue, reason and philosophy were the abbés Beauvais, Torné, Fauchet, Boulogne and Maury, and the Carmelite Père Elisée.[28] These clerics were far from being in the advance guard of radical political or philosophic ideas but they were prepared to raise the issue of the responsibilities that came with kingship. Such sermons could even, on certain prescribed occasions in the religious calendar such as the sermons given for Lent, be made to the king's face.

In February 1765 the rhetoric of virtue resounded in the pulpit when a barefoot Carmelite, the Père Elisée, a famous preacher of his day, used it in his address to the court. Elisée's own attitude towards virtue was somewhat ambiguous. He felt strongly that virtue without God was nothing but a fraud, but he was also shocked at the values of the court, and how far they diverged from true Christianity. The *dévot* party may well have had a hand in arranging for him to deliver an outspoken sermon in an attempt to capitalise on the death of Madame de Pompadour the previous year and recall Louis to his duty. Yet Elisée went beyond his remit to criticise the king's private morals. Louis was publicly castigated by the Carmelite for failing in his duty to give an example of virtue to 'the nation' and Elisée added, 'kings are put in place only in order to make men happy by their good deeds (*bienfaits*) and virtuous by their examples'.[29] Kingly virtue was no longer a matter of private conscience, but the justification for kingship itself and a matter for 'the nation' to judge, since it was the nation which was directly concerned. The sermon was reproduced in the *Mémoires secrets*, for the public to judge, with the ironical comment that the courtiers all has-tened to copy down the text assiduously as it was spoken, much to Louis's discomfiture.[30]

The criticisms of these clerics were couched in general terms: they were not, after all, involved in the niceties of government themselves. The clergy were in a privileged position whereby they were both part of established authority, and yet stood a little outside it, able to put for-ward alternative visions of society and political order based on moral order. Some clerics constituted themselves as spokesmen for the 'poor', the 'people' and the 'unfortunate', whose virtues were contrasted with the vices of the 'rich'. Wealth and noble birth in themselves did not make a person culpable, but being socially 'useless' and indulging in vice whilst the poor went hungry was seen as reprehensible and a betrayal of the duties of the privileged members of society. Most of these clerics would not be categorised as poor themselves, though some did come from humble backgrounds, and some, like the Père Elisée, chose to live austere lives.

The abbé Beauvais, who was considered by some to be the only preacher of the time to compare with Bossuet and Massillon for elo-quence, came from relatively humble origins. He also had a *parlemen-taire* background, being the son of an advocate in the *parlement* of Paris.[31] When still at the beginning of his career, he was chosen to deliver several sermons at court in 1760 and 1761. He took the oppor-tunity thus presented to draw attention to the miseries of the poor and to openly criticise the morals of the court. This attack on courtly vice won the congratulations of the dauphin. Despite the support of the *dévots*, it seems that the abbé in his eagerness had gone too far for some at court: it was 1768 before he spoke there again, when he was selected to give the sermons for Advent. He had previously delivered a sermon in Paris specifically on 'the social virtues', and he drew on this theme to argue for education and happiness, and against 'luxury'. Again his oratorical skills and his integrity were much praised but he did not receive the advancement he could have expected had he had better social connections. His most radical court sermons came in 1773 when he was selected to give the customary series of sermons for Lent. Once again, more openly than before, he spoke of the social virtues, giving sermons on such subjects as 'On the dispensation of good works (*bienfaits*)', 'On the misery of the poor', and 'On Christian chastity (*pudeur*)'.[32] This last subject particularly stunned the court, since they had sat back expecting the customary Annunciation Day panegyric of the Virgin Mary, but the abbé treated them instead to a sermon on the virtue of chastity, having somehow, he declared, not had time to complete the customary eulogy. He stressed the fact that chastity was an essential virtue, not only for women but also for men.[33] This was, he knew, taking the liberty of the pulpit dangerously far: 'Pardon my imprudence, which stems from the innocence of my motives and from my zeal for the purity of your souls.' He ended with calling upon the congregation to join with him in a prayer which linked the regeneration of 'chastity' at court with the regeneration of the nation itself: 'may we see the disappearance, along with the disorder of the senses, of all the vices, all the disorders and all the calamities which bring desolation to this nation'.[34]

In his sermon 'On the dispensation of good works', Beauvais spoke of the 'pitiless rich' who abused the 'unfortunate', and made a plea for a regenerated royal *bienfaisance* which would reward 'the virtuous men' and lead to 'the general happiness (*félicité*)'.[35] He set up the concept of virtue in opposition to the entire system of patronage by which the *ancien régime* functioned. He issued a general warning to all those involved 'in public administration', declaring that the practice of appointing people to official functions through favour, rather than as a means to 'recompense virtue' by appointing people of merit, engendered great distress, and was a calamity for the nation:

> Must it be then, that in order to satisfy the vanity of an ambitious man, that the happiness of an entire city, of a province, and maybe even of a whole nation be compromised? Must the good of all be sacrificed to the good of just one man? Fatal private advantages, which abuse the public good.[36]

He divided the nation into two parts, the 'rich' and the 'people'; constituting himself as the spokesman to the king 'in the name of his people', whose sublime loyalty he contrasted with the self-interest of the 'rich':

> Do not fear to hear murmerings from them: it is the rich who complain in the midst of their abundance. In the depths of their misery, and in ruined hovels, this people, this poor people bless your name. If they suffer injustices, they are convinced that someone else has misused your authority against your own wishes.[37]

Although his words were addressed to Louis XV, Beauvais apparently thought that little could be expected of so calculated a sinner, and he ended by turning his attention to the next generation, to the future Louis XVI, his brothers and their wives, entreating them to work to make the people virtuous and happy.[38]

Beauvais's last sermon, given on Easter Sunday, was the most daring of all, for instead of concluding with the customary 'compliment to the king', he launched into a dramatic prayer that Louis XV should resume the path of virtue:

> My God, save the king...and religion will take up once more its initial splendour; and public morals will recover their purity and innocence; and the nation will witness the flourishing of the ancient virtues and the lost honour of the French; and along with the interior felicity of the state, the monarchy will see a rebirth of its own power and external glory...let the king be reborn and at that very moment everything else, the happiness, the glory and the virtue of the nation, the entire nation, will revive along with its master. My God, my God, save the king, and everything is saved.[39]

This series of sermons, and particularly its dramatic conclusion, caused outrage in court circles; the *Mémoires secrets* reported that some courtiers had wanted proceedings to be taken against the abbé for having delivered what was tantamount to a public insult to the king, but that Louis had not permitted it. A rumour followed that the king would dismiss Madame du Barry, but nothing came of this.[40] A dispute then arose as to whether or not Beauvais should receive the customary reward for such a performance in the form of a bishopric.[41] This dispute thus followed the classic lines of the man of virtue (embodied by Beauvais himself) versus the privileges of noble birth. It was almost unheard of for bishops to come from any social class but that of the nobility and the question was as much about Beauvais's commoner status as about his uncomfortably moral sermons: a situation which appeared to support the idea that the court was a hostile environment for 'men of virtue'. It was said that the bishop of Carcassone, a man noted for his own 'virtues', intervened on Beauvais's behalf with the declaration: 'If I believed that nobility was the principal requirement needed for the episcopacy, I would trample my cross underfoot, and I would renounce the high office with which I have been invested'; but most of the bishops were openly hostile.[42] Beauvais eventually received his bishopric, an achievement which the *Mémoires secrets* attributed to the personal intervention of members of the royal family. This was seen by some as a qualified victory for the man of virtue over the social advantages of birth and nobility.[43] This appointment was an isolated instance, however, and was far from signalling the start of a movement to reform the episcopacy with appointments based on merit. On the contrary, at the beginning of the Revolution every one of the 139 bishops was of noble birth, a fact which contributed to the sense of grievance of the lower towards the higher clergy.[44]

Beauvais's appointment also signified a qualified victory for the rhetoric of virtue as a mode of criticising the values of the court. The following year, the abbé Beauvais spoke openly of the gulf between rich and poor in his sermon for Maundy Thursday and declared to the king: 'Sire, my duty as a minister of the God of truth obliges me to tell you that your people are suffering; and that you are the cause of their misery and that you have been kept in ignorance of this.'[45] The *Mémoires secrets* described the great impression made by Beauvais: 'His theme was the gulf between the idle and useless life of the rich and the active and useful life of the poor. On this occasion the orator presented a pitiful portrait of the misery endured by the people, and by means of an oratorical device claimed that he could depict their misery better than anyone, for he himself came from that class.'[46] Louis XV apparently accepted the rebuke, though without giving any indication that he meant to act upon it, and said with a smile that he hoped that Beauvais would remember that he had been engaged to deliver the Lent sermons in 1776 – despite being now a bishop.[47] It was rumoured that the *dévots* in general, and Christophe de Beaumont, bishop of Paris, in particular, had been the instigators of this particular sermon, once again in the hope of swaying the mind of the king.

The panegyrics of Saint-Louis

The 1760s also witnessed the revitalisation of the long tradition of praising past kings as a forum for the discussion of the virtues and duties of kingship. The foremost models of the great kings of France's past were Henri IV and St Louis (Louis XII also became the subject of eulogies, but not until about 1775, when he began to be associated with the Estates General).[48] These past kings were used as counters in political controversies and were often credited with various political reforms and a devotion to the 'nation' which bore scant relation to their historical existence. Henri IV had long enjoyed a posthumous popularity, but in the last years of the *ancien régime*, particularly during the Maupeou crisis of 1770 to 1774, a veritable cult grew up around him. According to La Harpe's eulogy of Henri IV, he was 'the best of kings' and 'the best of men'.[49] That Henri, who during his lifetime had enjoyed a somewhat flighty reputation for 'gallantry', could acquire posthumously a reputation for virtue illustrates the point that sexual continence was not in itself seen as a necessary kingly virtue. The essential point was that the king should not let himself be influenced by women either in his political decisions or in his dispensation of patronage.

The panegyrics of St Louis, which took place every 25th August in the chapel of the Louvre in the presence of the *Académie française* were to become a forum where it was possible to criticise the current values of government through the format of praising the virtues of a dead monarch. During the first half of the century this customary event had enjoyed a reputation more for dullness than for political fireworks: it was hard work, after all, for successive clerics to think up fresh things to say in praise of St Louis year after year. To their audience the whole procedure seemed outmoded and of little importance. The panegyrics were subject to censorship, which had been generally a formality, and were afterwards published. Typical of their style was the panegyric by Le Couturier given in 1746 which described in a straightforward fashion the traditional forms of kingly virtue, namely piety and military prowess. St Louis was said to unite 'the qualities of a great prince to the virtues of a Christian'. Louis XV was deliberately invoked and compared favourably with his ancestor – a comparison which would be avoided in later years.[50]

Signs of a change began from about 1750. One striking characteristic was the growing tendency to criticise the crusades: a sort of touchstone of clerical willingness to accept some of the basic values of the Enlightenment.[51] But, insidiously, the idea of kingly virtue also began to assume a greater significance both for speakers and auditors. The abbé Boismont was known for his interest in philosophic ideas. He referred to St Louis as a 'star of *bienfaisance*' in the heavens, who contributed to 'public felicity', but affirmed mildly that, 'the happiness of the virtuous Christian' could only be ensured by their being a 'submissive citizen'.[52] La Tour du Pin, who spoke in the following year, went so far as to praise St Louis's virtue as a civic quality, defining it as 'the virtue of citizens, as well as of kings; the virtue of man, as well as of Christianity'.[53]

In the 1760s and early 1770s, a number of the panegyrics were more overtly critical of the accepted basis of kingly authority, putting forward a new vision of an accountable monarchy. The members of the *Académie française* were largely responsible for this politicisation: it was they who appointed the clerics, sometimes applauded them (although sermons were not supposed to be publicly applauded as though they were indeed political events), and even made attempts for the sermons to bypass the obligatory censorship of the Sorbonne. The militancy of the panegyrics was part of the unofficial campaign undertaken by the *Académie française* for greater autonomy against the monarchy and the Church. In this, the academicians appear to have been motivated as much by the desire to modernise an institution which was felt to be so outmoded as to be almost an embarrassment, and the determination to control those events which came under their own corporate and institutional aegis, as by any deliberate desire to seriously rethink the basis of monarchy. At points the sermons became the centre of a political controversy, when it was felt that the speaker had taken advantage of having an official public forum to cast aspersions on the established order in what amounted to overt 'political discussions', by transforming the accepted boundaries of the political into a matter of public inquiry.[54] The subject which aroused most anticipation was how the clerics would handle the question of St Louis's involvement in the crusades, which the more radical of them attacked more or less openly, and even the more timid questioned the idea of a just religious war.[55]

One of the panegyrics which aroused the most controversy was that of the abbé Bassinet in 1767. He asserted that a king's authority can only be based on his virtue: 'power is only genuine in so far as it is established on the basis of virtue'. The virtues which Bassinet praised in Louis were not unique to kings but were common to all men. He claimed that his role as an orator was to praise, not St Louis the king (nor it appears the saint), but 'the man . . . decorated solely by his virtues'. Louis's principal virtues were to 'work for the good of men' and to 'serve the felicity of all people'.[56] When he came to the question of the crusades it is clear that Bassinet found it difficult to reconcile these with the model of St Louis's virtues which he had set out. He attributed Louis's participation to a victory of 'his piety over his politics', which implied that the latter quality was more necessary than the former in a monarch: strange language indeed from a cleric.[57] The *Mémoires secrets* gave an amused account of the 'great outcry' over this panegyric:

> He was reproached with having converted this eulogy, which was especially consecrated for the triumph of religion, into an absolutely profane ceremony. He did not even make the sign of the cross. No text, no citation from the holy scriptures, not a word about the good Lord nor his saints. He considered Louis IX only in relation to his political, warlike and moral virtues. He attacked the crusades, making his audience see the absurdity, cruelty, even the injustice of them.[58]

Duclos himself, the permanent secretary of the *Académie française*, supported Bassinet and arranged for him to give the same panegyric the following month at Saint-Roch.[59] When the panegyric was published the following year, Bassinet printed an introductory letter, defending himself against the charge that he had 'sacrificed the Christian to the Hero' in terms which make clear what was at stake for him in his definition of kingly virtue as political:

> I did not believe that it was needful to praise only the religious virtues of a sovereign and to neglect the civil and political virtues, nor that piety was the only quality needed to make a great prince.[60]

For Bassinet there was a clear distinction to be made between political or civic and religious virtues, and it was the former which were more necessary in a 'good' king. In the same letter he openly acknowledged his debt to 'the sublime author of *L'Esprit des lois*', adding that: 'The slight connection that people have claimed to trace between the work of this great Man and myself, infinitely honours me.'[61]

In 1769, the abbé Le Couturier delivered a panegyric which caused as great a stir as had Bassinet's two years earlier, and whose tone and language mark the extent of the changes in the customary rhetorical treatment of 'virtuous kings' since his own earlier effort in 1746. He launched into a fierce tirade against the inhumanity of the crusades, which he saw as the antithesis of Christ's virtue and Christian love. He painted a grim vision of 'the tomb of the God of peace, of the God of virtues, drenched in blood and sullied by crime'.[62] Le Couturier spoke less of civic virtue than had Bassinet, but much more of *bienfaisance*: the virtue of kings.[63] The priest emphasised to his listeners, 'Kings exist only in order to make their peoples happy'.[64] A furore broke out over how such a work came to be passed by the censor, and over the public applause which had greeted the abbé in the chapel. According to the *Mémoires secrets* Le Couturier was attacked for having 'given lessons in politics from a pulpit from whence only lessons in virtue should be given'. It was even reported of him that he was a supporter of the 'party of the encyclopaedia'.[65] The Archbishop of Paris forbade the abbé to preach again; but this penalty proved short-lived and only added to the culprit's reputation for daring outspokenness. When Le Couturier appeared again at a pulpit, the *Mémoires secrets* described how 'people hurried to go and hear this censured preacher, with the same eagerness with which they seek out forbidden literature which sells under the counter'.[66]

The shifting terms of the rhetoric which was used for the eulogies of St Louis was a matter to be negotiated by each cleric, a matter of choice, ambition and loyalties. In 1772, the abbé Maury was selected to deliver the panegyric. He was from a more obscure background than most of the panegyrists, the son of an artisan. It might be suspected that this would make him more political and more resentful of privilege, but the situation was much more complex. The relative weakness of his position, which was one more than usually dependent on patrons, and personal choice made him careful in his use of political language. The situation was complicated by the fact that in 1772 the exiling of the *parlement* of Paris was very much in people's minds. Defenders of the *parlements* had called for the summoning of the Estates General, a call which would be repeated in the final crisis of 1788. Maury was concerned both to please his audience and to avoid incurring official wrath.[67] The panegyric was scattered with copious references to such fashionable terms as '*bienfaisance*', 'patriotic virtues', 'nation', '*patrie*', 'the people's felicity'.[68] But Maury was careful to avoid making what might be interpreted as attacks on monarchy or religion, and chose to defend the crusades, an outmoded position by the 1770s, and one that aroused the derision of Voltaire.[69] On the other hand, Maury depicted monarchy as the appropriate defender of civic rights. He spoke of the obligations imposed by kingly *bienfaisance*: a king was 'a Man who is only elevated above the rest of humanity in order to be best placed to find out those people who are the most unfortunate'. He flattered himself that he had been the first to notice that it was St Louis who had first established the 'political existence of the Third Estate' by summoning its representatives to a public counsel at Languedoc. Thus, it was to the precedent set by Louis XV's ancestor that the Estates General owed its claim to 'completely represent the Nation'.[70] As a measure of how acceptable this form of rhetoric had become, provided that the speaker did not use it to criticise the existing regime, the *Académie* had little difficulty in procuring the customary benefice as his reward; even the reference to the Estates General proved acceptable in this context.[71]

Death of Louis XV and accession of Louis XVI, the *bienfaisant* king

The extent of the gap which had opened up between the ideal of kingly virtue and the popular perception of the actual condition of the monarchy is apparent in the funeral orations following the death of Louis XV in 1774.[72] The codes of language usable in such a situation was well understood, though not formally acknowledged, and the orations are most striking by what they leave out than for what they include. The orations are notable for the fact that by tacit assent, virtue is scarcely mentioned by the clerics who gave them, a telling absence which was in marked contrast to the funeral orations of Louis XV's own son, the former dauphin. The rhetoric of kingly virtue proved an embarrassment for the clerical orators as they struggled to find the words to present Louis as having been worthy of his high office without appearing to condone the way in which he had lived. They were in an unenviable position. What, after all, could a cleric say in expiation of a king whose reputation for vice rather than virtue was notorious throughout the kingdom, one who for so many years had not taken the sacraments? In terms of the rhetoric of kingly virtue the only function the dead king could serve was that of providing an ominous warning, both to his successor and to his people, of the consequences of abandoning kingly virtue and embracing all too human failings. Beauvais, who had been so courageous in delivering outspoken sermons before the living king, was now faced with the task of saying what he could on behalf of the dead one: 'man sees virtue,' he stated sorrowfully, 'he sees it, he loves it, and he lets himself be led astray by the vice which he himself condemns'.[73] According to Beauvais, Louis's greatest virtue was his 'amiable affabil-ity'.[74] This was hardly an impressive quality when set next to kingly *bienfaisance*, and it was even further removed from Bossuet's concept of kingly virtue as a partly divine quality. There were suggestions at the time that both this oration and Beauvais's sermon of the previous year had been engineered by members of the *dévot* party.[75] Most of the funeral orators followed suit and focused on the moral lessons to be learned from Louis's 'faiblesses' rather than straining their powers of imagination too far by thinking up virtues which could plausibly be attributed to the dead king.[76]

But a few clerics did take the opportunity to make projections for the new reign and to envisage a happy future under a new king. Torné, in particular, recalling the military disasters of the Seven Years War, spoke powerfully against war, caused, he said, by 'the passions of kings', and confidently predicted that the 'sublime class of thinking and virtuous men' would unite with the Church's ministers to bring about 'the happy revolutions which must restore peace, justice and liberty to the world'. Public opinion was, to his mind, composed of a league between the *philosophes* and the Church. He envisaged 'a united philosophic and Christian people' that would oblige monarchs to reign in accordance with public opinion: 'The combination of particular opinions gives birth to public opinion, whose indomitable force will make crowned heads bow to the morals of the age.'[77] Thus if kings could not be relied upon by themselves to act virtuously then it was legitimate that they should be constrained to do so by the force of public opinion, whose political virtue would uphold the integrity of the state even if kings proved all too human. Torné ended with a long and predictable assertion that Louis XVI and his wife were already giving signs of the virtue with which they would reign.[78] They and public opinion would doubtless be in accord with one another.

The opening of the reign of Louis XVI and Marie-Antoinette was marked by an outpouring of material on their virtues and on the happiness which it was eagerly assumed they would bring their people. The expectations aroused during this 'honeymoon' period between the new king and his people were heightened by the contrast presented with the last depressing years of Louis XV. Louis XVI also acquired some instant popularity for his initial interest in reform, and especially for his restoration of the *parlements*. The reasons why he did so are complex: it was partly (like so much of Bourbon policy) a consequence of ministerial intrigue and jostlings for power, but it was also an attempt on Louis's part to cultivate the approval of public opinion. This action was a great mistake from the point of view of monarchical interests, but it is a mark of the success of the new rhetoric of kingly virtue that the monarchy itself allowed its actions to be influenced by this image of itself. Some years earlier Louis had written in his *Réflexions*: 'I must always consult public opinion, it is never wrong.'[79] Louis wanted to see himself reflected in the eyes of his people as a virtuous king, who had made them happy. He would not be one of those kings who according to Fénelon, whose lessons he had taken in as a child, burn in hell for having oppressed the people.[80]

But it was a dangerous route for a king to take; it gave others the right to decide whether he was fulfilling his role. By slow stages the legitimacy of political power passed from his hands to where others, in the name of 'public opinion' or of 'the people' or of 'the nation', were ready to receive it. In Rennes (where the triumphant defender of the *parlements* during the Brittany Affair, La Chalotais, had recently been reinstated) a single performance took place of a highly subversive play entitled 'Le Couronnement d'un roi', written, it was said, by one of the lawyers of the Rennes *parlement*. It depicted the old king as surrounded by personifications of 'All the Vices that surround the throne...Luxury, Despotism, Voluptuousness, Flattery'. Although the virtue and *bienfaisance* of the new king were contrasted with the vices of the previous one, the

sacred aura of kingship was undermined by such representations. Nor
was Louis XVI's authority strengthened by verses which linked his virtue
to his having restored 'the senate' (the *parlement* of Paris).[81] The *parlements*, as we shall see, were serious challengers for the moral legitimacy
of virtue.

At the time of Louis XVI's accession to the throne he was greeted as a
bienfaisant king, an ideal man amongst other men, who possessed the
civic virtues and would lead his people to a new happiness on earth. The
virtuous king was now a *bienfaisant* king, as Claude Fauchet declared in
August 1774 when in the customary panegyric of St Louis he depicted
the king–saint as 'the model of all the virtues', who was credited by
Fauchet with being the instigator of what amounted almost to a Christian utopia in France. A virtuous king would now, in contrast to his
predecessor, be a living and active model of virtue to all his subjects.
There was a shift of emphasis from the older idea of the virtuous king:
the idea that a 'social pact' existed between the king and his people,
which it was the moral duty of the king to sustain. The voice of Fénelon
echoed once more, with greater resonance than it had done in his own
lifetime. He was invoked as an accepted authority on the duties of
kingship: a king 'only reigns in order to be a MAN OF THE PEOPLE;
and he is only worthy of royalty insofar as he forgets his own interests
for those of the public good.[82]

Thus, from a quality linked to the king's quasi-divine role, kingly
virtue was slowly but consistently being transformed into an essentially
secular quality. By the mid-1770s the king's virtues were held to be like
in kind to those of other citizens. The difference between a king and his
people was that God placed kings in an elevated position so that they
could put their virtue into practice. The legitimacy of kingly authority
was thus closely bound up with the extent to which a king could be seen
to be acting virtuously. The 'virtuous king' showed his active concern for
the people, especially those who were 'unfortunate', by his *bienfaisance*.
Virtuous kingship acquired elements of a civic discourse. A king's virtue
epitomised his essential humanity; he was one citizen amongst many,
albeit in an exalted position, and his first duty was to the 'nation'. The
source of the king's authority had shifted by imperceptible degrees from
the endorsement of God's will to that of the people. Kingly virtue was no
longer perceived as a matter for his private conscience and his confessor
alone, but as a fit subject for public concern and public judgement. Since
the king was responsible for government and the well-being of his
people, he ought not to have areas of his life which were unavailable
for public scrutiny. Not only were a king's private virtues the object of

legitimate public speculation, but also subject to examination was the way in which his private qualities affected his ability to carry out his public duties. If monarchical government was to be conducted virtuously the boundaries between private and public did not exist and the process of government should be transparent, its integrity apparent to all.

This altered definition of kingly virtue thus contributed to the wider process of desacralisation of the monarchy traced by Chartier and others. Interestingly, this particular form of desacralisation was not engineered by pamphleteers and those hostile to the monarchy, but was, on the contrary, led by certain members of the clergy, whose aim was not to undermine the institution of monarchy but to revitalise it, and secure its place within the hearts of the people. This reformulation of the nature and duties of monarchy was made necessary by the genuine popular unease felt by many of the clergy in particular at the way in which Louis XV conducted his private life and appeared to disregard quite flagrantly the precepts of Catholicism which he was sworn to defend. But Louis's critics were also inspired by two rather more positive influences: the philosophic concept of natural virtue and *bienfaisance*, and the Jansenist concept of kingly virtue first conceived by Duguet.

This language of active virtuous kingship did indeed help to regenerate the tarnished image of the French monarchy. The early years of the reign of Louis XVI bore witness to waves of optimism about the future. There was a sense of hope, of aroused expectation, but also an increased potential for disappointment. It was no novelty that kings should fall short of initial expectations of them, but the altered language of kingly virtue provided a linguistic and conceptual framework against which perceived shortcomings could be articulated and judged. The revitalised language of kingly virtue, whilst giving new legitimacy to kingship, was thus not without its negative side for the monarchy. There were two principal reasons for this: one of which related to the particular position of the king, the other to a more general ambiguity about the status of *bienfaisance* when it emanated from the rich. There was the acknowledged assumption that what would be a virtue in an ordinary person was, in a king, no more than a duty which might be rightfully expected of him, and therefore such moral qualities and concern for the public good were in him less intrinsically laudable. If the ideal was held that virtue did indeed, in Pope's words, bring 'happiness here below', and if the institution of absolute monarchy placed all the burden of active virtue in the person of the king, it was then his *duty* to love his people, to promote the 'public good' and to secure his people's happiness: an onerous burden indeed. More generally, there was the classic argument that since providence had given the rich so many material advantages, *bienfaisance* correspondingly cost them a great deal less than did the 'widow's mite' of the poor – an argument which could be used to undermine the *bienfaisance* of the king, even while it was officially being invoked and praised.

Marie-Antoinette: the queen as the corrupter of royal virtue

Public concern over whether or not the king was fulfilling his public role contributed to this desacralisation of the authority of the monarchy and ultimately to its destabilisation. Debates over the virtue of the monarchy in the 1780s focused, however, on its most vulnerable point, the virtues of the queen. Precedents for the harsh judgement of queens who were believed to have overstepped the perceived boundaries of their role can be found in the attacks on Anne of Austria and, before her, Catherine de Medici. Popular hostility towards queens combined two prejudices: distrust of women engaging in politics, and suspicion aroused by the presence of a foreign interest at the heart of the French government. The virtues of queens were different in character from those of kings, and the actions of queens had always been more circumscribed and held to be more publicly accountable than those of kings. The precept that the French public, being an 'enlightened people', was the rightful judge of the queen's actions, and could demand of her 'the virtues which it had the right to claim', was set out by (among others) Stanislas, the exiled king of Poland. A queen's virtues should include her resignation of any ties to her own people. The conduct of politics was also outside her sphere: she should not attempt 'to penetrate the veils which cover the secrets of the state'.[83] Stanislas's daughter Marie Leczinska, for her part, had obtained popular sympathy for her piety and devoutness, and long-suffering under the persistent neglect and chronic infidelity of her husband. She was the model of queenly or 'humble' virtues: devout, quietly suffering her husband's neglect and infidelity, with a chastity beyond question, and producing royal sons to whom she might impart her own virtues, and finally going quietly and uncomplainingly to her grave.[84] During Louis XV's reign, all the opprobrium lavished on 'political' women was reserved, not for the queen, but for his mistresses – above all, Madame de Pompadour and Madame du Barry. In the anti-monarchical propaganda of the time, Marie Leczinska stood for virtue: they stood for vice.

With Marie-Antoinette it was a different matter. Here the conditions were right, once again, for a queen to be held as the very personification of vice in the body politic. This was largely an unfortunate consequence of her husband being genuinely devoted to her, and taking no mistresses as his grandfather had done, thus laying himself open to accusations of uxoriousness. She combined the power of a queen with that of a mis- tress. She represented the vices of queenship: the very reverse of the 'humble virtues' of her predecessor. These vices were characterised as: sexual infidelity to her husband (and by extension, treachery to France), lavish spending, indifference to the sufferings of the poor and oppressed, the furtherance of corruption at court, and, of course, inter- ference in politics and the appointment of ministers. John Hardman has argued with authority that this image bore little relation to the truth, and that in fact Marie-Antoinette took little part in political decision- making until after the political disaster for the monarchy of the Assem- bly of Notables in 1787. But by that time her image had already been irreversibly damaged in the eyes of the public. Initially the hostile image of Marie-Antoinette was fostered by factions at court who were excluded from the circle of those who had ready access to the king and queen, and took revenge for the undoubted ineptness of the royal couple at hand- ling the system of patronage and faction which was the life-blood of the courtier.

Most damning of all for the queen had been the 'Diamond Necklace Affair'. This had begun in 1785 when an adventuress on the fringes of the court, Jeanne de la Motte, an obscure descendant from the ancient royal house of Valois, dreamed up a scheme to make her fortune. She persuaded the Cardinal de Rohan, currently out of favour at court, that the queen had asked her to entrust him with a secret mission to acquire on behalf of the queen a fabulously expensive diamond necklace. She told him that the queen dared not be seen to buy it openly, so that discretion was essential. The cardinal himself was hardly the conven- tional figure of the devout prelate, being somewhat susceptible to femi- nine charms, and a keen follower of mysticism (he was a patron of the magician Cagliostro). He proved to be a fairly gullible victim. To con- vince him of her good faith, Jeanne de la Motte arranged a secret meet- ing between the cardinal and a woman, disguised as the queen, at night in the gardens of Versailles. This woman, whose name was Nicole, was in fact a courtesan who happened to bear a superficial resemblance to the queen, but the susceptible cardinal was easily duped. The cardinal, believing that this would be a means to bring him back into royal favour again, used his personal credit to acquire the necklace which he handed over to Jeanne de la Motte. The necklace was broken up, its 579 diamonds disposed of and sold. The whole affair eventually came to light when the jewellers came directly to the queen and pressed for payment. Not knowing what was going on, the king and queen believed that Rohan had used the queen's name in an attempt at fraud, and to blacken her reputation. The king was badly advised by his minister Breteuil (who, for factional reasons was hostile to Rohan) to bring the cardinal to trial. The cardinal opted for trial before the Paris *parlement*. Along with him, Jeanne de la Motte and a motley collection of dubious characters processed through the courts, telling a series of implausible stories, which raised doubts in many people's minds about the queen's own role. The trial lasted for nine months and became an immense scandal, which assumed staggering proportions when the *parlement* acquitted the cardinal of any wrong-doing. The implication must be that the queen herself had been involved in the affair. Louis and Marie-Antoinette were devastated when they heard the verdict. Although she had not been directly accused, the virtue of the queen of France had been condemned by public opinion.

The Affair of the Diamond Necklace went far beyond court circles, and appeared to confirm all the rumours about the queen's conspicuous consumption and sexual corruption. More than any other single event, that particular scandal undermined the authority of the monarchy in the eyes of the public. The monarchy emerged from that sorry affair looking either depraved or ludicrous, depending on one's opinion. Either way, the contrast between the public image of the monarchy and the dignified language of kingly virtue could not have been more marked or more apparent to all observers, whether detractors or, more worryingly, to loyalists.[85]

6
The Maupeou Crisis and the Rise of Patriotic Virtue, 1770–5

may the light of your zeal never be extinguished in the hearts of the French, may you inspire people of every station, may you moderate their desire for riches, suppress the luxuries that entrammel us and lead us astray, recall the simplicity of good morals, and the taste for hard work, banish the exclusive love of self that destroys all society, inspire public and private virtues, and renew amongst us all the marvels that you are equipped to bring about!

Letrosne, exhortation to magistrates,
*Discourse on the present condition of the magistrature . . .
pronounced at the opening of the session for
the bailiwick of Orléans, 15th November 1763*

A virtuous man is a living law.

Servan, *Discourse on morals pronounced
before the Parlement of Grenoble, 1769*

The *parlements* of the *ancien régime* were the most powerful source of opposition to the monarchy, and on several dramatic occasions the magistrates of the *parlements* claimed to be the representatives of the nation in the absence of the Estates General.[1] Historians have long been aware of the importance of these struggles between *parlements* and monarchy, but in recent years the focus has shifted somewhat towards the study of the ideological arguments put forward by the *parlementaires*. Recent studies have examined how the *parlementaires'* rhetoric not only described but also structured and defined their sphere of authority.[2] Magistrates and lawyers were adept in the use of rhetoric acquired through their judicial training. All members of the judiciary spent a substantial amount of time familiarising themselves with the rhetorical

153

strategies of the most admired writers of antiquity. Of these, the best known of all were the declamations of Cicero, in which the process of law was frequently depicted as the struggle of virtue against despotism.[3] The concept of virtue was central to eighteenth-century notions of justice. This chapter will explore some of the codes and strategies involved in the use of the traditional *parlementaire* concept of virtue, and examine ways in which the concept of judicial virtue was taken up and used by lawyers and polemicists outside the *parlements*, writing in their support. What is perhaps most striking is the extent to which the magistrates themselves were wary of invoking the discourse of virtue too readily. They were well-aware of how unwelcome to themselves were its radical and egalitarian implications. They had other paradigms with which to justify their own authority and generally they preferred to use these, such as the traditional discourses of justice and service. The Maupeou suppression of the autonomy of the *parlements* offers a particularly significant example of how, in moments of crisis, the *parlements* themselves had recourse to the discourse of virtue. But it was left to others who were supporters of the *parlements*, journalists, lawyers and pamphleteers, to seize with real enthusiasm on the concept of virtue and use it as part of their strategic linguistic weaponry against the authority of the monarchy. It was a strategy which could be as alarming to the magistrates themselves as it was to the monarchy.

The sovereign courts occupied a complex and often ambiguous political position within the structure of the *ancien régime*. Although they owed their existence and offices to royal policy, they were far more than courts of law and their function of registering royal decrees frequently brought them into conflict with the monarchy. Whilst the monarchy recognised and had indeed delegated the right of the *parlements* to scrutinise royal decrees prior to registration, it would insist in critical instances on its sovereign right to obedience. The magistrates frequently tested this position by protesting and withholding the registration of decrees of which they disapproved. At several points between 1715 and 1771, the ritual procedure of disputation between the *parlements* and the authority of the monarchy escalated into open conflict. After 1753 the *parlements* argued that they had the right to judge for themselves the merit of putative laws, a right which they based on the claim that there had existed in Frankish times an ancient constitution which provided the basis of authority for contemporary law courts.[4]

Religious justifications were also employed: the part played by Jansenists in these disputes has been highlighted by several historians, of whom Dale Van Kley is the most prominent, who have argued that

Jansenists still formed a recognisable presence in *parlementaire* disputes during the period of the Maupeou coup and even up to the pre-revolution. This presence calls into question many of our assumptions about the relationship between political and religious thought. As we have seen, there was a growing strand of Jansenist thought whereby it could be claimed that men of virtue might justly engage in political life in defence of their faith. It was often Jansenist sympathisers such as Target, Mey and La Chalotais who made the most effective use of the notion of civic virtue.

Whilst no one would deny that struggles between monarchy and *parlements* were often intense, there is less consensus about the exact nature of the issues under dispute. Some historians, led by Keith Baker, have argued that there is a strong degree of intellectual coherence in the discourse of the *parlements* and that their quarrels with the monarchy were ideological in inspiration. Ideological opposition is said to have taken the form of a 'parlementary constitutionalism' which developed in the course of their disputes with Louis XV and his ministers.[5] The *parlements* and their supporters were increasingly prepared to align themselves with the concept of public opinion, which was depicted as an impartial judge of the monarch's actions, and which they claimed to represent. Public opinion was represented as moral authority – hence the centrality of the rhetoric of virtue. Without the justification of a moral basis, public opinion would be no more valid than more wayward and partial forms of judgement.

Various *parlementaire* discourses have been defined and examined, but to look at their language alone, without considering the intentions of the minds who created them, would be to take an unnecessarily reductionist approach to the idea of the past. The connection between discourse or rhetoric and intentionality, and how this connection can be studied, is a constant problem for the historian and one to which there can be no definitive answers. Historians of the *parlements* have tended to divide into those who thought that the *parlements* were selfishly undermining an enlightened and reformist monarchy, and those who see them as being, in a real sense, defenders of liberty against despotism.[6] To fall into either camp is to risk taking the rhetoric of either the *parlements* (that they acted in the public interest) or the monarchy (that the *parlements* acted selfishly at the expense of the public good) at face value. A third perspective emphasises not the *parlementaires'* rhetoric but their judicial role. According to this view, the magistrates' actions can best be understood as neither moral nor immoral but as the defence of their judicial function and corporate status.[7] Doubts have been cast on the idea that the *parlements* were ideologically opposed to the government, and on the existence of 'parlementary constitutionalism' as a recognisable and coherent contemporary ideology – at least in the period before the Maupeou coup. In terms of wealth, status, privileges, aristocratic pedigrees and, above all, official roles of responsibility, the magistrates were at the heart of the *ancien régime* rather than in opposition to it. If one accepts this claim, then the apparent conflict between the radical language of the magistrates and their privileged social status becomes yet more apparent.

The situation is complicated by the fact that a distinction should be made between those few magistrates who genuinely held reformist political views, and the great majority who appear to have been drawn along by the tide, whether through inertia or through a failure to appreciate the dangerous potential of the arguments which were being made in their collective names. Moreover, outside the ranks of the magistrates themselves existed a numerous camp of lawyers and polemicists ready to take up their pens on the magistrates' behalf. For these lawyers and other officials who depended upon the *parlements* for their livelihoods, the incentive to support them may have come from self-interest as much as ideology; for others who were outside the circles of the *parlements*, the motivation was more clearly ideological. This does not mean that supporters of the *parlements* necessarily believed the magistrates to be the champions of the nation, although some certainly did believe this to be the case; for most, however, in the absence of any more representative form of government, the *parlements* were simply the most powerful focus for opposition to the theory and practice of absolute government. Thus, whilst the *parlementaires* themselves proved reluctant to push the implications of their language to its possible conclusions, no such reticence existed on the part of many of those who claimed to speak on behalf of the magistrates. Some polemicists took up the defence of the magistrates in pamphlets couched in such vehement language that the magistrates themselves were on occasion driven to show their 'conservative' side by firmly repudiating such unwanted offerings.

Virtuous magistrates

As yet there has been no close study of the rhetoric of virtue within *parlementaire* circles, either as it was used by the magistrates themselves, or as it was adapted by those who wrote in their support, be they lawyers or other polemicists; yet this subject may throw light on some of the problems outlined above. In particular, an exploration of this utilisation of the moral rhetoric may help us to evaluate some of the complex interrelationships between intentionality and language. We need to understand why *parlementaires* and their supporters might choose to resort to such a rhetoric, the strategic use they made of it, and how in some ways it may have escaped their control with results far from those originally intended. First, we shall examine the importance of the language of virtue in political thought and polemics, and ask why and how it came to be associated with the *parlements*. Then we will focus on the specific example of the exploitation of the rhetoric of civic virtue in pro-*parlementaire* circles in response to the events known as the Maupeou coup.

The struggle between king and *parlements* which had begun in 1770 reached a crisis point with a series of dramatic events: the exiling of the Paris *parlement* in January 1771; a strike by the lawyers attached to the Paris *parlement* in support of the exiled *parlementaires*, which began in January 1771 and was to last until November; the edict of 23 February 1771, which provided for the establishment of new courts, *conseils supérieurs*, to hear cases which previously came under the jurisdiction of the *parlement* of Paris; the abolition of the *parlement* of Paris, and the setting up by Maupeou of a new *parlement*; the limited purging and reform of those provincial *parlements* that protested too vigorously.

These changes were accompanied by a storm of protests, from the *parlementaires* themselves, from the lawyers attached to the *parlements*, and from many observers of events who, partly as a result of the effectiveness of the pro-*parlementaire* or '*patriote*' propaganda, saw the coup not simply as a power struggle between king and *parlements* but as confirmation that the government was 'despotic' and that the *parlements* were heroic – and virtuous – defenders of the liberties of the nation.[8] These protests gradually diminished as people accepted the *de facto* situation, although this acceptance appears to have been based on pragmatism rather than a rejection of the opinion that Maupeou's actions had been 'despotic'. Following the succession of Louis XVI in 1774, the situation was unexpectedly reversed by the decision to reinstate the old *parlements*. This restoration was seen at the time, and subsequently, to have been a victory for 'public opinion'.[9] Here we will examine the use of the concept of virtue in the polemics engendered by the supporters of the *parlements*, together with the ways in which this concept developed into a wider politicisation of public opinion.

Parlementaires made judicious use of the rhetoric of political virtue to legitimise their taking up a position that appeared to infringe the king's legislative rights. Thus speakers for the *parlements* tended to play down the more radical civic and egalitarian aspects of the rhetoric, concentrating more on its strong associations with justice, impartiality and public service. Their notion of virtue echoed the traditional idea that the *noblesse de robe* possessed virtue through public service. The link between justice and virtue stretched back to antiquity. But the *parlements* also gave an explicitly political resonance to this concept of judicial virtue by using it as the basis of their claim to be impartial representatives of the true interests of the nation. Their crisis opened up a forum in which it was possible to talk openly of politics. And in the course of this crisis, many observers received an education in the politics of the *ancien régime* and the importance of words and rhetorical strategies. Ideas of despotism, illegitimate authority, the rights of the nation and the role of virtuous citizens in defence of the nation were publicly expressed and reached new audiences. The crisis provided an opportunity for a new level of political awareness.

We need to consider the rhetorical uses of concepts of political or civic virtue in *parlementaire* circles, both by magistrates and lawyers and by polemicists writing in support of them: a group which came to be known loosely as the *parti patriote*. Whilst the idea of political virtue did not in itself constitute a theoretical argument against absolute monarchy, it did play a vital role. It served to validate and legitimise other arguments – such as that of national sovereignty – by attesting to the moral integrity and disinterestedness of the speaker. At a time when the king's own magistrates, let alone members of the public, had no acknowledged right to speak on political matters, the claim to be motivated by civic virtue could provide a moral right to speak out. Magistrates used the notion of disinterested judicial virtue to claim that their motives for opposing the wishes of the monarch were based on devotion to the public interest rather than to the self-interest of their *corps*. The magistrates themselves were generally selective and circumspect in their rhetoric, and made little reference to the wider egalitarian and democratic implications of civic virtue. But some of the more radical polemicists who wrote on the *parlementaires'* behalf stressed these very implications, by extending the notion of civic virtue to include not only the nation's judicial representatives, but members of the nation themselves. This extension of civic virtue to the wider public served to endorse the legitimacy of public opinion as the supreme arbiter of political authority by basing that legitimacy on the moral authority of civic virtue. Both rhetorical strategies were careful and deliberate exploitations of some of the possibilities inherent in the discourse of political virtue.

Virtue was a customary term in a specifically *parlementaire* vocabulary of opposition from at least the early eighteenth century; indeed, many of the so-called 'new' discourses attributed to the 1750s or later appear to have been employed long before that time.[10] The ideal of the 'good magistrate' dated back to before the beginning of the eighteenth century. This was the model of the magistrate as virtuous, impartial and incorruptible.[11] The 'good magistrate' also carried an element of self-consciously 'patriotic' rhetoric about it, as expressed, for example, in the famous *mercuriales* of d'Aguesseau with their proud claim that 'the perfect magistrate only lives for the republic.'[12] The ideal of the 'perfect magistrate' was consciously elitist in the sense that those who wrote of it drew attention to the importance of family, nobility and exclusive education in fashioning the ideal magistrate. Nevertheless, the model of judicial virtue was not confined exclusively to magistrates, but could, by extension, be applied to anyone who exercised official functions within the corporate environment of the *parlements*. Theorists on virtue whose ideas fed into the parlements included Duguet, Bolingbroke and, of course, Montesquieu.[13]

Rhetoric in support of the *parlements*, 1770–3

When we come to the circumstances of the Maupeou coup of 1770 to 1774 we may begin with the remonstrances put forward by the *parlements*. Political arguments expressed in the remonstrances are particularly significant because their influence was felt beyond legal circles.[14] The remonstrances were drawn up according to a carefully prescribed formula, in which the overt framework was that of humble subjects respectfully reminding the monarch of some difficulties which appeared to have escaped his attention: the language was deferential, even where the meaning was not. From the 1750s these remonstrances, whilst still supposedly a confidential matter between the king and his law courts, were being widely circulated as part of a deliberate attempt to enlist the support of public opinion. The remonstrances helped to provide a political education for people previously excluded from such knowledge, and the political language employed by the *parlementaires* helped to shape the terms of reference within which the nature of politics was comprehended.

In issuing the remonstrances that preceded their exile in 1771, the magistrates of the *parlement* of Paris did not speak of their own virtue: they declared only that they had been acting solely on behalf of 'the public good'.[15] Part of the accepted code for using the rhetoric of virtue was that one could not oneself claim to be virtuous, for this would suggest arrogance rather than genuine concern for the public interest: one could say at most that one 'loved virtue'. Nothing, however, prevented the supporters of the threatened *parlementaires* from making such a claim on their behalf. When other *parlements* took up the cause of the magistrates of Paris in remonstrances and formal letters of protest to the king they made frequent references to the civic virtues of the exiles. The *parlement* of Paris was likened to the Roman Senate. Its members had acted selflessly and only in defence of the liberty of their nation and their fellow-citizens. They were said to be 'virtuous magistrates', their vicissitudes those of 'virtue', their cause that of 'the Nation'.[16] The *Parlement* of Toulouse spoke of 'the virtuous Magistrates, torn from their posts, for having refused their consent to the destruction of the Laws of the Country'.[17] Only the virtue of the magistrates appeared to stand between the nation and disaster. Without their exemplary selflessness, declared the *parlement* of Rouen:

> The love of the public interest, this sacred flame, seed of honour and the virtues, will be extinguished in all hearts, crimes will be just minor flaws and virtue will be known only by the persecution it suffers.[18]

Most of the remonstrances went no further than asserting that the exiled magistrates were virtuous, as part of a general expression of moral outrage. It is evident that *parlementaires* well understood the risks to themselves in investing their protests to the king with the rhetoric of civic virtue, and most showed an appropriately judicial circumspection in their choice of language, perhaps because the number of genuine would-be political reformers within their ranks was so few.

One set of remonstrances, however, was notably outspoken; they were produced by the *Cour des Aides* in February 1771, and drawn up by its *premier président*, Malesherbes. Whereas most of the *parlementaires* were conservative in their instincts, Malesherbes was a moderate reformer, whose rhetoric contained aspects of both conservatism and radicalism. He identified the cause of the magistrates with that of 'the nation', and made reference to its 'inviolable rights' and France's 'fundamental laws'.[19] These were being defended by 'these virtuous magistrates', whose cause was not one of self-interest, despite the privations engendered by their exile: their sufferings represented 'the completion of the destructive system that threatens the entire Nation'.[20] The courts were depicted as being, in the absence of the Estates General, 'the only protectors of the weak and unfortunate' and the only place in which it was permitted 'to raise one's voice in favour of the People'.[21] The people, the nation itself, depended on the virtue of the magistrates:

> It is even needful that the People should really suffer; that the rights of the Nation be violently attacked; it is needful too that the senti- ments of honour and of virtue are strong in the hearts of the Magis- trates, so that they will expose themselves to imprisonment, to exile, to the upsetting of their fortunes which will result, the loss of their health, and even the loss of their lives.[22]

The civic virtues of the *parlementaires* were contrasted with 'the personal virtues of a King', which were insufficient in themselves to safeguard France from 'a total subversion'.[23] Malesherbes used the lan- guage of virtue in order to characterise the affair of the *parlement* of Paris as a matter of moral politics, which concerned not only the interests of the *parlements* as a whole but also those of 'the people', arguing that the *Parlements* represented the poor as well as the powerful of France, and that they, rather than the king, were the upholders of law. The effect of Malesherbes's arguments was greatly increased by the fact that he was prepared to shape his actions to his rhetoric, in a cause for which he was himself prepared to suffer exile. These remonstrances were accepted as the work of a man who himself possessed 'great virtues' and who meant what he said.[24] The *Mémoires secrets* announced that they were a work of sublime patriotism.[25]

Malesherbes was an exception, however, and on the whole the magis- trates themselves evinced great caution and proved reluctant to employ the rhetoric of virtue against the authority of monarchy. But some of the lawyers attached to the *parlements* were prepared to wield the rhetoric of virtue on behalf of the magistrates, or rather, on behalf of the principles they appeared to embody. One of the most prominent of these was Target, once a defender of Jansenist rights, now increasingly a propon- ent of overtly political and philosophic causes.[26] In his 1771 pamphlet, *Lettre d'un homme à un autre homme sur l'extinction de l'ancien Parlement*, Target admitted that the *parlement* of Paris had not been without its failings, but claimed that taken overall it presented an example of a virtuous magistracy in defence of constitutional rights:

> Nothing is finer than the spectacle which France has given to Europe; all is calm and respectful; there is no cabal, no personal interest, no *esprit de corps*, everything in our motives is pure, everything is

courageous in our conduct, each of us is armed only with honour, patience, firmness; there is no league except that of virtue and the public good which we all feel, and on which we are all in accord.[27]

By promoting egalitarian notions of virtue as the only valid distinction between men, such arguments undermined the value system of a society based on privilege. Target's denial of political factions and conceptualisation of politics as a transparent process guided solely by virtue was in some respects already evocative of the conceptualisation of politics put forward by the revolutionary assemblies.[28]

The *Maximes du droit public* by the Jansenist abbé Claude Mey was one of the best known and most influential of the pro-*parlementaire* works. He went so far as to claim that 'the nation' had the right to summon the Estates General.[29] He also extended the concept of virtuous citizenship beyond that of virtuous magistrates who acted on behalf of the people, to incorporate a much broader (though vaguely defined) stratum of French society. Virtuous citizens could take on rights and responsibilities for the form of government themselves. In effect, they had the right to national sovereignty. Mey contrasted the 'base slaves' who supported despotic (arbitrary) government with the following model:

the virtuous Citizen . . . cherishes his Prince, he is submissive to his orders, he observes the Laws, he is concerned for the *Patrie* and the public good, but this is because reason and religion which are guides, demand it of him. He is all the more obedient as a Subject, all the more sincere as a Citizen, because he is motivated by his conscience and not by his own self-interest. He studies the limits of Royal Authority in order to better understand the extent of his obligations, and in order to fulfil them more completely. If he wishes to know what is not due to the Public Authority, this is so as not to be mistaken over what is demanded of his fidelity, in order not to give himself up to a blind and servile obedience.[30]

Some of the most radical arguments for national sovereignty were made by a relatively obscure lawyer from Bordeaux, Guillaume-Joseph Saige in his 1775 pamphlet, *Le Catéchisme du citoyen*. Saige's earlier work of 1770, *Caton, ou Entretien sur la liberté et les vertus politiques*, which was modelled on Mably's *Entretien de Phocion sur le rapport de la morale avec la politique* (1763), had taken the form of a lengthy discussion between Cato, Cicero and Favonius (the narrator) on the nature of citizenship and virtue as the supreme political quality.[31] Virtue was completely incompatible with autocratic government: 'Liberty and virtue...are inextricably connected, they give each other mutual force; and the downfall of one always leads to the downfall of the other.'[32] Saige characterised 'the true citizen' as inspired by 'the holy love of virtue' so that, in whatever situation he found himself in life, 'the good of the patrie will be his first, or, rather say, his only motive'.[33] In itself, *Caton* was a forceful though hardly original exposition of the importance of classical republican virtue. But, inspired by the Maupeou coup and the stirring example of the *parlementaires* resistance to the monarchy, in his *Catéchisme* Saige used this concept of moral politics as a legitimation for actual resistance to autocratic government. Not surprisingly perhaps, the *parlementaires* of Bordeaux and of Paris were to disassociate themselves from such a position and ordered the ritual destruction of the *Catéchisme*.

Following the implementation of Maupeou's coup, much of the outcry against it came from the clandestine and scurrilous press. Such publications, with their racy journalism, were an inappropriate forum for the self-consciously imposing rhetoric of virtue. But they did make frequent references to vice and corruption at court, a subject full of satirical possibilities. The king, his mistresses and his ministers were frequently depicted as both politically and morally corrupt, and in this context pointed contrasts were drawn between the behaviour of the court and models of civic virtue.[34] Such works as the *Maupeouana* contained many knowing references to the private vices of the king and his ministers, especially Maupeou himself. Sometimes the humour took the form of heavy irony. For example, there is an extended joke in which the naive figure of Sorhouet, a member of Maupeou's reformed *parlement*, repeats his conviction that, contrary to all appearances, Maupeou is a model of virtue and disinterested patriotism. Here the rhetoric of virtue itself served as a foil against which to highlight the machinations of the demonised Maupeou.[35] In its notice of the first appearance of the *Maupeouana*, the *Mémoires secrets* repeated this satirical theme, 'this excellent Citizen ... this Chan****, so virtuous, so wise, so attentive to the good of the *patrie* and the conservation of its rights'.[36]

The association of the court with vice went back at least as far as La Bruyère. But the difference here was that the notion was being put forward as part of a deliberately political polemic, the purpose of which was to convince readers of the integrity of the *parlements* as opposed to the court. Readers were invited to identify the supporters of the *parlements* and also, most importantly, identify themselves, with the side of virtue, and to judge the court as corrupt. In reality, however,

what pro-*parlement* polemicists called 'corruption' could in other circumstances be used to characterise what were customary and accepted
practices of patronage and venality in the *ancien régime*, in which the
magistrates themselves were as implicated as anyone.

The public discussion of political arguments of the early 1770s was
not entirely one-sided: apologists of absolute monarchy also were beginning to be obliged to submit propaganda in the attempt to win over
public opinion. One of the most prolific of the polemicists on behalf of
Maupeou was Voltaire, who took pains to point out the irony of the
parlements' setting themselves up as defenders of liberty. Models of
'virtuous heroes' such as Henri IV, l'Hôpital and d'Aguesseau were used
by anti-*parlementaire* polemicists to illustrate the dangers of giving
excessive authority to the magistrates. Where virtue was spoken of,
however, it was generally confined to the idea of virtuous kingship.
Civic virtue, with its basis in classical republicanism, was, as we have
seen, a particularly awkward notion to exploit on behalf of the monarchy.[37] On the whole, however, apologists of the monarchy often
proved wary even of enlisting the idea of kingly virtue as a moral
justification for divine right. To lean too heavily on the idea of the
moral rectitude of the monarchy might actually undermine the position
of a monarch who in his own life fell dramatically short of such standards. Even Louis XV's most loyal subjects did not consider him to be a
model of virtue. The most noted apologist for the monarchy, Moreau, in
his *Leçons de morale*, avoided speaking of virtue except in his prefatory
remarks to the dauphin, where he went no further than to repeat the
standard formula for kings that 'their virtues have been the happiness of
men, whereas their vices have been the scourge of humanity'.[38]

Victory in 1774: vindication of the magistrates as defenders of the nation

Providing the resolve of the government remained unshaken, *patriote*
propaganda could do little to actually change the situation. By 1773,
many of the most powerful figures who had supported the cause of the
parlements, including the *frondeur* Princes of the Blood, had cut their
losses and became reconciled to the monarchy; appeals to their sense of
virtue were patently futile.[39] The sudden death of Louis XV and the
decision of his successor to reinstate the former *parlements* were fortuit-
ous events. It was ironic that the most significant success of the rhetoric
of civic virtue was the influence which it appears to have exerted over
the new king. There are indications that Louis XVI was impressed by the

idea of a virtuous and *bienfaisant* monarchy and desired to cultivate public opinion, at least in the early years of his reign. Nevertheless, the *parlements* and their supporters made the most of their victory. The history of the last four years could now be officially rewritten as the story of how the civic virtue of the magistrates in defence of their *patrie* had gained its inevitable reward through the establishment of liberty.

On the reinstallation of the *parlement* of Paris, one of the lawyers attached to it, Henrion de Pansey, gave a well-received eulogy at the public reception of the lawyers of the *parlement*. He used the language of virtue to mythologise the events of the last four years. Although he hoped that 'the true Citizens' would spare some of their sympathy for the lawyers who had also suffered during the period of suppression, the main subject of his eulogy was the virtues of the magistrature in general: 'perhaps these virtuous Citizens [the returning magistrates] are too close to us to be properly appreciated. There are certain actions whose true importance can only be understood from the distance of centuries'.[40] These virtuous citizens had brought about a peaceful and happy political revolution: 'a memorable Revolution, which gives back to the Nation its constitution, its liberty; and, that which assures for ever its happiness, safeguards the defenders of both constitution and liberty'. The magistrates were thus the defenders of the nation, the constitution and liberty. The guarantee of integrity in their motives was their civic virtue. Whilst the magistrates had reached such heroic proportions, the king was demoted: he was a citizen, a man: 'A crowned Citizen, he knows that his subjects are men; he sees in mankind his own likeness.'[41]

The main subject of the eulogy was the life of Matthieu Molé, who had been the *premier président* of the Paris *parlement* during the Fronde. This use of a long- dead hero enabled the speaker to develop the political issues of his theme in a manner impossible when speaking of the present. In the process, Henrion was rewriting the history of the *Fronde* as well as that of recent events. Had he wished to present a more radical account of the *Fronde* he would have used a figure like Broussel. But Molé had significant advantages: first, that his family were still very much powerful figures in the *parlement* of Paris, to whom the picture of their virtuous ancestor would be likely to appeal; secondly, Molé was a figure of law and order, who stood for reconciliation and the restoration of law and order rather than the more subversive and radical magistrates of the time of the *Fronde*.[42] By selecting him as the hero, the identification of the restored *parlement* with the authority of the *ancien régime* rather than with opposition to the monarchy was reasserted.[43] Molé was described as 'a Magistrate who could unite the courage of a hero with all the virtues that form the Citizen and public Man'.[44] Molé's public virtues included defending 'the public good' against the machinations of courtiers, ministers and 'les great'. The court was the source of 'politics' and 'the art of governing men', but it was a 'cold and calculating politics...where one no longer finds any national spirit'.[45] This courtly view of politics was contrasted with the *parlement*. It alone during the *Fronde* was 'without any personal interest, and saw nothing, desired nothing, but the general good'.[46] Not only was Molé a paragon of public virtue, he also offered, in the tradition of classical heroes, an example of private virtue: 'His house is the sanctuary of all the domestic virtues: he is open handed towards all the unfortunate.'[47] Molé was thus an example, not only of civic, but of *bienfaisant* virtue. His sympathies for the poor did not, however, extend into any question of their entitlement to civic rights: 'the people' are described as wayward, often unjust and 'more changeable than waves on the ocean'.[48] According to this discourse, the *parlementaires* could claim to represent 'the nation', but 'the people' did not possess sufficient virtue to represent themselves.[49] The account of Molé was designed to assert the authority of the *parlementaires*, based on their virtues, but it was an authority which was identified with that of the monarchy and the *ancien régime* itself rather than with any attempt to oppose it.

The Brittany Affair had been one of the political *causes célèbres* of the eighteenth century. Over ten years there had been hostility between the monarchy and the *parlement* of Brittany, which had begun in 1765 with the arrest by royal troops of the attorney-general, La Chalotais, a leader of the Brittany *parlement*. This affair was now rewritten as the inevitable triumph of virtue. La Chalotais was allowed to resume his office. The *Mémoires secrets* printed an official 'compliment' from the prior of the Benedictine abbey of St Mélaine at Rennes to La Chalotais and reported how the prior had said to La Chalotais that he had defeated his enemies 'by your own virtue', claiming that Louis XV had respected 'these virtues' even whilst succumbing 'to the machinations of the cabal'. Had Louis's life not been cut unexpectedly short he would no doubt have listened to 'the voice of justice and the cry from his own heart' and reinstated the attorney-general. Happily, the new king was now paying the debt of his predecessor:

> in acceding to the wishes of the Nation and reinstating you, he announces to the whole of Europe, that has concerned itself so intensely with your misfortunes, that his reign will be the scourge of injustice, the triumph of innocence and the era of public felicity.[50]

The prior then addressed La Chalotais's son, M. de Caradeuc, 'you enlighten your enemies by your wisdom, as you have disconcerted them by your firmness'. It was, he said 'the triumph of virtue'.[51] In the case of the younger La Chalotais, the appellation of 'virtuous hero' was particularly ironic, since it was his unfortunate simple-mindedness which had constituted one of the more pressing motives behind the attempt to deny him the family office in the *parlement*. This text was not officially printed, but the *Mémoires secrets* was zealous in making good the omission and publicising the reevaluation.

Such accounts of the Brittany Affair constituted a fictional rewriting of the actual events. But this 'mythologising' went deeper than a propagandist attempt to win over public opinion. The rhetoric of political virtue would not have been so important, or so influential, if it had been only a matter of the cynical exploitation of a discourse in order to achieve power. In private accounts, not meant to influence an audience, one also encounters the framework of civic virtue being used to give meaning to political events. In his private memoirs, Robert de Saint-Vincent, Jansenist and *parlementaire* veteran, characterised the Brittany Affair as a struggle between virtue and oppression. Interestingly, of 'all the good citizens' who supported that cause, he chose a woman as the symbol of that virtue, Mlle de La Chalotais, who came to Paris to seek help for her father's defence: 'this girl who is matchless in her merit, her talent, her zeal, her modesty, her virtue' attracted the support of 'all the virtuous people' who flocked to defend 'virtue oppressed'.[52] Like the models of women in antiquity, she could exhibit civic virtue if this was expected in her capacity as a daughter.[53] Here, in this private source, without any idea of influencing public opinion, the idea of virtue could pass beyond rhetoric into the very framework of thoughts within which political consciousness is articulated.

Public opinion on the resolution of the crisis

The image of the victorious *parlementaires* was reflected in much of the press, which showed an air of lively expectation about the prospects for the future. It was assumed that the restoration of the *parlements* would mean political change rather than the reimposition of the old system. The public might now participate in some sense in the business of politics. Not through the franchise, of course, because that was denied them, but indirectly, through the pressure they could exert on events, a pressure made legitimate by their virtuous citizenship. The idea of virtue thus reinforced and legitimised the concept of public opinion. The members of the public had the right to judge those who ruled them, not simply because they were the public or the majority (for then they would be no more than the mob) but because public opinion was more virtuous than the monarchy, and the public were virtuous citizens. Most tellingly, perhaps, the rhetoric of virtue was also taken up by defenders of royal policy. In the early years of his reign Louis XVI inclined towards administrative reform and this was reflected in his choice of ministers and officials. D'Angiviller became *Directeur des bâtiments du Roi* in 1774, effectively putting him in charge of official policy for commissioning works in the arts. He was a friend of Turgot, whose brief period in administrative power also began in 1774. D'Angiviller was sympathetic to the physiocrats and to attempts to reform the administration of the government. He attempted to use the rhetoric of virtue, through history painting and the commission for the statues of 'great men', to put the state back on the high moral ground, and especially, following the reinstatement of the *parlements*, to counter some of their versions of history and the part played in it by men of virtue in France's past. As in the prize essays of the *Académie Française* in the early 1770s, L'Hôpital was a key figure, but it was claimed that his loyalty was to the monarchy rather than to the *parlements*. [54]

In 1775, revitalised by the victory of the *parlements*, the relaxation of censorship and the air of reform around the new king and queen, a loose network of 'frondeur' journalists collaborated in a radicalisation of the legitimate press itself and used it to portray themselves as virtuous citizens who loved their *patrie*.[55] One of the most prominent of these was Mercier, who in 1775 took over the *Journal des dames* and used this innocuous-sounding journal to put forward radical political views – for example, to publicise and discuss Henrion de Pansey's eulogy.[56]

Amongst some of the lawyers, in particular, the Maupeou coup seems to have brought about greater politicisation.[57] Amongst these men, virtue was used even against the magistrates who had vaunted their 'civic virtue'. In 1775, the radical lawyer Delacroix published a defence of the publication of lawyers' *mémoires*, and accompanied this with a general call for the opening up of the process of the law to the public. His reasoning was that the practice of secret legal hearings before only a magistrate tended to benefit the 'great', the rich and privileged – that the integrity of the magistrates could not be guaranteed by their virtue. The law, far from being the province of virtue, was the prerogative of those who could afford it. Taking Montesquieu's classic distinction between virtue and honour, Delacroix claimed that France was 'a Nation where honour counts for everything, and virtue for hardly anything'.[58]

The nobility and the wealthy were not motivated by virtue but by honour, he said, therefore the only way that they could be made to act as though they had integrity was for law suits to be conducted 'under the eyes of the Public, whose opinion is the censor of Magistrates, Ministers and Kings'.[59] Thus magistrates were here included with the king and his ministers in the category of people whose virtue was no longer certain: it was through the judgement of public opinion that virtue was guaranteed. Mercier lavished praise upon this work, summarising Delacroix's arguments about the different kinds of justice dispensed to 'the rich' and 'the poor' and defending the importance of 'the voice of the public... which is rarely led astray'. His defence of public scrutiny of the virtuous man emphasised the notion of politics as a transparent process in which there was no division between private and public morals: 'The *honnête homme* does not fear enquiries into his private life. Like the virtuous Roman, he chooses to live in a diaphanous house.'[60]

These complex and ambiguous relationships between motivation and language defy easy explanations. It is clear that *parlementaires* and their supporters were highly selective in their use of rhetoric, choosing what was most appropriate to their aims in particular circumstances, but also encouraging the growth of public opinion without realising that this could have consequences far beyond those intended. Contemporary observers were often highly cynical about the integrity of the magistrates themselves, and showed a sophisticated grasp of the ways in which the rhetoric of virtue and devotion to the public interest constituted a legitimising discourse which was prone to exploitation by would-be political manipulators, who were, after all, in pursuit of their own interests. Diderot evinced a reluctant and qualified support for the *parlements* as the only bastion against autocracy, but their moral rhetoric was greatly at odds with the spectacle of the magistrates of the *parlement* of Paris 'ceaselessly opposed to the good, or only lending themselves to it for bad motives'.[61] Mercier in *Le Tableau de Paris* expressed his irritation at the way the *parlements* had exploited the rhetoric of virtue and patriotism through their remonstrances, 'which sometimes sport a masculine and patriotic eloquence, worthy of republics, yet which are entirely without substance'.[62]

It may well be that the motives of the *parlementaires* and of their supporters were often at variance with their professed devotion to the public interest. This in itself would hardly be a surprising revelation of the nature of political life. Moreover, it would be difficult to try and generalise since individuals' motives and thoughts were clearly much

more complex than the umbrella term '*parlementaire*' can express successfully. The magistrate or lawyer was also a landowner, churchgoer,
client or patron, and a member of the cultural elite, and these several
roles might generate conflicting motives. The historian of language
needs to be aware of the difference between discourse and motives,
but this does not make the study of discourses or ideologies in itself
irrelevant. Magistrates were obliged to shape their actions to a certain
extent in line with the ideologies which legitimised them: they both
shaped the discourse and were shaped by it. Their rhetoric itself had the
effect of politicising them and hardening their own position. Although
the magistrates themselves were cautious and judicious in their use of
the inflammatory discourse of virtue, outside their own elite ranks, their
supporters, lawyers, polemicists, pamphleteers, were often much more
enthusiastic in invoking this rhetoric. Ideas such as civic virtue, service
to the *patrie*, and incorruptibility in public life as legitimising bases for
participation in political life, could be taken up and used by those whose
political convictions were rather more egalitarian than those of the vast
majority of the magistrates. This in turn was to have its effect on the
development of public opinion.

For the great majority of the magistrates, the issue of 'parlementary
constitutionalism' seems to have been one towards which they retained
a strong degree of ambiguity, as is suggested by their relative calm in the
years after 1775 when their own jurisdictional authority was left relatively secure.[63] But it is nevertheless evident that from the time of the
Maupeou coup, the jurisdictional quarrel between *parlements* and ministers had generated in the minds of people who followed the debate,
the idea of the legitimacy of civic virtue as an authority for political
participation.[64] The egalitarianism and moral authority implicit in the
concept of civic virtue became, in the context of the final crisis of the
ancien régime, a veritable Pandora's box.

7
The Triumph of Virtue, 1774–88

> *To be a man, to love one's fellow men, that is to bring together all the virtues . . . only the love of humanity can inspire great actions and create true heroes.*
>
> Brissot, *De la Vérité* (1782)

> *Virtue triumphs straight away;*
> *to be a great man, in effect,*
> *one needs only its decree.*
>
> From a satirical royalist verse on the
> duc d'Orléans, *Actes des Apôtres*, no. 179 (Summer 1790)[1]

The years of the absolute reign of Louis XVI witnessed considerable fluctuations in political fortunes and royal policies, but the language of virtue retained a consistent place in the conceptualisation of political ideas. The main elements of this language had been invented long before Louis came to the throne. It was a versatile form and could be adapted to different arguments and contexts. It was not yet a revolutionary language. Nor can it be argued that the language of political virtue caused the Revolution. But it did provide a linguistic framework through which it was possible to criticise some of the shortcomings of absolute government on the grounds of civic responsibility. Few of the writers who used the concept of political virtue in the 1770s and 1780s were to support the Revolution of 1789, and scarcely anyone anticipated it before the event. If their choice of language helped to undermine respect for the institution of absolute monarchy this was, for most of them at least, an unintended, unforeseen and unwanted development. This was to change in 1789. As the last political crisis of the *ancien régime* tightened its grip, political virtue would provide a means through which

171

revolutionary politics could be conceived and expressed. But the connection between political virtue and revolution would only become apparent when a massive political and financial crisis finally brought down the *ancien régime*.

In this period there was both a widening of the popularity of the rhetoric of political virtue and its accompanying concepts and an extension of the kind of uses to which the rhetoric might be put. There was a remarkable degree of consensus about the terms of political language in the 1780s, which in turn led to a shared political consciousness, a space within which political ideas took shape. The 'idiom of virtue' occupied a primary position within this language, and had become a rhetorical commonplace, familiar to everyone in educated circles from bishops to journalists, lawyers to novelists.[2] Although writers of the 1770s and 1780s who invoked virtue, together with connected concepts such as *patrie* and 'nation', were largely relying on meanings imparted by earlier generations, this period did see a considerable expansion in the use of such terms. A broader category of people had grown accustomed to speaking of political virtue, and to applying this discourse in a range of social and political contexts.

Despite the constraints of censorship, the last years of the *ancien régime* witnessed a growing influence of journalists and the written word. The concept of 'public opinion' was fast gaining ground with the reading public. This was the well-established idea of the public as a source of moral judgement, an impartial body which constituted a legitimate source of authority, the equal of that of the traditional sources of authority; king and Church. The rhetoric of civic virtue played an essential role in the formation of public opinion, for it served to bolster the belief that the people could form impartial moral judgements on the basis of their virtue. Thus, their devotion to the public good itself gave legitimacy to public opinion. Public opinion could not be bought off by material advantage, or swayed by inadequate arguments. The legitimacy of public opinion, therefore, stemmed not from the sanction of God, which endorsed the authority of absolute monarch and Church, but from humanity's natural moral integrity and its universal conscience.

Not everyone was won over: the values that virtue embodied never found universal favour. Some writers were intrigued by such ideas and incorporated them into their work, others did not. Some people found the rhetoric overblown and distasteful; many reacted cynically to the boundless optimism of the discourse; some thought it implied too great a confidence in the integrity of man at the expense of God; others suspected its more political resonances as tending to undermine respect for absolute monarchy and to puff up the vanity of the populace, which might take pride in the thought that it too might aspire to virtue. Nevertheless, the language was generally familiar to a widening circle of the reading public, most of whose newer members were bourgeois. They understood its resonances, regardless of whether or not they agreed with its implications. The rhetoric of virtue thus formed an active component of the political consciousness of the pre-revolutionary era.

The politicisation of natural social virtue

Before we consider specific circumstances in the 1770s and 1780s we need to look more closely at the point of intersection between the discourse of virtue and political ideas. How did a moral rhetoric become political? The kind of virtue that featured in classical republicanism had always been part of an explicitly political tradition and naturally lent itself to political critique. But the political content of discourses of natural and social virtue was more oblique and problematic. The years from 1771 to 1787 saw a flowering of ideas of social virtue, patriotism and *bienfaisance*. Interest in social virtue and its related vocabulary co-existed alongside the more formal political language of classical-republican virtue.

Since natural virtue and the humanitarian impulses of *bienfaisance* were not overtly 'political' in the sense that classical-republican virtue was, their importance for the development of a more radical form of political thought, particularly in these last twenty years of the *ancien régime*, has tended to be overlooked as a factor in the rise of politics. It was not a language that leaps immediately to mind as worthy of a political study. Baker, who has made a close analysis of the invention of a new political language, has not included the vogue for natural or social virtue as part of that language, possibly because it was not a precise political language and not symptomatic of one specific ideology or doctrine. Darnton notes its popularity, though he claims that this was no more than a passing fashion and that much about the movement was conservative.[3] But it was certainly more than a passing vogue: as we have seen, the rhetoric of social virtue had a long and intellectually imposing pedigree. And whilst some aspects of the language could appear conservative, it was more often radical. Such radicalism was a relative factor and stemmed, not from the discourse as such, but from the ways in which it was used and the contexts in which it appeared. The very fact that it did not seem to provide a threat and did not arouse the unease of the censors helped to facilitate its wider acceptance. In a country where there was no accepted framework for the discussion of politics, social virtue and *bienfaisance* facilitated the growth of the idea of virtuous citizenship. Through its provision of a vocabulary with which to express social concerns, natural virtue evolved gradually into an increasingly explicit political language which laid out an active role for citizens to play within the *patrie*. Embedded in the language of social virtue were many of the same political elements and concepts that were already explicit in classical republicanism, such as 'love of the *patrie*' and the concept of the 'public good'. The most fundamental of these political ideas was the conviction that virtuous citizens could and indeed ought to participate actively in creating a *patrie*, and that the king in turn was answerable to the *patrie*. By 1774, moral legitimacy could be claimed to rest with 'the nation', 'the *patrie*' and 'the people'. The whole balance of the conceptualisation of politics was tilting, and the language of virtue (in its various forms) played a pivotal role in making such a change possible.

The path-breaking work of an historian of an earlier generation, Daniel Mornet on *Les Origines intellectuelles de la Révolution française*, set out much of the territory which historians are still considering. He contended that 'social and political morality' was of key importance, not because it could be said to have *caused* the Revolution, but because it supplied many of the ideas and approaches that revolutionaries were to use to create a vision of the future.[4] In its early years the Revolution was a profoundly optimistic movement, and many of its projects had their origins in the 1770s and 1780s and the belief in the efficacy and facility of natural virtue. Mornet traced the origins of this moral discourse to the attempts made by the *philosophes* to instil a secular morality into the public consciousness. Mornet could have taken this argument further, however, and asked how far the existence of this new ideology was an essential precondition for the Revolution itself. Virtue not only provided a language of political opposition but also stood for a system of moral values and legitimacy that were an alternative to the traditional pillars of Church and king. The revolutionary context is mostly beyond the scope of this book, though we shall come back to this problem in the 'Conclusion'. The task of this chapter will be to examine how the language of virtue became more overtly political in the last years of the *ancien régime*.

The question remains how the rhetoric of social virtue could acquire an explicitly political orientation and form the linguistic basis of a challenge to the existing political system. There were several stages along the way. The first rested on the assumption that man is naturally good and that the individual is inspired by natural feeling, to give happiness to others by means of good actions. The next stage was the belief that happiness itself was a social right, both for individuals and, by extension, for the rest of society. From there it was but a short step (though one that was shattering in its implications) to the contention that some kind of political system ought to be created whereby such rights could be guaranteed. Many commentators in the 1780s could happily go along with the first step, the idea of virtue as a natural inclination to create happiness. Once the discourse moved from individual human nature to mankind's social rights, it became more problematic. But it was the third stage, the idea of happiness as a political right, which was to define revolutionaries. Not everyone would take the arguments to their logical conclusion: whether they chose to or not depended both on their individual temperament and on their circumstances. Before 1788 the language could form the basis of a challenge to the political system; after 1789 it could form the basis of a social and political programme.

The later 1780s provided a set of circumstances against which the rhetoric of political virtue stood out in sharp relief against the background of an *ancien régime* that was perceived to be in political and economic crisis. Even more significant was the perception that the government had lost much of its moral authority and was staggering under the weight of allegations of political, financial and sexual corruption. The first of these circumstances was the perceived recrudescence of despotism in the form of a number of government measures and intentions. The second was the attempt to reassert the censorship laws, an attempt which backfired on the authorities. This was the period when writers such as Latude, Linguet, and Mirabeau won over a popular audience in their declamations against the Bastille and what it stood for – arbitrary and despotic government – and the authorities began steadily to lose ground in the propaganda war. The third circumstance was a series of scandals involving members of the court nobility and even the king's own family. Such scandals (whether founded on truth or not) were intensely damaging, and lent credence to the popular belief that the court was a haven of decadence and vice. The most damaging of all these was, as we have seen, the Affair of the Diamond Necklace. All these circumstances were enthusiastically exploited by pamphleteers and journalists. Some put their energies into satire, pornography and the traditional *libelles*; others, who saw themselves as more 'serious' writers, seized the opportunity for more lofty and ambitious analyses of the weaknesses of the ruling elite – and here the rhetoric of virtue added force to their arguments.

The rest of this chapter will explore how, within the constraints of the *ancien régime*, what was by now a potentially revolutionary language could be exploited to legitimise opposition. We shall concentrate on three areas. First, there was an increasing polarisation in class terms of the themes of vice and virtue. The second area is the extraordinary proliferation of public writings about social virtue and *bienfaisance* in the 1780s and the diversity of authors who were attracted to this theme. The last area is a consideration of how the rhetoric of virtue in the later 1780s could serve as a deliberate political strategy amongst those jostling to retain power or manoeuvring to attain it.

Was virtue a bourgeois rhetoric?

The question of how far the rhetoric of political virtue was attached to one particular social group or estate in these years presents a number of problems. In striking contrast to the ideal of noble virtue which had held sway in the first part of the century, by the 1770s a clear antithesis had emerged between the concept of nobility and that of virtue. A nobleman could still be described as a 'man of virtue' but this was *in spite of* his noble status, not because of it. The old links between virtue and nobility, honour, and glory had fallen into disrepute. This change in meaning had even found its way into standard dictionary definitions. It had been customary in dictionaries at the beginning of the century to illustrate the nature of virtue using the story of Marcellus, who constructed the temple of Honour in such a manner that one could only gain access to it via the temple of Virtue, so that virtue led directly to honour. After about 1770 this anecdote still appeared in dictionary definitions but now its meaning was ironic. Nowadays, it was said, the way to achieve 'honour' was not through 'virtue': 'It would be truer to say that nowadays the temple of Honour is commonly entered by the secret gate; the route that leads by way of Virtue is certainly the least frequented.'[5] Noble status, hereditary rank and affluence made the attainment of true virtue more difficult. Virtue was to be met with most often in the ranks of the Third Estate – or at least, so advocates of the Third Estate liked to claim. One might note by contrast that the association between 'honour' and nobility remained tenacious long into the nineteenth century.[6]

Clearly certain sections of the nobility provoked more hostility than others. In the popular imagination the court had long been associated with vice – sexual and financial – rather than virtue. The court and the values that sustained it appeared as the antithesis of both classical-republican virtue and natural virtue. Courtiers sought honours and advancement and their mode of life was inimical to the austerity and selflessness of republican virtue; whilst the artificiality, luxury and duplicity of courtly life provided barren soil within which natural virtue was stifled. Although this association of the court with vice went back many years, by the 1780s it had crystallised into an assumption to be met with everywhere, even amongst the ranks of the courtiers. Years later, the marquise de la Tour du Pin was to attribute the Revolution itself quite literally to the contempt that her own class, the court nobility, showed for virtue as bourgeois and provincial. 'Virtue in men and good conduct in women became the object of ridicule. . . . The Revolution of 1789 was only the inevitable consequence and . . . the just punishment of the vices of the upper classes.'[7] In the 1780s even the queen indulged in the vogue for the natural life, removed from the artificiality of the court. Most notoriously (and ironically) she even had constructed her *Hameau*, a model village in the grounds of Versailles, where she and her friends could play at being virtuous peasants as a respite from the stultifying formality of the court.

What was little more than a pleasant pastime for Marie-Antoinette was a much more serious and deeply-held belief for others. Virtue went far beyond a rhetorical device, informing private as well as public discourse and helping to shape people's conceptions of the institutions at the pinnacle of the *ancien régime*. The abbé Fauchet first made his public name through preaching at court. When he first visited Versailles in 1774 he wrote in a private letter to his friend, the writer Bernardin de Saint-Pierre, that despite his success there, he was relieved when he left:

> These people are very honest (*honnêtes*); but God forbid that a poor man like me should come to live amongst them! Compliments cost them nothing; but as for virtue, that is out of the question. Everyone is bored here, even in the midst of splendour, and true sentiment has been stifled by superficial politeness. Long live nature, simplicity, candour and friendship.[8]

Fauchet's fears that he might prove susceptible to the temptations of court life were well-founded. Despite his private reservations he soon became somewhat notorious for the number of pensions and benefices, along with the honorary title of 'preacher for the king', that he accumulated as a result of his fashionable preaching at court. His declamations included a sermon praising 'virtue' and 'the feeling soul' of Marie-Antoinette at a 'meeting of ladies for charity' at which she presided.[9] There was nothing unusual in Fauchet's turnaround. It was the customary recognition that one must live in the real world, not in a political utopia – a compromise of which Montesquieu would have thoroughly approved.

Nevertheless, it would be hard, and unwise, to try to predict from the way in which people were speaking or writing about virtue, nation and patriotism in the 1780s, which political path they would take once a revolution began to seem a distinct possibility and the political tension escalated dramatically. For example, we have seen how the magistrates of the *parlements* had adapted the idea of noble virtue as the administration of justice, to the defence of their corporate position. By claiming to be representatives of 'la nation' they had drawn ever closer to the concept of civic virtue. This involved many of the more politically active magistrates, such as Robert de Saint-Vincent and D'Eprémesnil, in a paradox. They spoke of defending the rights of 'la nation' and inspired many outside the privileged ranks of the *parlements* to agitate on their behalf, while continuing to defend their own rank and corporate privileges as members of the judicial nobility. This gap between the aims and the language of many of the *parlementaires* became increasingly evident towards the end of the 1780s as leading *parlementaires* took up widely differing positions with regard to the emerging Third Estate, and in 1788 Robert de Saint-Vincent and D'Eprémesnil rapidly found themselves on opposing sides.[10]

Nobles were just as likely to be familiar with the language of moral politics as were the bourgeoisie. Many had been eager participants in the spread of new ideas, and constituted a high proportion of the members of masonic lodges and academies. Even in the early stages of the Revolution, nobles were often no more averse than commoners to using the language of virtue, patriotism and nation to make political points – chiefly at the expense of the monarchy and the royal ministers. The *cahiers de doléances*, or books of grievances, compiled by nobles (most of them provincial) for the summoning of the Estates General that ignited the Revolution, consistently showed hostility towards the court nobility. They spoke out against 'political despotism', which they depicted as the fault, not of the king, but of successive ministers and the system of court patronage whereby self-advancement was deemed preferable to public service.[11]

But this did not mean that significant numbers of the nobility were ready yet to give up the system of privilege for a more egalitarian society.[12] Ironically, some of the most outspoken – and most influential – speakers against 'political despotism' and Calonne in the late 1780s were themselves members of the higher court nobility, such as Mont-morency-Luxembourg, La Rochefoucauld and the Noailles family. One can be cynical about this too, and note, as Wick has done, that many of these men and their families were out of royal favour at court and had found their paths to self-advancement through the usual network of patronage, blocked at court. Positions, offices and pensions which they felt that they had a right to expect in order to maintain the expensive life-style demanded at court were being diverted to favourites of Louis and Marie-Antoinette such as the Polignacs. But principles too played a part, especially for noted humanitarians such as Liancourt and La Rochefoucauld, who remained as members of the Party Patriot in 1789 and were firm supporters of the earlier liberal stages of the Revolution.[13]

Could virtue be compatible with Christian doctrine?

The variety of responses made by members of the clergy in the 1770s and 1780s to the rhetoric of virtue illustrates its complexity. We have seen that some of the best known preachers – though by no means all – were increasingly willing to incorporate the language of virtue into their sermons and writings. Variants of Jansenist thought, most impor-tantly Richerism, made great inroads into clerical thought, particularly amongst the lower clergy who were drawn to an ideology which sought to take the Church back to its early simplicity, equality and purity, and attacked the excessive power and wealth of the upper clergy, most of whom came from the ranks of the nobility. But theological discourses were not the only influence. Some clerics were attracted to aspects of the Enlightenment. This was particularly the case amongst certain members of the higher clergy. It is difficult to be certain of the extent to which some may have had doubts about conventional Catholic beliefs – they would naturally have been loathe to admit to it. Probably few were deists, but many had an interest in natural virtue, reason and mildly philosophic speculations, and did not consider these ideas to be incom-patible with Christian doctrine.[14]

Among thinkers, it was Rousseau, rather than religious sceptics like Voltaire, whose ideas might prove attractive to the clergy, although Rousseau's reluctance to accept revealed religion made it difficult for the more conventionally devout to accept him. But it would be difficult and possibly misleading to try to isolate different strands of influence. Even Rousseauism and Jansenism – though in some ways poles apart –

resembled each other at certain points. As Dale Van Kley has pointed out, the Jansenist work *L'Ecclésiastique citoyen* (1787), which called for radical church reform and denounced the wealth and privilege of the higher clergy, made much of the idea of the virtuous parish priest who lived a simple life close to nature and was a 'useful' citizen, an ideal not far removed from that of Rousseau's Savoyard curate.[15]

The vision of a more egalitarian society based on social virtue, patriotism and *bienfaisance* recalled Christian ideals as well as antique utopias and Rousseauist idylls. The age of Enlightenment was still profoundly religious in many ways – although the nature of that religious belief was changing. Ideas associated with the Enlightenment were to be encountered everywhere, but they mingled with quite different traditions. Even Fauchet, who greatly admired Rousseau, was selective in his debt. He interpreted Rousseau's doctrines in line with his own inclinations, and thought that Rousseau had been unnecessarily pessimistic about human nature and the natural capacity for virtue.[16] There is a possibility that Fauchet was also inspired by Jansenist thought, but again, this is hard to prove.[17]

The idea that virtue was natural to mankind, rather than a gift from God, put all but a few hardy clerics into a difficult and paradoxical situation, for it called into question the fundamental belief in original sin. Conventionally devout Catholics found it difficult to credit the idea of a 'secular morality'. But others were less resistant to the picture of a more egalitarian society where the poor were succoured and people helped rather than oppressed each other, which after all, recalled the ideals of the early Church. It was too effective a vision to leave to the 'irreligious', to deists, let alone to atheists. Some clerics tried to combine the vision of beneficial social effects of natural virtue with a continuing insistence that such virtue stemmed ultimately from God. This could be a difficult juggling act.

Père Elisée, for example, was a staunch opponent of the idea that virtue could exist without God's intervention. The son of an advocate in the *parlement* of Besançon, he was educated by Jansenists but later joined the Carmelite Order. Ironically, it was said that he owed his fame to Diderot who heard one of his sermons, delivered in an obscure Parisian church, and was so struck by the Carmelite, whose preoccupation with virtue paralleled his own but whose religious ideas were so different, that he told his friends and acquaintances about this humbly-dressed, simple but eloquent preacher. Elisée subsequently became one of the most renowned preachers in Paris.[18]

Elisée's hostility towards the ethics of Diderot and the other *Encyclopédistes* continued unabated. He voiced his opposition in a series of sermons 'on the Falsity of Probity without Religion'. True integrity could stem only from awareness of eternal justice and fear of eternal punishment. Without this the most dazzling virtues were 'no more than refinements of self-love (*l'amour-propre*)'.[19] It was an argument that echoed the attitude of Jansenists such as Père Nicole at the end of the previous century. Elisée placed the blame for contemporary vice and moral laxity firmly on the shoulders of the *philosophes* who had extolled secular morality and irreligion, and encouraged the erroneous belief that excessive passions could lead to virtue. He believed strongly in original sin, and attacked head-on the idea that virtue was natural to human nature. True morality was impossible to attain without the intervention of God. Nevertheless, such terms as 'patriotism', 'social virtues', 'public good' and 'citizenship' had crept into the discourse of even this devout and austere Carmelite, though he argued that these ideals stemmed from love of God. Indeed, for him the devout Christian was a better and more virtuous citizen than was the devotee of the *philosophes*. The origin of virtue was different, but its effect was the same: the amelioration of human existence and the bringing together of people in a common humanitarian bond:

> How easily, oh my God! does the Christian practise the social virtues, when he meditates on the law which sets out all his duties; which recommends to him ... the love of the public good and all the qualities that form the citizen![20]

Other popular preachers went further than the Père Elisée to embrace the discourse of virtue and seemed to anticipate no conflict between religious doctrine and natural morality. Some spoke of the happiness that would come with the growth of virtue, and linked this to the theme of an earthly community of patriotic citizens. There was the abbé Cormeaux, who gave a sermon which set out to prove that 'the charms of virtue are indeed ravishing' and that they led to peace, tranquillity and serenity.[21] A Dominican monk, Père Richard, wrote an anti-philosophic (specifically anti-D'Holbach) work, which laid claim to morality, virtue and politics for the side of religion, and in 1785 he produced a compendium of *Annales de la charité et de la bienfaisance chrétienne*.[22] In 1782, the abbé de Boismont, a member of the *Académie française*, addressed an assembly for the setting up of a royal hospital (*maison de santé*), on the subject of patriotism and *bienfaisance*. Addressing his audience as 'Citizens and Christians', he defined 'the *patrie*' as:

a common mother that Providence gives those great families
which we call nations. ...It is in vain that it has recently been
claimed that [patriotism's] influence is only felt in republics. ...Let
us state with confidence, in the midst of this assembly which is
both patriotic and Christian, that one can be a citizen in a monarchy,
and that in loving the head of State it is one's country that one
loves.[23]

He went on to contrast 'private charity' with 'public *bienfaisance*':
whilst the former did good, its benefits died with its bestower, whereas
'public *bienfaisance*' was 'this political lifeblood' which benefited 'the
mass of the nation'.[24] Boismont was known for his 'philosophic' sympathies, but still, this was daring stuff. Yet it seems to have raised no
eyebrows in 1782 although it might well have done twenty years earlier.
Such language was almost commonplace. The sermon proved a great
success and won much praise for Boismont, as noted by the *Mémoires
secrets*. The collection afterwards for building another hospital raised the
impressive sum of 150,000 livres.[25]

Sermons preaching social virtue and *bienfaisance* did not always pass
without challenge. When in April 1786 Fauchet preached a sermon on
Christian charity at the church of the Filles-Pénitents du Sauveur in Paris
there was outrage from some senior clerics and a feeling that he had
gone too far. He was accused of having justified 'pagan philosophy' and,
under the cover of speaking about Christian charity, spoken only about
'philosophical *bienfaisance*'. The sermon was referred to Fauchet's superiors, but it is notable that they did not view his language as a serious
matter and he was let off with a caution.[26]

Such sermons played their part in making the rhetoric of virtue and
bienfaisance seem more acceptable to the kind of audiences who were
resistant to ideas associated with the *philosophes*. They contributed to an
atmosphere in which the idea of a better society of virtuous citizens was
seen as a desirable and possible political goal. Of course, this does not
mean that even these progressive clerics saw themselves as being advocates of Enlightenment ideas of secular morality. But it does suggest that
they believed that human existence could be made happier, and that
society might so be organised as to facilitate the expression of natural
virtue. This does not make them future revolutionaries: most were very
far from anticipating or wanting major political change, and certainly
not an end to the monarchy or the authority of the Catholic Church. We
cannot predict from the rhetoric that they used before the Revolution
what would be their political choices in the traumatically transformed

context of 1789 and 1790, when the Civil Constitution of the clergy forced them to decide where their loyalties lay.

Fauchet was one who did choose the Revolution. He came from an affluent family, and during the course of his career had accumulated a number of benefices. He was both successful and popular as a preacher. Yet when another possibility was to open up for him Fauchet chose a different route. He was present at the storming of the Bastille and became a committed revolutionary. He strove to reconcile his religious beliefs with his political commitment and later became the constitutional bishop of Calvados. According to Fauchet himself, his ideas had been established long before the Revolution, in the culture of the *ancien régime*. In July 1790 he wrote to the editor of the *Journal de Paris* declaring that:

I am dedicated to the Revolution; I will be loyal till death. It is not events that have given me my principles. I have always had the same ideas of liberty, legislation, and the public happiness.[27]

Like so many others he was not to survive the Terror. He was executed in October 1793.

As we have seen, education at secondary level offered much potential for the instilling of progressive ideas about virtue and citizenship. Much of the discussion of social virtue in the 1770s and 1780s continued to develop the theme of education (both formal and informal) for virtue. After the departure of the Jesuits the Oratorians had begun to dominate the teaching of boys in the *collèges*. They were seen as more progressive than the Jesuits, taught more often in French, and were less wary of imparting to students the republican attitudes of many of the classical authors who were the mainstay of the curriculum, such as Livy, Tacitus and Cicero.[28] One should not exaggerate, however, the extent to which members of the revolutionary generation were being subjected to a diet of republican virtue during their formative years. There was still a preponderance of religious works which downplayed virtue, ignored the idea of social improvement and concentrated on the issue of individual salvation.

Typical of such devout works intended for impressionable young minds, was *L'Ecolier vertueux* by the abbé Proyart.[29] This was introduced as the true account of the life of Décalogne, a schoolboy at Louis-le-Grand, who had died aged sixteen after a life devoted to prayer, piety, chastity, hard work and humility. It was intended as an inspirational work, to instil students with the more traditional forms of Christian virtue. Décalogne's last months had been filled with meditations on heaven, hell, death and judgement, the futility of this life, and anticipations of the next. He had died of a putrid fever, but his virtue was such that, wondrous to relate, no smell of corruption came from his body. This edifying narrative was a typical example of so many devout works where human virtue could change nothing on this earth, but only make for a better death. Proyart composed it largely for the benefit of the schoolboys in his charge at Louis-le-Grand. His pupils there included such future revolutionaries as Camille Desmoulins and Maximilien Robespierre, who arrived at the school shortly before Décalogne's death. What they made of this work and its vision of the futility of the search for earthly happiness is not recorded, although J. M. Thompson was probably right to contend that such works were read under compulsion and often with derision and helped to turn Robespierre and some of his contemporaries at Louis-le-Grand against revealed religion. They chose instead a quite different kind of virtue. Not surprisingly, Proyart did not regard Robespierre as one of his educational successes. He later was a probable contributor to a hostile account of Robespierre's life which claimed that, even as a boy, he had shown villainous tendencies and paid little attention to the admonitions of his tutors.[30]

Bienfaisance, social virtue and philanthropy

In the secular world the abundance of works on the themes of social virtue and *bienfaisance* was striking. There was a profusion of treatises offering models of good conduct through instruction in the ways of virtue and *bienfaisance* with titles such as *Bienfaisance françois* and *La Morale en action*.[31] Such works were more notable for their enthusiasm than their originality. The journalist Brissot seized the opportunity when reviewing one such book, a translation of Dragonetti's *Traité des vertus et des récompenses*, to condemn the genre: 'This is an overworked and exhausted category of ideas and maxims on virtue, which we have heard repeated a hundred times before.'[32] This repetition of ideas to the point of banality which so exasperated Brissot emphasises the extent to which social virtue had established itself with the reading public. Often the ideas of social virtue and of *bienfaisance* were watered down into anecdotes of virtuous and *bienfaisant* actions. Such anecdotes frequently appeared in the 'respectable' national press such as the gazettes and the *Mercure de France*, which were subject to censorship, but were more freely available than illicit works like the *Mémoires secrets*.[33] The provincial journals, or *affiches*, which proliferated from about 1770 were forbidden to discuss political subjects, but there was nothing to prevent their spreading similar ideas of social virtue, which they did enthusiastically. It has been argued that the bourgeois readers of the *affiches* were able to imbibe political ideas therein and develop a political consciousness in the last years before the Revolution.[34]

These accounts of virtuous actions, sensibility and *bienfaisance* which appeared in the popular press were in turn gathered up and republished in collections and yearbooks such as the *Annales de la bienfaisance* and the *Etrennes de la vertu*. The *Annales de la bienfaisance*, for example, encouraged its provincial readers to participate as virtuous citizens by sending in examples of 'acts of *bienfaisance*' from their own local *affiches*.[35] Lourdet, the censor of this particular work, used the formal notice of 'approbation' to voice his agreement with the aims of the author, whom he characterised as 'an excellent Patriot' whose work would encourage 'his fellow citizens' to emulate the 'models of religious and social virtues' which he offered.[36] The *Etrennes de la vertu*, which appeared annually from 1782 to 1792, was another work which was compiled to a large extent from newspaper sources, of which the principal one was the *Journal de Paris*.[37] This work was specifically directed towards the 'young people of both sexes' with the express intention of making them '*bienfaisant*, generous, humane, in a word . . . Virtuous Citizens'.[38] In accord with this preamble, the number of stories of virtuous and *bienfaisant* women in this work compared very favourably with the number of men. It is notable also that, in order to show the egalitarian character of virtue, most of these virtuous women were chosen from the poorer classes. Often such women were depicted as caring for orphaned or abandoned children when already burdened with children of their own.[39] Such stories invited a favourable comparison of the virtues of the poor with those of the rich: 'Show me the Great or the Rich in Paris who, having four children of their own, would assume responsibility for the care of three poor children of strangers for three months?'[40] Another story extolling the virtuous poor was that of a woman servant who, when her mistress lost her fortune, gave her own savings to her employer.[41] Such writings were not political as such, but they did help to confirm the egalitarianism of social virtue, and the idea that *bienfaisance* outside the circle of their own families was a virtue at which women, especially poor women, excelled.

Bienfaisance, or philanthropy as it might now be termed, was more than a rhetorical device by the 1780s. It had begun to affect actual policy and played a role in the development of provision for the poor in a manner which has been brought to light by historians such as Colin

Jones, Olwen Hufton and Catherine Duprat.[42] By the 1780s some of the most well-respected political minds of the day had come to believe in the efficacy of social virtue. Writings on *bienfaisance* had diverse aims – or rather, various projects were caught up in the common language of *bienfaisance*. Practical projects for hospitals, poor relief, sanitation etc., employed a similar vocabulary to that used to relate individual acts of kindness and sensibility, a vocabulary which in turn was often used to conceptualise a regenerated society or *patrie*. The Christian language of charity and the tradition of almsgiving was gradually superseded by this new secularised language, but it was not a matter of a straightforward polarisation between clerical and secular approaches to poverty for, as we have seen, some clerics were also enthusiasts for the new ideas. The discourse of *bienfaisance* ran a gamut of social responses to the poor which ranged from visualising them as equals in human dignity, though unfortunate, through condescension, to overt attempts to control their behaviour. At its most conservative, *bienfaisance* was redolent of over-bearing philanthropy and the desire to mould and educate the indigent classes rather than to learn from their example. But where the language of virtue and citizenship was also employed it tended to mitigate these more patronising aspects of *bienfaisance* and to emphasise its egalitarian implications, that is, the notion that 'the less fortunate' were fellow-citizens of the benefactors. Though unfortunate in their lives they were equal in rights.

The virtuous poor as the nation: virtue rewarded

Whilst the higher nobility laboured under the popular association with vice and corruption, the image of the virtuous poor and humble abounded in social and political writings as well as novels and plays. The man of low origins, with nothing to recommend him but his virtue, basked in the light of public approval as never before. Virtue was identified with the popular image of the Third Estate: the humble, poor and obscure. Even the marquise de la Tour du Pin, though hardly a democrat, was proud to claim that she was taught virtue by the simple illiterate peasant woman who was her nurse in her early years. Her simple virtue was in striking contrast to the irreligion and immorality of the household in which the young Lucie lived, that of her grandmother and her uncle the Archbishop of Narbonne.[43] As an image it was to be wielded most successfully to legitimise the growing social and political significance of the bourgeoisie, who were the chief practical beneficiaries of this discourse. But most often it was the peasantry who were idealised in books and images, though they themselves derived little practical benefit. This association of the workers in the countryside with the virtuous and best part of the nation made possible such a work as Rétif de la Bretonne's *La Vie de mon père* (1779), which would have been unthinkable at the start of the century. The hero of Rétif's semi-autobiographical, expiatory, idealised portrait of his childhood in Burgundy was his father, a peasant (although admittedly an unusually wealthy and educated one). Edmé Rétif leads an exemplary life of 'an everyday kind of virtue' as a hard-working man, in his family life and in the local community with his 'fellow-citizens'.[44] Edmé dominated successive wives, children and farm servants in patriarchal manner. His son had, as a young man, rebelled under the constraints of this paternal authority and departed to experience the decidedly less austere climate of Paris and the company of women who were far from virtuous. In later life he repented some of his youthful frivolity and saw in his father's life the epitome of a good man. He decided to vindicate his father's way of life and make expiation for his own filial lapses. His reconstructed literary memories of peasant life probably owed as much to Rousseau as they did to genuine peasant values, but it was a powerful portrait none the less. He quite deliberately constructed this triumphant account of a humble but virtuous man to contrast with tales of the old heroes of glory and renown. Rétif began the Preface to the work by stating:

> Some celebrate warriors who have triumphed in armed combat; academies bestow prizes on writers who have enhanced the reputation of former ministers and of distinguished men of letters. I, on the other hand, shall pay tribute to the memory of an honourable man whose virtue was of the ordinary 'everyday' kind, one might say. He was simply upright and hardworking, and it is qualities such as these that are the bedrock of every society and without which heroes would die of hunger.[45]

The virtuous common 'people' were generally to be encountered in abstract form on the page or the canvas rather than in any more physical manifestation. The ranks of the great unwashed were usually excluded from the salons, masonic lodges and literary circles. But there were exceptions. Sometimes the people themselves were invited to partake in events that celebrated the more egalitarian versions of virtue. When they did appear they were expected to be clean, decent, respectful – like Greuze's idealised peasants – and to keep their opinions to themselves.

In the *Discours sur les sciences et les arts*, Rousseau had advocated the offering of prizes for virtue: 'Rewards are lavished upon fine minds, whilst virtue goes unacknowledged. There are a thousand prizes for well-composed discourses, and not one for a fine action.'[46] In the 1770s this idea began to be taken very seriously and examples proliferated.

The growing vogue for offering 'prizes' for virtue led to some surprising encounters between the virtuous poor and their benefactors. In 1783, for example, the *Mémoires secrets* recounted how, at that year's public session of the Académie française, an event customarily attended by some of the most prestigious members of French society, the gaze of the public met the rather surprising spectacle of a 'woman of the people' sitting in the gallery where women from the highest ranks of the nobility customarily sat. She was 'a woman of between thirty-five and forty, fairly plain; dressed in the worker's Sunday best', and she was accompanied by other men and women of the same social class. It was announced that this woman, named Lespalier, had won the newly-established 'Prize for the people's virtue' for having cared for a poverty-stricken sick woman.[47] Some points here are worth noting. The Academicians sought here to make the ideal of civic equality more than an abstraction, though what the woman herself thought of being thus paraded for her virtue was naturally not recorded: her role was entirely symbolic. But it was a somewhat challenging event for three reasons. First, she was not a peasant or the embodiment of uncorrupted rural values, but a member of the urban lower classes – not traditionally known for their association with virtue. Secondly, she had neither youth nor beauty to make her virtue sentimentally appealing: this was virtue without the sugary coating. Thirdly, her virtue went beyond the narrow range usually ascribed to women, those of chastity, or maternal or family love. Indeed, it was reported that the Academicians had given the prize to this particular woman rather than to one of the other nominees precisely because her virtuous action had not been directed simply to a member of her family, but to 'a stranger'. She had been a good patriot for an act of *bienfaisance* to a fellow-citizen.

Many similar prizes were set up as 'Prizes for *bienfaisance*' or 'virtuous actions', often given by private donors but distributed by provincial academies following the example of the *Académie française*.[48] The provincial academies also encouraged the growth of ideas of virtue amongst the reading public by continually extending their prizes for essays and eulogies on heroes of virtue and explorations of the political meaning of virtue and citizenship. Many future revolutionaries developed their political ideas partly through entering such contests, such as those of the *Académie des Jeux floraux* of Toulouse, where the young lawyer, Barère wrote eulogies of *bienfaisant* kingship, and the virtues of Rousseau.[49]

Dozens of festivals of virtue (often known as *rosières* after the rose wreath which constituted part of the prize) which offered prizes for virtuous conduct, were set up in the period from the late 1760s to the Revolution, modelled on the original festival held at Salency, in Picardy.[50] Traditionally at this annual festival the most virtuous (i.e. chaste and filial) girl in the village was given a rose wreath and a dowry which would enable her to make a good marriage. This was originally a small affair organised by the local community. It was brought to the attention of polite society by Madame de Genlis in 1766. She had resided in the neighbourhood of Salency for many years though she moved in the very different circles of the court nobility, and only became aware of the festival at the age of eighteen when the growing idealisation of rural virtue made her see in a positive light an event hitherto thought of little importance. Madame de Genlis herself participated in the festival. She played her harp for the edification of the peasants, and her friends partook of a rustic supper and danced innocently under the stars. Salency, was thus 'discovered' by fashionable society, many of whom began to attend the festival, eager to experience the charms of rural virtue for themselves.[51]

The festival at Salency soon became a contested event, played out before the eyes of public opinion. William Everdell and, more recently, Sarah Maza have recounted how in 1773 the local seigneur, Danré, attempted to curtail the Salency festival, resenting the intervention of outsiders on what he considered to be his territory. The community went to court to appeal against the seigneur's judgement and the matter became a *cause célèbre*, defended by two of the most prominent *patriote* lawyers and supporters of the then exiled Paris *parlement*, Target and Delacroix, and played out against the backdrop of the continuing exile of the *parlement*. The two lawyers exploited to the hilt the discourse of natural rural virtue on behalf of the peasants and against the hapless seigneur, cast in the role of the villain of the piece, the overbearing noble opposed to virtue. In their hands Salency appeared as an earthly paradise, the equivalent of Sparta or *La Nouvelle Héloïse*. Danré eventually lost his case. Maza gives a compelling account of the ways in which the discourse of rural virtue was appropriated by a legal rhetoric which associated the virtues of the villagers with the virtues of the 'nation'. She goes on to link the symbolism of the *rosière* girl's chastity with the integrity of the nation, an idea which she claims found its full expression in the reduction of women to symbols of chastity during the Revolution.[52]

A number of the festivals that were set up at this time went beyond the more limited concern with young girls' virginity and emphasised popular virtue as *bienfaisance*. Other festivals of virtue were set up, often by sympathetic clerics, nobles and affluent bourgeois, as part of a desire to spread ideas of social virtue. As the festivals were extended, so were the categories of people who might receive prizes. The festival 'des Bonnes-Gens' for example, inaugurated at Canon in Normandy by the celebrated lawyer Elie de Beaumont and his wife, provided prizes for a 'good old man', a 'good father' and 'a good mother' as well as 'une bonne fille'.[53] The elaboration of such complex systems of reward for acts of individual virtue operated on many levels: it was far more than an attempt to exert some form of 'social control' to ensure 'good' behaviour, though that was sometimes part of it. On the whole, people seem to have been singularly free of cynicism and to have believed that society could genuinely be 'made happier' by the proliferation of virtuous actions.

But some of the inspiration for such festivals may have derived from more politically contentious models. The example of the American Revolution had encouraged the idea that a society of virtuous citizens was an achievable possibility. Works such as Crèvecœur's *Lettres d'un cultivateur américain*, together with Franklin's much publicised visit to France, helped to spread the myth that in America natural patriotic virtue truly existed, and that the Americans were a nation of independent virtuous citizens, living in the vast rural areas, far from the corruption and hierarchy of old European cities.[54] The Quakers in particular were seen as a community that lived according to nature and to virtue. This was not something out of a bygone classical age, but a real and contemporary society. The portrait thus painted of American life was certainly an idealised one, though Crèvecœur did at least discuss the horrors of slavery in unflinchingly grim detail. But this vision of America encouraged the belief that society was capable of improvement: if people became more virtuous they would be able to act as independent citizens. The virtue of the Americans had enabled them to shake off the political systems that dominated the Old World. They had emancipated themselves from a hierarchical State Church, from an exploitative nobility, and from monarchy itself.

There was very little call, as yet, for political change. But in some quarters, there was the expectation, or at least the hope, that giving prizes for private virtues would inculcate virtue and might lead to the first step, the moral regeneration of society. When in 1787 Mathon de la Cour wrote a *Discours sur les meilleurs moyens de faire naître et d'encourager le patriotisme dans une monarchie* for a contest offered by the Academy of Châlons-sur-Marne, he argued that prizes for virtue should be established in each town in France. This, he said, was the best way to influence 'public opinions' and encourage patriotism. He distinguished between 'love of the *patrie*' and 'patriotism': the former was 'a natural inclination', based on self-love and limited to love of family, friends and the familiar; whilst 'patriotism' was an ardent desire to help those we do not know, our compatriots: it was, in short, 'a virtue'. This more profound virtue grew out of the love of humanity, which in turn could be nurtured by the encouragement of the practice of individual virtuous actions. From 'the domestic virtues', he said, grew 'the public virtues' such as patriotism. Here he was paraphrasing Mably, who had claimed that the love of humanity was a superior virtue even to the love of the *patrie*, and that without it, the Greeks and Romans, for all their patriotism, were barbarians who oppressed their neighbours and enslaved them.[55]

Others went further and used the idea of the natural virtues of 'the people' as an indictment of the ruling classes. When Fauchet spoke in August 1788 at Surenne, a village near Paris, where a new *rosière* festival had just been set up, he contrasted the virtue of the peasantry with the corruption of the seigneury. 'The public good, my brothers, is the happiness of peoples. This happiness consists of national virtue, and national virtue is based on the perfection of rural morals.'[56] He went on to speak optimistically of the forthcoming 'National Assemblies', ordered by 'Our King, the people's friend', but followed it with a scathing attack on the landed nobles whom he accused of exploiting the peasantry:

These oppressors of human Nature in the countryside do not sit on Thrones; they are in closer proximity to the people, and press upon rural families more suffocatingly with their riches, their corruption. They have no sense of justice, they own people; they have no soldiers, they have values; they have no rights, they have gold. Who could count the means they use ceaselessly to harass people of no account, as they term them; to corrupt the lower orders, as they dare to designate almost the whole of the Nation? There is nothing impressive about their physical nature; most of them are so ravaged by hereditary corruption as to be amongst the least of the human race: nor is there anything admirable in their moral nature; almost all of them are so personally depraved as to be the lowest kind of human beings in their tastes, and the most degraded in the mire of Vice. Pride and money, this their majesty; this their power; these are their only titles by which they oppress Humanity.[57]

It was a sweeping indictment of the ethics of the seigneurial system, and the rhetoric of natural virtue imparted legitimacy to this critique. It was the poor who constituted the 'nation' through their virtue, not the rich who oppressed them. This was not an expression of simplistic class conflict. Among the many distinguished members of the nobility present was the comtesse d'Artois, wife of the king's brother. By this date the system of censorship, like almost every other aspect of the administration of the *ancien régime*, was beginning to break down, but even so it was striking that such outspokenness seems to have drawn no formal complaints, though many must have been disconcerted at what they heard. It may be that Fauchet's privileged audience heard him out in uneasy silence because of the power of the rhetoric of virtue, so strong was the desire to identify oneself with the side of the virtuous. Few people wanted to be seen, or to see themselves, as opponents of virtue. Fauchet's sermon was given its official royal approbation and duly published. One passage was suppressed but this, significantly perhaps, was not a passage that used the rhetoric of virtue but a specific indictment of the difficulties which the poor encountered in obtaining legal redress when the offenders against them were often themselves also the administrators of justice and often attached to the court 'by high birth or important office'.[58]

Virtue as a political strategy: the virtuous king, Louis XVI

The rhetoric of virtue was not confined to dead heroes, obscure peasant women or fictional characters, it was also being enlisted to reinforce deliberate political strategies, to attribute moral qualities to leading players on the political stage. The rhetoric of political virtue, strategically applied, could give moral authority to those who wanted to substantiate their political credentials, though it necessitated some tricky manoeuvring and was a tactic that could easily backfire. In the uncertain and highly charged political atmosphere of the last years of the absolute reign of Louis XVI most players in the public arena, from bishops to journalists, showed a keen awareness of political rhetoric, including that of virtue. Many such examples could be fruitfully explored. For our purposes three examples must suffice here: the first is Louis XVI himself, the second is his cousin the duc d'Orléans, and the third is Jacques Necker, one-time minister of finance.

The king himself was in a unique position. His legitimacy stemmed from quite other sources, above all from the doctrine of divine right, as well as long tradition and acceptance. So it is a measure of the success of the rhetoric of virtue that the staunchest supporters of absolute monarchy were increasingly having recourse to it in writings and speeches as an attractive and popular way of appealing to public opinion. But this sometimes resulted in a somewhat awkward juxtaposition of traditional loyalties with egalitarian rhetoric. Such awkwardness is illustrated by remarks made in defence of Louis's rights by the abbé Maury. Maury was one of those noted by Mornet as an enthusiast for natural morality, and it is true that he included discussion of politics and the condition of society in his sermons, even those which he gave before the king. Nevertheless, he was moderate enough to know when to hold back and he avoided bringing recrimination on himself. In the early stages of the Revolution he was to sit in the Constituent Assembly where he strongly defended the *ancien régime*, especially the privileges of the higher clergy and the nobility, in spite of the fact that he himself came from a humble artisanal background of Protestant origins. His loyalty to his king was clear in remarks made before the *Académie française* in 1785 where he struggled to reconcile the rhetoric of virtue with that of absolute monarchy:

> This Prince has invented a way of honouring talents and the highest virtues which was unknown before his reign. Up until now...the People have raised statues to Sovereigns; but no Monarch had ever accorded a similar honour to his subjects. Louis XVI is the first Sovereign in history who has acquitted himself of this important debt to the Patrie, by elevating statues in his palace to the great men of the Nation.[59]

The king was to be admired for honouring the virtue of his subjects, his role had subtly altered to a passive one, that of recognition of the virtue of the humble 'people'. The attribution of this change in perception to Louis's own initiative was no more than a polite form of words. It was the reading public which had changed its perception of the relationship between king and the people and their expectations of Louis. Members of the reading public, with no responsibility themselves for the education of kings, wrote with confidence and authority on the role of kingship, and the need of kings to be virtuous and *bienfaisant*.[60]From a quasi-divine concept, kingly virtue had become an expression of the king's fundamental humanity.

Even the most loyal apologists for the monarchy invoked the new concepts of kingly virtue, albeit often with reluctance. Astute propagandists such as Gin, formerly a *conseiller* in the *parlement* established by Maupeou, and then, after its dissolution, a *conseiller au grand-conseil*, recognising the power of the new language of natural virtue and *bienfaisance*, attempted to turn it into a reinforcement of the political authority of Louis XVI. He had gone to the heart of the matter in his *Les Vrais principes du gouvernement françois* (first published in 1778), in which he had defended absolute monarchy as the best form of government, concentrating his fire on one of the fundamental tenets of the politics of virtue: Montesquieu's concept of virtue as the selfless love of the *patrie*. He argued in cogent fashion and using Montesquieu's own words against him, that political virtue was an inadequate basis for sound government, for it was based on the people being selfless public-spirited citizens, whereas everyone knew in truth that the people were ignorant, vacillating and ill-fitted to play a political role.[61]

In a eulogy of Louis's father, the previous dauphin, written some time after his death and with the intention of strengthening Louis's authority rather than making a belated valediction to the father, Gin re-stated the principle of kingly virtue in an attempt to make the new language of virtue work in support of the sovereignty of the monarchy. Gin contrasted the superior Christian virtues of the dauphin with the pagan virtues of another model, Marcus Aurelius, who was 'this idol of the Roman people', but whose pagan virtue was the result of 'pride' which could be corrupted.[62] Gin used the model of Christian virtues to argue that only a Christian king had the authority and genuine disinterestedness to bring together 'particular interests' with 'the general interest'. Such sovereign authority, he continued, could not be given to the *'peuple'*, whom he described as 'this hydra', wayward and easily led. Nor could it be wielded by 'the alleged representatives of the Nation' (the *parlements*), of whom he said: 'The more they identify themselves with the people, the more particular interests they will have to satisfy, and the more will the public good be sacrificed.'[63] But Gin's attempt to bestow upon Louis XVI the soubriquet of 'Louis the *Bienfaisant*' which he said 'the Nation' had already conferred upon him, and which had been originally intended for Louis's father was problematic and did not find wide acceptance. Public opinion proved recalcitrant on this point: a living reigning monarch was seen very differently from a dead one who had never ruled. The assertion that the king was *bienfaisant* and the emphasis on his humanity and kindness as credentials for respect left him more vulnerable in the long-run to counter-assertions that he and his queen were lacking in humanitarian qualities.[64]

Virtue as a political strategy: the virtuous noble, d'Orléans

In contrast to Louis's supporters were the actions of his cousin and unofficial rival the duc d'Orléans and his propagandists. The extent of his political ambitions both before and during the Revolution has always been subject to much speculation both at the time and since. Documentation is lacking to prove conclusively that d'Orléans sought to oust Louis and gain the throne for himself in the early years of the Revolution. What is not in doubt, however, is that d'Orléans, and his father the old duke, used their vast power, wealth and connections to set themselves up as leaders in an unofficial *fronde* or opposition to the Bourbons. They had opposed the Maupeou coup, aligning themselves with the magistrates as 'defenders of the nation' for which father and son underwent a brief period of exile. But it was not until the late 1780s, when the monarchy embarked on its last fatal collision course with unruly members of the elite in the *parlements* and the Assembly of Notables, that d'Orléans went beyond customary family rivalry and *frondeur* politics and emerged as a focus for overt opposition. As Kelly puts this, of all the unruly princes of the blood, only d'Orléans anticipated the change from closed *frondeur* politics to 'open' politics.[65] The Palais-Royal became an alternative court and centre of power in the heart of Paris. D'Orléans gave little sign that he was capable of thinking out and creating a successful political persona for himself. He was something of a 'playboy', with a dissolute reputation facilitated by his extensive possessions, land and wealth. His main interests were women and horse-racing. He was out of his depth in complicated political exchanges. Although he hitched himself to the discourses of liberty and equality, it was liberty for himself rather than for the populace that concerned him. On the other hand, he could well afford to pay for some of the most sophisticated propagandists of the day to influence public opinion on his behalf. This 'machine' was headed firstly by his former mistress, Madame de Genlis, and the Ducrest family. She had made herself an authority on models of virtue and appears to have been behind some of the attacks on the virtue of Marie-Antoinette at the time of the Diamond Necklace Affair.[66]. Later the 'machine' was taken over by Choderlos de Laclos, more famous now for a novel which played on the popular image of a court nobility devoted to vice and the overthrow of virtue. He entered the household of d'Orléans in late 1788. The pleasure-loving and self-indulgent duc d'Orléans was far from being the ideal candidate for an austere and selfless 'hero of virtue'. It says much for the ingenuity and resourcefulness of his propagandists that they managed to manufacture a fairly credible image for him in this respect.

The tangled strategies of Orléanist political propaganda of this later period take us into the new arena of the Revolution itself. But one example from the earlier period of the mid-1780s illustrates the way in which the rhetoric of virtue was being enlisted to cultivate a political image for the d'Orléans family. This was the occasion of the rival and contrasting funeral eulogies given to mark the death of the old duc d'Orléans (known informally as 'Louis the fat') and which signalled his son's first serious forays at creating a public image.

The first funeral eulogy of the dead duke was pronounced by Maury, who was selected specifically for this task by Louis XVI. Maury's approach to his task fitted in with the will of his royal patron and was hardly intended to appeal to the d'Orléans clan. The extent to which the dead duke's virtues were praised was far more than a matter of form: it had a political dimension. Maury walked a difficult tightrope here. He could not, of course, be seen to be attacking overtly the posthumous reputation of the dead duke, but the tenor of his words served to undermine subtly the image of the present one, who was already establishing himself as a thorn in the flesh of his royal cousin. In his oration Maury, whilst formally praising the virtues of the old duke, managed to negate the effect by airing the popular belief that the nobility now no longer stood for virtue (especially military virtue) but for vice, especially sexual vice. He did this by a subtle combination of excessive praise undermined by insinuation. The *Mémoires secrets* reported that Maury 'expounded too freely on the general opinion of his hero, whose memory he was powerless to rehabilitate after having degraded it'. Maury made sidelong references to the duke's many sexual liaisons interspersed with such overblown praise of the duke's virtues, in particular 'warrior virtues', as actually to provoke his audience to ironic laughter. Most importantly, Maury also implied, in a way that was perfectly understood by his audience, that the old duke had not been able to bequeath to his son such virtue, his piety or *bienfaisance*, as he possessed. Maury expressed the pious hope that the old duke's grandchildren would inherit his virtues, but managed to omit the present duke entirely, insinuating instead that the new duke had only the *vices* of his father, by means of some dark references to 'the respect' which princes ought to have for 'the public' and how they ought not to 'shock opinion'.[67] Incidentally, the author of the commentary in the *Mémoires secrets* seems to have shared this scepticism concerning the new duke's *bienfaisance* for he commented scathingly on the meanness of the facilities provided for his father's funeral service.

The new duke was reportedly furious. His response was to suppress the publication of Maury's eulogy and to appoint his clerical rival, the abbé Fauchet to give an alternative eulogy. The choice was politically significant. Maury and Fauchet, both came from similar, fairly humble origins, but whilst Maury had grown more conservative with the passing years and was now firmly in the camp of the court, Fauchet was developing in quite other political directions. He gave a fulsome eulogy of the deceased, which downplayed or discreetly ignored the matters which Maury had brought up to the duke's discredit. Fauchet built up a very different model, of a man whose distinguishing qualities were his 'sensibility', 'bienfaisance', but above all, 'his national virtues'.[68] This last arresting phrase was a development of the phrase 'public virtues' and elsewhere Fauchet had also applied it to the peasantry. In a prince, said Fauchet, such virtues consisted of 'attachment to the Sovereign, courage in the defence of the *Patrie*, respect for the Laws, love of the People, and fidelity to Religion'.[69] It was the duke's respect for the laws which had caused him to defend the proscribed *parlements* during the Maupeou coup. The duke had simply defended the fundamental and unalterable elements of monarchy, which were: the sovereign authority of kings, the security of property, the sacred rights of 'venerable institutions, and the magistratures' and 'the great power of Opinion, or the voice of the People'.[70] In defending these rights, observed Fauchet, the duke was not challenging the authority of the king, but asking only for 'equity', which was 'a sacred right; it honoured the King as much as the Nation'. Thus, the old duke's 'national virtues' involved the defence of the rights of the nation, even when Louis XV had been inclined to neglect them. By insinuation, the duke had shown more of a sense of the public good than the king had done. When Fauchet came to the duke's 'domestic virtues' he lingered on his *bienfaisance* and his care for the unfortunate. Here indeed was a political model to challenge that of the *bienfaisant* king: when a portion of the royal debt was suspended, and charitable works temporarily lapsed, it was the duc d'Orléans who showed himself: 'The Friend of the Poor... he is no longer a Prince, he is only a man. Ah! Say rather that he is even more of a Prince, because he is more of a man: he is the father; he is the King of Humanity.'[71] Fauchet had his sticking point, however: he found himself unable to lie outright and praise the new duke's virtues. Instead he concentrated principally on the virtues of the new duke's long-suffering wife – with the implied reproof that the duke, being a fallible man, might in time-honoured fashion learn virtue from her example.[72] Nevertheless, the new duke was said to be well-satisfied with this second funeral eulogy, which obtained a wide circulation amongst the public. Fauchet himself had many copies printed, including six hundred alone for d'Orléans' own household, for which d'Orléans apparently neglected to pay him.[73]

The propaganda machine acquired by the new duke set to work to create for him such a reputation for *bienfaisance* and virtue as Fauchet had accorded his father. Brissot (who worked for d'Orléans during the time of the Ducrest ascendancy) later described how he and the other writers in the pay of the duke deliberately tried to win over public opinion. One strategy was to appeal to men of letters and the learned societies by having the duke set up an impressive number of philanthropic societies and workshops for *bienfaisance* in the area of his 'apanage'. Brissot added that to prepare the Revolution one needed 'good morals' but that D'Orléans's efforts to present himself in this light were sporadic and half-hearted.[74] Such instances were then assiduously reported to the press and contributed to the creation of the duke as a model of virtue, the number of whose reported instances of *bienfaisance* rivalled those of the king. The *Etrennes de la vertu* described how the duke provided 150,000 livres a year for pensions for 'pauvres gentilshommes' on his estates and several other projects for *bienfaisance* in 1787, including schools for the children of the less well off, as well as his founding of several 'philanthropic societies'.[75] The winter of 1788 was exceptionally cold, hard and deadly for the poor. Madame de Genlis urged the duke to court popularity by selling his picture gallery and announcing that the money raised should be used to help women in childbirth, and to distribute bread to the poor.[76] The vast wealth and privileged status of the duke was of importance only in so far as it could be made to benefit the public good. Thus, on the brink of Revolution, some of the most skilled propagandists of the day worked to manufacture the image of the duc d'Orléans as a model virtuous citizen and representative of the Third Estate. It was an attempt at early political image-making, but it was a formidable task and it met with only limited success amongst the public. It was one thing to construct the model of the man of virtue, it was another to persuade people to believe in it.

Virtue as a political strategy: the virtuous minister, Necker

A final example of virtue as a political strategy is that offered by the Genevan banker and former finance minister, Necker. He had shown himself to be an astute manipulator of political rhetoric some years before with his publication in 1781 of the *Compte rendu au Roi*. This had broken new ground in its promotion of the principle that the hitherto sacrosanct mysteries of government should be subject to public scrutiny. During much of the 1780s he was an outside observer of the growing financial crisis which loomed over the monarchy. Both he and his supporters believed that, given the opportunity, he could do better than his beleaguered successors, Calonne and Brienne. In 1788 he published *De L'importance des opinions religieuses*. This work was in part a defence of the idea of an innate sense of virtue which worked for the happiness of all, very much in the mould of Shaftesbury. Necker's version of virtue was one which stemmed from God, whom he frequently invoked in deist terms, either as divine providence or as the Supreme Being. But virtue's primary purpose here lay in its temporal applications – to unify society and alleviate poverty. Even for so sophisticated a financial analyst as Necker, it was virtue that offered the means to a better society.[77] It was through virtue that people respected the rights of others. He went so far as to declare that the '*bienfaisant* virtues' were indispensable if the fabric of French society was to hold together:

> in present-day society, it has become impossible to do without these virtues. It is not enough to be just when the laws of property reduce the majority of men to dire necessity, and the least accident can have a disastrous impact on their meagre resources: thus, I am not afraid to assert that such are the extremes of inequality established by these laws, that the spirit of *bienfaisance* and of charity must now be considered as a constitutive part of the social order.[78]

Unlike Shaftesbury, however, he was more concerned with the particular opportunities that existed for those who held public office to act with virtue. *Bienfaisance* was a desirable quality for the rank and file of society, but it was indispensable for those who wielded political power, 'the morality of princes, that of ministers, that of governments in general, is the primary source of the happiness of peoples'.[79] Public opinion could have some impact as a judge of public figures, but it was not infallible. It could be deceived by clever political manipulation.[80] Thus it was all the more important, Necker argued, that ministers have virtue: 'ministers without virtue are more to be feared than sovereigns who are indifferent to the public good', for they were closer to the crowd, and more skilled at manipulating its passions and encouraging its vices.[81]

Whether or not it had been his original intention, this book contributed to its author himself being depicted as an example of that
rarity, the virtuous minister. As a piece of political image-making it
was well-timed. On 26th August of that year he would be recalled to
public office in a last desperate attempt to avert financial disaster. The
Opinions religieuses had many admirers, one of whom was Robespierre,
soon also to be launched abruptly onto the political stage. He praised
Necker as a new Sully who, inspired by 'the eloquence of virtue', had
now been recalled to serve the descendant of Henri IV.[82] Necker and
Robespierre, so far apart in their political loyalties, had this, at least, in
common: they shared the belief that only through virtuous government
could France's political future be assured.

Conclusion: Virtue and the Creation of Revolutionary Politics

We have seen that the rhetoric of political virtue took several forms throughout the eighteenth century. Some aspects of this rhetoric were to prefigure to a striking degree the contours of the revolutionary debate about virtue. However, the link between the pre-revolutionary and revolutionary understanding of virtue was not a simple or inevitable matter of linear progression. Just as there had been competing ideas before the Revolution about the role of virtue in public life, so this disagreement about the scope of political virtue continued into the Revolution itself. None the less, we can see that the revolutionaries' underlying premises about the nature of virtue were drawn from a long political tradition which had its roots far back in the eighteenth century and even earlier.

It was not the meaning of 'virtue' that was transformed in 1789 so much as the meaning of 'politics'. The context in which the debate about virtue was held changed drastically. This book has concentrated on the politics of virtue before the Revolution, but in this last section we shall consider some of the transformations brought about by the impact of the Revolution. The fate of virtue in the shifting and traumatic context of revolutionary politics would make a book in itself, if not several. Here, we only have space to make some preliminary points and to speculate a little about the paradoxical relationship between theories of universal happiness, selfless citizenship, and the often violent realities of revolutionary politics. Three points need to be made about the relationship of virtue to the Revolution. First, political virtue was central to the conception of revolutionary politics: it was through the rhetoric of virtue that the Revolution could be articulated and given meaning. Secondly, the theme of political virtue and the need to inculcate virtue provided revolutionaries with projects and plans for the future and the idea of moral regeneration. Thirdly, the rhetoric of political virtue provided the necessary justification for turning rebels into revolutionaries. It gave revolutionaries moral legitimacy and from that sprang their claim to authority. To be a 'man of virtue' meant that one was engaging in revolution not to profit from it, not to overthrow one ruling class in order to replace it, but for the public good.

By 1774 the main elements of the discourse of virtue as it was to be applied during the Revolution were already apparent. This book has charted that process. Political virtue originated from much earlier sources, above all from the traditions of classical republicanism, though also from Christian theology, discourses of kingship, and of nobility. Equally important had been the belief that the inclination towards virtue was natural to an uncorrupted humanity. This idea, which originally came from English philosophers, crossed over into French thought shortly before the mid-century. It served as a starting point for a new generation of *philosophes*, associated with the *Encyclopédie*, to reformulate their ideas about the relationship between mankind and society, and the potential of virtue to contribute to the development of projects for the improvement of humanity.

During the period of the pre-revolution (from early 1787 to May 1789) great political changes took place which brought virtue into the forefront of debate. The most fundamental shift (which took place from about September 1788 with the decision to summon the Estates General according to the form of 1614) brought growing disillusion – and dissatisfaction – with the role played by leading nobles in the *parlements* and at court, and began the process that launched the Third Estate into consciousness of its political self. Up until that point, 'politics' in so far as it existed in practice (and according to the theory of absolute monarchy it did not exist at all outside the remit of kingship), was still very much 'closed', that is, it was very much confined to the world of the elite, disputing amongst themselves and seeking unofficial confirmation of their status, whether they were magistrates in the *parlements*, courtiers out of favour and conducting *frondeur* politics, or leading Jansenists denied the right to determine their religious loyalties. From September 1788 began the shift to 'open' politics, that is, to a popular participatory politics within a forum where public opinion could no longer be denied a voice. Within that forum the rhetoric of political virtue was to resonate as never before.

The rhetoric of virtue came to be associated particularly with the bourgeoisie, and thereby played a role in the creation of public opinion as a source of moral authority. The idea of public opinion, which stemmed from Jansenists and the *philosophes*, was taken up by journalists, lawyers, clerics and other writers and reached a much wider audience in the later eighteenth century. Virtue was fundamental in lending moral authority to public opinion: the public was a source of legitimate opinion precisely because it was said to be virtuous, that is, disinterested, and motivated only by a desire to bring about the public good.

Ultimately, however, the power of the discourse of political virtue stemmed from the fact that it was much more than a 'mere' political language. It retained its philosophical and moral basis. Any man (and even any woman) could aspire to virtue as a way of being, of creating meaning, and of having value in the world. Virtue could be easily assimilated, adapted and manipulated by different classes and social groups. Its appeal was ubiquitous and it had proved extraordinarily versatile.

The language of virtue was not universally spoken in the last years of the *ancien régime* but it was, amongst the educated classes, universally understood. It formed an important component of the conceptualisation of political theory. At its most radical, the rhetoric could imply that virtue, not wealth, power or privileged status, was the only true measure of a man's worth, and thus it bore democratic and egalitarian implications. It was not always the intention of the speakers of the rhetoric to emphasise these egalitarian undertones. Many of those most vociferous in their assertion of their own virtue were concerned with far more parochial issues than were implied by the grandeur of the language. The reception of the rhetoric was therefore equally as significant as the intentions of the speakers. Thus the magistrates of the *parlements* posed as Roman senators virtuously and selflessly defending the rights of the 'nation', but in practice they were rather more interested in defending their corporate status and privileges; and they were indignant at those supporters who took the ideals of civic virtue literally.

It was the cracking apart of the *ancien régime* that brought the language of virtue to the centre of the political stage and revolutionised it. Here it was not the bourgeoisie who were the prime movers. They could revel in literature extolling humble heroes of virtue, but this had no impact on their actual political status, which was one of relative powerlessness. It was not the bourgeoisie who first took up the rhetoric of virtue in political challenge. Furet was surely right to emphasise the importance of language in the construction of categories of supporters and opponents of the Revolution – the virtuous and the enemies of virtue – but the relationship between the discourse and the kind of people who used it was not one of straightforward identity. One of the ironies of the Revolution is that it was initiated by members of the highest-ranking nobility even though the rhetoric at its heart, the rhetoric of virtue, was anti-aristocratic.[1] A high proportion of the politically dissenting literature that circulated up until 1788 stemmed from the elite themselves, who often acted as secret sponsors of subversive writers and pamphleteers. Many of those men held positions of authority within the *ancien régime*, including leading courtiers and younger members of the judiciary. Whether motivated by disaffection, *parlementaire* constitutionalism or idealism, men of privilege and wealth in the *ancien régime* had recourse to a language whose political radicalism went further than they themselves actually desired. By deliberately courting public opinion and promoting pamphlets and other subversive literature, such men inadvertently but recklessly encouraged the less privileged to see the language of political virtue as a means of political conceptualisation which could also include them.

The discourse of virtue at the outbreak of the revolution

Political virtue was a familiar term to educated participants in the early stages of the Revolution, but if we consider what they understood by the phrase it is clear that it stemmed from much more than 'Rousseau's concept of virtue'. In terms of strictly political definitions it would be more accurate to call it 'Montesquieu's concept of virtue' but this too would fail to do justice to the complexity of the idea. Only a small minority of active participants in the early stages of the Revolution were directly influenced by Rousseau's political ideas. Nor does the so-called 'radical' Enlightenment appear to have exerted a particularly influential force. The men of the late 1780s owed an intellectual debt to a much wider body of ideas than the Enlightenment narrowly defined. Jansenism played a part in the formulation of political thought which has been well-charted in recent years.[2] Classical republicanism and the civic concept of virtue that emerged from it were part of a common tradition familiar to all the deputies from their secondary education. Studies of the political culture of the deputies of the National Assembly – the men who forged the Revolution – have shown that in its early months the deputies made more references to classical republicanism than to Rousseau's political ideas (of which most were very wary) or the more radical elements of Enlightenment thought.[3]

Together with classical republicanism, the idea of natural virtue found favour amongst adherents of the Revolution. This was translated into the revolutionary term 'fraternity' popularised by the abbé Fauchet and members of the *Cercle Social*, the educational society set up in 1790. More than one commentator has remarked on the paradoxical capacity of revolutionaries to show open emotion and even shed tears when they witnessed those scenes of sensibility and *bienfaisance* that emphasised the shared nature of humanity. They clung to the idea that humanity was brought together by natural emotions of fellow-feeling, even when shortly after such outbursts of sentiment they would be violently opposing one another once again.[4] Their idea of natural sociable virtue owed much to themes of 'virtue rewarded' and 'common happiness' popularised in the 1780s, and relatively little to the philosophical complexities with which Diderot and Rousseau had endowed the concept of virtue. The principles of popular sovereignty and the concept of 'the general will' provoked both confusion and uneasiness in most political participants in the early years of the Revolution, but the idea that the goal of government was to ensure the happiness of the people and that, to that end, those in political power ought to act with virtue, was much more widely acceptable and easily assimilated. Even so, virtue was not something that took people over and determined their ideas for them. Some were enthusiasts, others more cynical, but it was a common linguistic resource or strategy that could be used to negotiate a way through political minefields.

There are other indications that the rhetoric of virtue had found its way into the mentalities of provincial representatives of the Third Estate in the early stages of the Revolution. The *cahiers de doléances* were written in the traditional judicial style and deferential language of the *ancien régime* even though the grievances listed in them were often new and forcefully expressed. In the main catalogues of grievances there was little mention of virtue or other terms from the new political vocabulary. Significantly enough, this kind of language came into use when the writers of the *cahiers* addressed the king and voiced their expectations of how the monarchy would act in this situation. A considerable degree of loyalty to Louis XVI remained but it was being expressed in terms somewhat different from the traditional emphasis on the sanctity and remoteness of monarchy. Louis was praised for his 'patriotic virtues', addressed as 'the *bienfaisant*' (particularly in the cahiers of the Third Estate); he was the heir to 'the virtues of Louis IX, Louis XII and Henri IV'.[5] Such terms as 'kingly virtues', 'citizenship', 'patriotism', *bienfaisance*, had crept into the rhetoric of the *cahiers* on the basis of the assumption that the role of the king was to ensure the happiness of his people. The French people themselves were often referred to as 'citizens'. The emphasis in the *cahiers* was no longer on the exclusively sacred character of monarchy (for the nation and its citizens were also held to be sacred) but on the essential humanity of the monarch. Although the word 'sacred' was still used in a minority of cases, when it did appear it referred to the nation or to individual rights as often as it did to the king.[6] There were suggestions, too, that the virtues of an individual monarch were no longer in themselves sufficient to guarantee the integrity of the State. Thus, the *cahier* of the nobility of Provins admired Louis's virtues but stated that the power of the king ought 'to be limited by law so that a prince less virtuous than Louis XVI or an unfaithful minister can never cross that limit'.[7]

In the language of the pamphlets of 1788 and 1789 one finds many instances of the term 'virtue', as well as 'patriotism', '*bienfaisant* monarchy', the need for virtuous ministers, the corruption and vices of the court and, above all, the virtues of the people.[8] Virtue stood for the Third Estate, for 'the people' and 'the nation', not for the nobles. As one pamphlet writer expressed it in literal terms: 'Eighteen million virtuous men suffer, and the two million who oppress them are not satisfied with that.'[9] The assumptions behind such language were familiar but, like keys fitting into place, the abstract models of vice and virtue had became specific. Virtuous ministers and corrupt nobles acquired names and faces. Thus when Duport, a founder of the Society of Thirty and prominent radical in the Paris *parlement*, led an attack on the financial mismanagement of Calonne, he justified this as a defence of 'the social virtues, public morals' against the 'men of corruption'.[10]

The abbé Sieyès is held by many historians to have been the commentator who was best able to understand the deeper significance of the political upheavals of late 1788. His famous pamphlet *What is the Third Estate?* (which appeared in early 1789) was seen as being radical in the extreme when it first appeared, and it took some time for the ideas expressed in it to gain wider acceptance. It was only through the failure of both the monarchy and the opposing factions in the Estates General to achieve a compromise that his argument that the Third Estate must itself act to constitute the nation came to be seen by a significant number of the deputies as the logical step out of the impasse. *What is the Third Estate?* was in many ways emblematic of the route that revolutionary ideology would follow in 1789. In it Sieyès set out what would become some of the fundamental principles underlying the Revolution. He depicted the political struggle that was beginning as one in which the aristocracy (who pursued only the empty goal of honour) were pitted against the people (who sought only virtue and the public interest). The people were already virtuous citizens (because they were productive and not parasites) and therefore they had the moral right to political representation. If this was denied them, then they were justified in seizing it for themselves. By contrast, the nobility were concerned only with their own self-interest, which they furthered under the guise of defending their honour. He took Montesquieu's distinction between virtue and honour and used it to distinguish between the virtuous bourgeoisie and the self-seeking nobility.

> While the aristocrats talk of their honour yet watch out for their self-interest, the Third Estate, that is to say, the nation, will develop its virtue, for if corporate interest is egotism, national interest is virtue.[11]

The key words in this text served a political purpose. They were not intended by Sieyès to be taken literally: they were a way of constructing and legitimising an argument, the aim of which was to give the bourgeoisie political representation.[12] Virtue had an explicitly political meaning: since the Third Estate was virtuous, what the Third Estate willed was by definition right. He had slipped skilfully from the word 'nobility' to the word 'aristocracy', a term which constituted everything that was opposed to virtue and the people. The 'people' were the nation, because the people were virtuous. In talking about the 'people' Sieyès meant, not the common people, but the propertied and educated part of the Third Estate, the bourgeoisie. In talking about the 'aristocracy', he meant, not the nobility as such, but those who were opposed to the people.

> There was once a time when the Third Estate was in bondage and the noble order was everything. Today the Third Estate is everything and the nobility is only a word. But concealed beneath this word and based only on the influence of false opinion, a new and intolerable aristocracy has illegally established itself; and the people has every reason not to want any aristocrats.[13]

It is generally accepted that Sieyès' pamphlet was sponsored by the Society of Thirty, the great majority of whom were from long-established noble families, of the robe and of the sword.[14] Sieyès himself (possibly at the instigation of Madame de Genlis) also assisted the duc d'Orléans in drawing up one of the most influential of the model *cahiers* which helped to establish the duke's political credentials as a man of virtue.[15] These were further examples of the egalitarian rhetoric of virtue being exploited by some of the most privileged individuals of the *ancien régime*. Sieyès was not advocating a wholesale denunciation of the principle of nobility. Rather, his anti-noble rhetoric was inspired by specific political circumstances – the decision to constitute the Estates General as in 1614 and the failure of Necker to intervene to establish a workable alternative. But his discursive strategy escaped from his control and had unforeseen consequences. Sieyès, somewhat isolated on the extreme left at the opening of the Estates General, soon found himself outflanked and surpassed by the rapid process of political radicalisation which resulted from the failure to establish a viable compromise. He was opposed to the revolutionary attacks on the position of the Catholic Church and he withdrew altogether from active politics during the period of the ascendancy of Jacobinism. The implications of his discourse, which set the 'virtuous people' against the 'corrupt and self-seeking aristocracy', were to take on a tangible and blood-soaked significance in 1793 which appalled him.

This radical language current in the 1780s did not itself bring about the end of the *ancien régime*. For that we have to look to the financial and administrative crisis and the inability of successive ministers to reform the *ancien régime* although it was acknowledged that reform was needed. The reasons for this were manifold. The vacillations of the last two kings, ministerial ineptitude, the resistance of the first two Orders to financial reform, and the factional politics and intrigues that contributed to the intransigence of the Paris *parlement* and the Assembly of Notables, all played a contributory part. But once that final crisis had been made public, the speed with which revolutionary political ideas came to the fore in pamphlets and public writings, above all in the period between September 1788 and May 1789, shows how much of the rhetorical basis for revolutionary politics was already in place. Virtue, citizenship, nation and patriotism provided a strategic vocabulary with which to articulate political dissent. Even so, the Revolution was not inevitable. Few deputies to the Estates General actively sought an end to the *ancien régime*. Responsibility for the crisis becoming a revolution must rest in part with the lack of leadership from the monarchy, the continued intransigence of a large part of the First and Second Estates, and their opposition to even limited reform, which made compromise impossible. The resultant undermining of political compromise left virtue, as the logical consequence, as the 'purest revolutionary discourse'.

Virtue was enshrined in the Declaration of Rights of Man and the Citizen (26 August 1789), the self-conscious and defiant statement of revolution. Article 6 of that document stated that there should be no distinction between men except that of 'their virtues and talents'. After an intense and heated debate this had replaced the earlier phrase, that distinctions could be permitted amongst men 'according to their capacity'. This phrase, which had anti-egalitarian aristocratic overtones, had been proposed by Mounier, a barrister in the *parlementaire* constitutionalism tradition. His proposal had been greeted in the Assembly with 'cries against the aristocracy'.[16] The Declaration set the tone of revolutionary language: virtue would be essential to the revolutionary concept of citizenship. It would not be enough to say of someone that he was simply 'a citizen': he needed to be a 'virtuous citizen'. It was a point made continually by revolutionary journalists from the early years of the Revolution as they used the phrases 'good' and 'bad' citizen to distinguish between those whose policies they approved and those they suspected of corruption.[17]

The republic of virtue

But it was in the first, most radical period of the republic, from September 1792 to July 1794, that the rhetoric of virtue reached its apotheosis through the formulation of a 'republic of virtue'. Furet was surely right here to emphasise the terrible power of a language of moral politics, its capacity to bring power to those who defined themselves as 'moral' and to destroy those deemed the enemies of virtue. There has long been a recognition of the power of rhetoric in revolutionary politics; as Michelet put it, 'there were words that saved and words that killed'. But, inspired in part by Furet's reassessment of the centrality of language to the process of achieving and maintaining political power, questions of revolutionary language and rhetoric have been taken up with renewed vigour and attention in recent years.[18] Together with this there has been a new interest in the writers of rhetoric and in revolutionary journalism and political culture which has transformed our understanding of how 'public opinion' was forged and manipulated during this period.[19]

Furet's challenge to the traditional way of seeing revolutionary politics in terms of economic class has brought invaluable new insights into the nature of language – and the present study is much indebted to this new emphasis. But Furet's close focus on discourses of power even to the exclusion of the political context and the individuals who participated in politics, has led to revolutionary virtue being interpreted in a very particular light which tends to obscure two important points which the present study has sought to redress. The first point is that of continuities in political rhetoric. The language of 'moral politics' – the language of political virtue – was well-established long before 1789, as the present study has demonstrated. It was not in itself a 'new dynamic' as Furet claimed. The revolutionary politics of virtue must be understood in terms of eighteenth-century ideas and not solely in terms of the birth of a modern conception of politics.

Secondly, there is the problem of intentionality. Whilst language played its part in shaping ideas, it was by no means the final determinant. The emphasis on discourse itself, on rhetoric as a 'motor' that determines history, rather than on rhetoric as a strategic choice by individuals, tends to obliterate the importance of other contributory factors. It was not the rhetoric of virtue that determined people's choices in becoming adherents or opponents of the Revolution, but rather more tangible factors, such as family and friendship networks and loyalties, corporate ties, and individual choices and personalities, maybe even moral choices. It is difficult to predict which way someone would turn when the Revolution itself took place by looking at people's language during the *ancien régime* alone. It is not discourses but people who commit violent acts. Of the enthusiasts for virtue featured in this book who lived into the revolutionary era, only a minority supported the Revolution of 1789, far fewer the republic of 1792. Very few were supporters of the Terror, and a significant proportion perished from it. For every Mathon de la Cour or Fauchet who actively participated in the Revolution (and in their cases met their deaths as a result), there was a Maury who actively opposed the Revolution, or an Henrion de Pansey who lay low, and re-emerged later into a political world and a social hierarchy that seemed remarkably similar in some ways to what it had been before the Revolution.

To take Furet's approach to its logical consequence would mean to risk falling into the assumption of dismissing the rhetoric of virtue as an 'inherently totalitarian' discourse, that is, one that led inevitably to the Terror. Furet himself was much too subtle to attempt to give so twentieth-century a label to Jacobin politics.[20] But other historians have been less careful. The only full-length study of the politics of virtue during the Revolution, Blum's *Rousseau and the Republic of Virtue: the Language of Politics in the French Revolution*, tends to take that approach. She prefers to focus on a narrow range of Jacobins who were leading terrorists, most particularly Robespierre and Saint-Just. This is a valid approach, but it leaves out so much that is important to the wider culture of the revolutionary politics of virtue. For example, Blum is very dismissive of Claude Fauchet, who did so much to spread the vocabulary of Revolution through key terms such as 'fraternity'. For Fauchet, virtue meant universal love. Blum states only that he rejected Rousseau's concept of virtue as too difficult to achieve, for Fauchet held to the view that men were naturally loving, sociable, and wished to do good to one another. The abbé Grégoire is also dismissed as 'seeming not to understand what Rousseau had said about virtue'. But this is exactly the point. The revolutionary concept of virtue was much wider than that of Rousseau.[21] By defining virtue as she does, and by concentrating on Rousseau as interpreted by Robespierre and Saint-Just, particularly during the period of the Committee of Public Safety, and arguing that their understanding of Rousseau's concept of virtue was peculiar to themselves, Blum uses selective ammunition to confirm her thesis that there was an essential link between virtue and terror.[22] Certainly Robespierre repeatedly claimed to be the true spokesman of virtue (something that tells us a lot about Robespierre and about revolutionary politics), but this does not mean that historians have to agree with him or assume that he had a monopoly on the discourse. That would be to succumb to the power of the rhetoric rather than to analyse it impartially. Indeed, it is very debatable whether Robespierre's and Saint-Just's concepts of virtue were the same as Rousseau's or even whether, in the context of 1793 and 1794, Rousseau's idea of virtue was very relevant or helpful to their political situation, but that is another story and beyond the confines of the present work.[23]

Virtue in the republican period needs to be studied not just in terms of a personal link between Rousseau and Robespierre but as part of a wider political culture. The influence of civic virtue through the tradition of classical republicanism (a theme not much covered since H. T. Parker's still very relevant study) would merit closer attention. The revolutionary obsession with natural virtue also needs reevaluation. Many of the plans and projects of the revolutionaries, from the open-air festivals to the comités of *bienfaisance*, owed much to ideas current in the 1780s regarding the natural impulse to virtue, and the innate virtue of the common people. Events that seemed innocuous and somewhat anodyne in the 1770s and 1780s, such as the annals of virtuous deeds in the popular press, prizes for virtuous peasant girls and virtuous peasant couples, reports in the *affiches* of deeds of *bienfaisance*, were destined to take on a different meaning in the context of the Revolution. The problem of innate virtue and the question of how to fashion good citizens was at the heart of the intense debates waged over education and the need to instil virtue. Bourgeois revolutionary thinking here was based on a paradox at the heart of the idea of 'natural' virtue. For if the common people were naturally virtuous, why did they not always act virtuously?

And why should they need education to make them good revolution-aries? As Mona Ozouf has shown, men who took part in the debates on revolutionary education took up the idea of 'regeneration' and sought to find a way out of the paradox by arguing that the natural virtue of the people had been corrupted by hundreds of years of oppression by kings.[24] It was far from being an easy dilemma for them to solve.

Along with key words such as *patrie*, 'citizen', 'nation' and *bienfaisance*, virtue was a familiar term, part of the way in which people conceptualised society, progress, responsibilities and rights. It was at the heart of the revolutionary conception of the Republic. Such words were fought over. The questions of who were the 'people' and who was a 'citizen', were essential to establishing one's political credentials. Increasingly these categories were defined not in economic terms (e.g. the 'active citizen' as a property owner, the 'people' as the common workers) but in moral terms. Set against these terms, the word 'aristocracy' was less a specific definition of nobility than a broader one of political allegiance, by means of which 'aristocrats' were defined as those who supported the system of hierarchy and privilege and opposed the 'republic of virtue'. The rhetoric of virtue was necessary to give moral authority to the Jacobin government and to establish its credentials to rule.[25] It was the more necessary since its hold on power was otherwise of dubious legality and legitimacy, lacking the centuries of tradition that kept the Bourbons on the throne, and with the support of only part of the Convention (and that only out of desperation) and the vital support of the *sans-culottes*, and incurring open hostility from many sections of society and much of the provinces. There were obvious reasons why the Jacobins appealed to the rhetoric of political virtue to legitimise themselves, despite the problems and difficulties of adopting a language never meant to describe concrete politics but only political ideals, a fact of which the Jacobins, through their classical education, were all too well aware. It was an impossible rhetoric for them, but it was a natural step to take.

The one major transformation in linguistic meaning for the concept of virtue which took place during the revolutionary period was the forging of a link between terror and virtue in the Jacobin rhetoric of 1793. This development followed on from, rather than led, events. But it was a traumatic shift. The perspective of the Jacobin leaders became intensely polarised in the uncertain and tense atmosphere of a political situation where no one was sure of loyalties and affiliations. The language of virtue had always carried the potential to divide political participants in terms of the righteous and the unrighteous, patriots and conspirators, the virtuous against the morally corrupt. From late 1793 this tendency came to the forefront and influenced political conduct at the high point of the Jacobin Terror in a way inconceivable in more stable circumstances.

One consequence of the Terror was the subsequent discrediting of the rhetoric of political virtue. Never again would its premises be accepted as a way of structuring politics. Across the Channel in England, commentators watched horrified at the playing out of the Terror. Burke led the thunderous attack on the principles of 'universal benevolence' and his chief target was Rousseau, although these principles had originally stemmed from his countrymen.[26] Indeed, a surprising amount of the rhetoric of virtue had originated from English sources, including Bolingbroke, Shaftesbury and Hutcheson. In England, where there were other ways of articulating political dissent, together with a regime that was perceived as being less autocratic and absolute, political virtue did not become the language of revolution. But in France where there was neither legitimate political opposition nor a language with which to articulate such an opposition, then the rise of political virtue was much more explosive and potentially dangerous – given the right set of circumstances. At once vague, absolute and all-encompassing, the language of virtue had the potential to be deadly. It did not have to be a language of terror, but in the context of the political trauma of 1792 to 1794, that is what happened.

Index

differs from Jansenism 124;
emergence 51–2; formation of
arguments 78–9; influence on
Revolution 204; and religious
ideals 179, 180; Rousseau's place
in 84–5
*An Enquiry into the Origin of Our Ideas of
Beauty and Virtue* (Hutcheson) 76
*Entretien de Phocion sur le rapport de la
morale avec la politique* (Mably) 94,
98–9
Entretien sur les romans (Jacquin) 74
Entretiens sur Le Fils naturel
(Diderot) 117–19
Eprémesnil, D' 178
equality: in possession of virtue
18–19; Rousseau's *Contrat social* 90;
Rousseau's *Emile* 91
Ernaud: *Discours de la noblesse et des
justes moyens d'y parvenir* 33
Esprit, J. 47, 123
Essai d'éducation nationale (La
Chalotais) 123
Essai sur le bonheur (Beausobre) 124–5
Essai sur les règnes de Claude et de Néron
(Diderot) 127
*An Essay Concerning Human
Understanding* (Locke) 53–4
Estates General 160, 202; fail to
compromise 206; Louis XII 141;
nobles' grievances 178; opening
of 208; panegyrics of St Louis 145
Etrennes de la vertu 185, 198
Everdell, William 189

Fable of the Bees (Mandeville) 72,
125–6
Faret, N.: *L'Honnête homme* 34
Fauchet, abbé Claude 137, 148, 180,
210; angers religious superiors 182;
criticism of court life 177–8;
dedication to Revolution 183;
enlisted by duc d'Orléans 197–8;
fraternity 204–5; fraternity and
universal love 210–11; on virtuous
peasantry 191–2
Fénelon, François de Salignac de la
Mothe 25; chosen by the *Académie*
as hero 114, 116; fall from

favour 30; *Télémaque* 29–31, 90;
utopia 45; virtuous
monarchy 131; voice echoed in
young Louis XVI 136–7, 148
Le Fils naturel (Diderot) 117–19
Fleury, Cardinal de: bans Duguet's
book 50
fortune 41
Foucault, Michel: discourse and
power 10, 11
Franklin, Benjamin 190
fraternity: meaning to Fauchet
210–11; natural virtue 204–5
French Revolution: abbé Sieyès's
principles 206–8; clergy make
choices 182–3; Cold War
historiography 5; discourse of
virtue at outbreak 204–9;
establishes a republic of
virtue 209–13; modern politics
5–7; not anticipated 171–2;
Rousseau's influence 82–3
Furet, François 5; centrality of
language to politics 209–11;
language 203

gender: feminine virtue 3–4;
masculine virtue 26–7, 40–1
Genlis, Madame de 195, 207; festival
of rural virtue 189
Gin, P. L. C.: *Les Vrais principes du
gouvernement françois* 194
government: Montesquieu's forms
of 62
Gracchi brothers 39
Greece: *arete* 24; barbarity 67;
classical influence on French 37;
oppression of neighbours 191;
virtue and politics 2
Greuze, Jean-Baptiste 187
Grotius, Hugo 53

Habermas, Jürgen 3; public
sphere 11
happiness: goal of *bienfaisant* king for
people 132; not necessarily
connected to virtue 126–7;
political goal 205–6; as a social
right 175

Notes

Introduction

1. Some of the most important works in recent years to have examined pre-revolutionary political culture and its relationship to revolutionary politics include: K. M. Baker (ed.), *The French Revolution and the Creation of Modern Culture*, vol. 1: *The Political Culture of the Old Regime* (Oxford, 1987); K. M. Baker, *Inventing the French Revolution* (Cambridge, 1990); R. Chartier, *The Cultural Origins of the French Revolution* (Durham and London, 1991). There are also many older but classic studies whose influence is still greatly felt, including: D. Mornet, *Les Origines intellectuelles de la Révolution française: 1715–1787* (1933; republished, Paris, 1954); R. Mauzi, *L'Idée du bonheur dans la littérature et la pensée française au XVIIIe siècle* (Paris, 1960); H. T. Parker, *The Cult of Antiquity and the French Revolutionaries* (1937; republished New York, 1965); J. Ehrard, *L'Idée de nature en France à l'aube des lumières* (Paris, 1970); E. Carcassonne, *Montesquieu et le problème de la constitution française au XVIIIe siècle* (1927; republished Geneva, 1970); and R. R. Palmer, *Catholics and Unbelievers in Eighteenth-Century France* (New York, 1961).
2. Amongst the many studies on this subject one should include: R. Darnton, *The Literary Underground of the Old Regime* (Cambridge, Mass., 1982); J. R. Censer and J. D. Popkin (eds), *Press and Politics in Pre-Revolutionary France* (Berkeley, Cal., 1987); N. R. Gelbart, *Feminine and Opposition Journalism in Old Regime France*, (Berkeley, Cal., 1987). On the cultural politics of fine art production, see T. E. Crow, *Painters and Public Life in Eighteenth-Century Paris* (New Haven, Conn., 1985).
3. J. Habermas, *The Structural Transformation of the Public Sphere*, trans. T. Burger and F. Lawrence (Cambridge, Mass., 1989).
4. Works which have analysed the relationship between gender and virtue include: D. Outram, *The Body and the French Revolution* (New Haven, Conn., 1989); C. Blum, *Rousseau and the Republic of Virtue* (New York, 1986); J. B. Landes, *Women and the Public Sphere in the Age of the French Revolution* (New York, 1988); D. Outram, 'Le langage mâle de la vertu: Women and the Discourse of the French Revolution', in P. Burke and R. Porter (eds), *The Social History of Language* (Cambridge, 1987).
5. My research on the relationship of women to the politics of virtue is forthcoming in Marisa Linton, 'Virtue Rewarded? Women and the Politics of Virtue in Eighteenth-Century France', parts I and II, *History of European Ideas*, 26, 1 (2001), pp. 35–49; 51–65.
6. On the political impact of the Kornmann case see R. Darnton, 'Trends in Radical Propaganda on the Eve of the French Revolution, 1782–1788' (DPhil, Oxford, 1964). Two recent major studies of legal cases and of lawyers respectively are: S. Maza, *Private Lives and Public Affairs: the Causes Célèbres of Pre-revolutionary France* (Berkeley, Cal., 1993); and D. A. Bell, *Lawyers and Citizens: The Making of a Political Elite in Old Regime France* (Oxford, 1994).

7. Works on Britain and America which have studied political virtue in the context of classical republicanism include: J. G. A. Pocock, *The Machiavellian Moment: Florentine Political Thought and the Atlantic Republican Tradition* (Princeton, N.J., 1975); J. G. A. Pocock, *Virtue, Commerce and History* (Cambridge, 1985); S. Burtt, *Virtue Transformed: Political Argument in England, 1688–1740* (Cambridge, 1992); M. M. Goldsmith, 'Public Virtues and Private Vices: Bernard Mandeville and English Political Ideologies in the Early Eighteenth Century', *Eighteenth-Century Studies*, 9, 4 (1976), pp. 477–510; G. Bock, Q. Skinner and M. Viroli (eds), *Machiavelli and Republicanism* (Cambridge, 1990); I. Hont and M. Ignatieff (eds), *Wealth and Virtue: the Shaping of Political Economy in the Scottish Enlightenment* (Cambridge, 1983). On politics and political theory in early eighteenth-century Britain there is also I. Kramnick, *Bolingbroke and his Circle: the Politics of Nostalgia in the Age of Walpole* (Cambridge, Mass., 1968).
8. For example, this is the approach of Blum, *Rousseau and the Republic of Virtue*.
9. See, above all, the speech Robespierre gave in February 1794, 'On the principles of public morality', which may be consulted in several places, including the edition of his speeches edited by M. Bouloiseau, *Discours et rapports à la Convention par Robespierre* (Paris), e.g. p. 216.
10. J. L. Talmon, *The Origins of Totalitarian Democracy* (London, 1952).
11. See Alfred Cobban's comments in 'The Enlightenment and the French Revolution', in A. Cobban, *Aspects of the French Revolution* (first published 1968; this edition, St Albans, 1971), p. 24.
12. F. Furet, *Interpreting the French Revolution* (1978; this edition, trans. E. Forster, Cambridge, 1981), p. 26. Amongst the many works to owe a debt to Furet, some of the most prominent include: L. Hunt, *Politics, Culture and Class in the French Revolution* (Berkeley, Cal., 1984) on the revolutionaries' invention of a new language, see esp. p. 34; F. Furet and M. Ozouf (eds), *A Critical Dictionary of the French Revolution*, trans. Arthur Goldhammer (Cambridge, Mass., 1989); *The French Revolution and the Creation of Modern Culture*, 3 vols, eds K. M. Baker, C. Lucas and F. Furet, respectively (Oxford, 1987–9); K. M. Baker, *Inventing the French Revolution* (Cambridge, 1990); C. Lucas et al. (eds), *Rewriting the French Revolution* (Oxford, 1991).
13. A. Cobban, 'The Fundamental Ideas of Robespierre', in *Aspects of the French Revolution*, pp. 138–41.
14. On the derivation of Robespierre's concept of virtue and its place in his political ideas, see M. Linton, 'Robespierre's Political Principles', in C. Haydon and W. Doyle (eds), *Robespierre* (Cambridge, 1999), pp. 37–53.
15. Robespierre, *Discours*, p. 214. On the extent to which Robespierre's concept of political virtue derived from Montesquieu rather than from Rousseau, see Cobban, *Aspects of the French Revolution*, pp. 137–58, esp. pp. 141 and 152. For a comparison with Montesquieu's concept of virtue as the principle of the republic see his *Oeuvres complètes*, ed. Roger Caillois, 2 vols (Paris, 1949–51), vol. II, book III, p. 251.
16. See, above all, K. Baker, 'French Political Thought at the Accession of Louis XVI', together with the other articles in *Inventing the French Revolution*.
17. Of the many works of Foucault one of the most pertinent in this context is M. Foucault, *The Archaeology of Knowledge* (New York, 1972). For Pocock, see his 'Introduction: the State of the Art', in *Virtue, Commerce and History*, pp. 7–34.

18. This was the conclusion Quentin Skinner reached when confronted with a similar difficulty in assessing the sincerity of Viscount Bolingbroke's espousal of the rhetoric of patriotism and virtue when he opposed the ruling Whigs in the 1720s: Q. Skinner, 'The Principles and Practice of Opposition: the Case of Bolingbroke versus Walpole', in *Historical Perspectives: Studies in English Thought and Society in Honour of J. H. Plumb*, ed. N. McKendrick (London, 1974).

19. J. Habermas, *The Structural Transformation of the Public Sphere*, p. 89. Habermas's approach has generated much further discussion, including D. Goodman, 'Public Sphere and Private Life: toward a Synthesis of Current Historiographical Approaches to the Old Regime', *History and Theory*, 31 (1992), pp. 1–20; and K. M. Baker, 'Politics and Public Opinion under the Old Regime: Some Reflections', in Censer and Popkin (eds), *Press and Politics in Pre-Revolutionary France*, pp. 204–46.

20. On 'public opinion' as an eighteenth-century term, see Baker, 'Public Opinion as Political Invention', in *Inventing the French Revolution*; and M. Ozouf, 'L'Opinion publique', in Baker (ed.), *The Political Culture of the Old Regime*.

21. Amongst the best studies of eighteenth-century politics is P. R. Campbell, *Power and Politics in Old Régime France, 1720–1745* (London, 1996). For insights into the politics of patronage and faction in the seventeenth century, one should consult S. Kettering, *Patrons, Brokers and Clients in Seventeenth-Century France* (New York, 1986); and R. Mettam, *Power and Faction in Louis XIV's France* (Oxford, 1988).

22. This definition is from the 'Avertissement' to the 1757 edition of Montesquieu's *L'Esprit des lois*: Montesquieu, *Oeuvres complètes*, ed. R. Caillois (Paris, 1949–51), vol. II, pp. 227–8.

23. Baker, 'On the Problem of the Ideological Origins of the French Revolution', in Baker, *Inventing the French Revolution*, p. 24.

Chapter 1   Concepts of Virtue before 1745

1. In the article on 'virtue' in A. Furetière, *Dictionnaire Universel* (The Hague and Rotterdam, 1690); see also the articles on 'virtue' in the *Dictionnaire Universel, François et Latin, 'Le tout tiré des plus excellens Auteurs, des meilleurs Lexicographes, Etymologistes, et Glossaire'* (Paris, 1704); and in A. Furetière, *Dictionnaire Universel, 'Revû, corrigé, et considérablement augmenté par M. Brutel de la Rivière'*, 4 vols (The Hague, 1727).

2. Furetière, *Dictionnaire Universel* (1690); also P. Richelet, *Dictionnaire françois contenant les mots et les choses, plusieurs nouvelles remarqués sur la langue françoise*...(Geneva, 1680).

3. *Dictionnaire Universel, François et Latin.*

4. Richelet, *Dictionnaire françois.*

5. For example, Richelet, *Dictionnaire françois*; and the *Dictionnaire Universel, François et Latin.*

6. *Dictionnaire Universel, François et Latin*; and repeated in Furetière, *Dictionnaire Universel* (1727).

7. Richelet, *Dictionnaire françois*; Furetière, *Dictionnaire Universel* (1690).

8. *Dictionnaire Universel, François et Latin.*

9. See J. G. A. Pocock, *The Machiavellian Moment: Florentine Political Thought and the Atlantic Republican Tradition* (Princeton, N.J., 1975), p. 37; and J. G. A. Pocock, *Virtue, Commerce and History* (Cambridge, 1985), pp. 41–2.

10. In practice, of course, the authority of the kings of France had distinct limits: see P. R. Campbell, *Louis XIV* (London, 1993).

11. J.B. Bossuet, 'Pensées Chrétiennes et morales', in *Oeuvres oratoires de Bossuet*, ed. J. Lebarq, 7 vols (Paris, 1890), vol. VI, pp. 520–1.

12. See, for example, Bossuet, 'Sermon sur l'Honneur' (1666), *Oeuvres oratoires*, vol. V, pp. 55–7.

13. See, for example, Bossuet, 'Sermon sur les devoirs des rois' (1662), in *Oeuvres oratoires*, vol. IV, p. 273. G. Budé used the kingly virtue of justice (inspired in part by Plutarch's examples of virtuous leaders) to underpin his justification of absolute monarchy in his work dedicated to François I: *De l'Institution du Prince* (1547; this edition, Farnborough, 1966), pp. 20–1.

14. J.B. Bossuet, *Politique tirée des propres paroles de l'Ecriture sainte* (1709; this edition, Geneva, 1967), book III, article I, pp. 64; 70–1.

15. Bossuet, 'Sermon sur les devoirs des rois' (1662), *Oeuvres oratoires*, vol. IV, pp. 272–3; 'Pensées Chrétiennes et morales', ibid., vol. VI, p. 532.

16. Jean-Baptiste Massillon, *Sermon pour le quatrième dimanche de Carême. Sur l'Aumône* (1709).

17. See P. Burke, *The Fabrication of Louis XIV* (New Haven, Conn., 1992), pp. 23, 122.

18. J.B. Bossuet, *Lettres sur l'éducation du Dauphin* (Paris, 1920), pp. 39–57.

19. 'Oraison funèbre de Monseigneur Louis Dauphin', in J.B. Massillon, *Sermons sur les Evangiles du carême*, 6 vols (Trevoux, 1723), vol. VI, pp. 130–76.

20. 'Oraison funèbre de Monseigneur le Dauphin et de Madame la Dauphine', ibid., pp. 206–11.

21. For an account of Fénelon as a politically contentious model in the *Académie Française* in the early 1770s, see M. Linton, 'The Concept of Virtue in Eighteenth-Century France, 1745–1788' (DPhil, University of Sussex, 1993), chapter 5.

22. Fénelon, *Télémaque* (1699; this edition, Paris, 1966), pp. 276–322.

23. Ibid., pp. 392–7.

24. Much of this material came from courtiers unfriendly to the regent, notably Saint-Simon. See C. Duclos, *Secret Memoirs of the Regency*, trans. E. Jules Meras (London, 1912), pp. 8, 39.

25. Jean-Baptiste Massillon, 'Sermon pour le dimanche des Rameaux', *Petit Carême*, cited by E. Carcassonne, *Montesquieu et le problème de la constitution, française an XVIIIᵉ siècle* (1927; republished, Geneva, 1970), pp. 4–5.

26. G. Huppert, *Les Bourgeois gentilhommes* (Chicago, 1977); A. Jouanna, *Ordre social: mythes et hiérarchies dans la France du XVIᵉ siècle* (Paris, 1977); A. Jouanna, *L'Idée de race en France au XVIᵉ siècle et au début du XVIIᵉ siècle, 1498–1614*, 3 vols (Lille, 1976); E. Schalk, *From Valor to Pedigree: Ideas of Nobility in France in the Sixteenth and Seventeenth Centuries* (Princeton, N. J., 1986).

27. Schalk, *From Valor to Pedigree*, pp. 145–73.

28. N. Faret, *L'Honnête homme, ou l'art de plaire à la cour* (1630; this edition, Geneva, 1970), pp. 22–4.

29. Molière, *The Misanthrope and Other Plays*, ed. and trans. John Wood (Harmondsworth, 1959), Act 1, Scene 1, pp. 28–9.

30. La Rochefoucauld, *Maximes, suivies des Réflexions diverses* (1678; this edition, Paris, 1967), No. 187, p. 48.
31. La Bruyère, *Characters*, trans. Jean Stewart (London, 1970), pp. 129, 156.
32. See H. A. Ellis, 'Genealogy, History and Aristocratic Reaction in Early Modern France: the Case of Henri de Boulainvilliers', *Journal of Modern History*, 58, 2 (1986), pp. 414–51.
33. Carcassonne, *Montesquieu et le problème de la constitution*, p. 25.
34. In addition to the works cited in the 'Introduction', see F. Venturi, *Utopia and Reform in the Enlightenment* (Cambridge, 1971).
35. H. T. Parker, *The Cult of Antiquity and the French Revolutionaries* (1937; republished, New York, 1965), pp. 11–21.
36. F. Lebrun, M. Venard and J. Quéniart, *Histoire générale de l'enseignement et de l'éducation en France*, vol. 2: *De Guitenberg aux Lumières* (Paris, 1981), pp. 512–19.
37. On the influence of classical authors on rhetorical training, see P. France, *Rhetoric and Truth in France: Descartes to Diderot* (Oxford, 1972), pp. 3–33; also J. Starobinski, 'Eloquence antique, éloquence future: aspects d'un lieu commun d'ancien régime', in K. M. Baker (ed.), *Political Culture of the Old Regime* (Oxford, 1987), pp. 311–29.
38. See Bossuet, *Lettres sur l'éducation du Dauphin*, pp. 39–57.
39. See Parker, *The Cult of Antiquity*, esp. pp. 21–4.
40. For example, Tacitus, *Histories* (London, 1956), vol. I, ii, LXIX, p. 271; vol. I, iii, LI, p. 413; *Annales*, vol. II, i, IV, p. 249; vol. II, i, LXV, p. 625; Livy, *Histories* (London, 1961), vol. I, book i, Preface, pp. 5 and 7; Sallust, *The Conspiracy of Catiline* (London, 1963), pp. 178–83.
41. Plutarch, *Lives: The Dryden Plutarch*, 3 vols (London, 1910), vol. I, pp. 84, 86 and 88.
42. Cicero, *On Moral Obligation* (*De Officiis*), trans. Walter Miller (London, 1913), pp. 99, 101, 163.
43. Cicero, *Philippics* (London, 1957). See, for example, Plutarch's account of the virtues of Cato the Elder: Plutarch, *Lives*, vol. I, pp. 516–41; also Cicero's denunciation of Mark Antony in the 'Second Philippic': Cicero, *Philippics* (1957).
44. See, for example, Sallust, *The Conspiracy of Catiline*, pp. 181–2.
45. Plutarch, *Lives*, vol. I, p. 543; also, pp. 226–8.
46. Sallust, *The Conspiracy of Catiline*, p. 120.
47. Cicero, 'Pro Balbo', in *Cicero: The Speeches* (London, 1958), p. 697.
48. Plutarch, *Lives*, vol. I, pp. 327–8 and 339.
49. This tension between civic and Christian virtue is explored in Pocock, *The Machiavellian Moment*, part 1.
50. Montaigne, 'De la Vanité', *Oeuvres complètes* (Paris, 1965), book III, chap. IX, p. 970. For a further discussion, see I. D. McFarlane, 'The Concept of Virtue in Montaigne', in I. D. Mcfarlane and I. Maclean (eds), *Montaigne* (Oxford, 1982), pp. 77–100; and R. A. Sayce, *The Essays of Montaigne: A Critical Exploration* (London, 1972), pp. 142–8 and 162–7.
51. P. Hazard, *La Crise de la conscience européenne, 1680–1715* (Paris, 1961), pp. 266–73.
52. Q. Skinner, 'The Principles and Practice of Opposition: the case of Bolingbroke versus Walpole', in *Historical Perspectives: Studies in English Thought and Society in Honour of J. H. Plumb*, ed. N. Mckendrick (London, 1974).

53. For an account of Bolingbroke's influence on Montesquieu, see R. Shackleton, *Montesquieu: a Critical Biography* (Oxford, 1961), pp. 126–30, 152, 297–
301. On Bolingbroke's relations with the *Club de l'Entresol*, see I. Kramnick,
Bolingbroke and his Circle: the Politics of Nostalgia in the Age of Walpole (Cambridge, Mass., 1968), pp. 13–17.

54. See Pocock, *Virtue, Commerce and History*, pp. 32–4 and 48–50; and A. Hirschman, *The Passions and the Interests: Political Arguments for Capitalism Before its
Triumph* (Princeton, N.J., 1977), esp. pp. 16–19.

55. See, for example, the introduction to J. Dwyer, *Virtuous Discourse: Sensibility
and Community in Late Eighteenth-Century Scotland* (Edinburgh, 1987).

56. On Montesquieu's intellectual debt to the practices and concerns of the
Bordeaux *parlement*, see R. Kingston, *Montesquieu and the Parlement of Bordeaux* (Geneva, 1996), chap. 2.

57. 'From Montesquieu to the Revolution', in Venturi, *Utopia and Reform in the
Enlightenment*.

58. Montesquieu, 'Voyages', *Oeuvres complètes*, ed. R. Caillois (Paris, 1949–51),
vol. I, pp. 553–4, 547–8, 559; on the Dutch republic, see pp. 863–4, 872.

59. Montesquieu, *Oeuvres complètes*, vol. I, p. 47.

60. Ibid., vol. I, p. 132.

61. Ibid., vol. I, p. 174.

62. Ibid., vol. I, pp. 145–53. Montesquieu later wrote a more 'Mandevillian'
version of this story, which he suppressed, but which suggested that private
vices had their place in society: see M. Richter, *The Political Theory of Montesquieu* (Cambridge, 1977), pp. 41–3.

63. Carcassonne unearthed a vast amount of material on *parlementaire* disputes,
but took the constitutional language at its face value, and neglected the
impact of Jansenism. See *Montesquieu et le problème de la constitution*, pp. 25–
63. For recent analyses of the early eighteenth century, see C. Maire, 'L'Eglise
et la nation: du dépôt de la vérité au dépôt des lois, la trajectoire janséniste au
XVIIIe siècle', *Annales: Economies, Sociétés, Civilisations*, 5 (1991), pp. 1177–
205; and P. R. Campbell, 'Aux Origines d'une forme de lutte politique:
avocats, magistrats et évêques. Les crises parlementaires et les jansénistes',
Jansénisme et Révolution (Paris, 1990).

64. D'Aguesseau, *Oeuvres* (Paris, 1759), vol. I, pp. 207–8.

65. Carcassonne, *Montesquieu et le problème de la constitution*, pp. 50–2.

66. J. Esprit, *La Fausseté des vertus humaines* (originally 1677–8; this edition, Paris,
1693); P. Nicole, *Essais de Morale, contenus en divers Traités sur plusieurs Devoirs
importants*, 14 vols (originally 1715; this edition, Paris, 1781). This may well
have influenced Rousseau's conception of 'amour-propre' in the *Discours sur
l'inégalité*.

67. B. Pascal, *Pensées* (Paris, 1964), No. 485, p. 197.

68. Esprit, *La Fausseté des vertus humaines*, 'Conclusion', esp. pp. 488–90; Nicole,
Essais de Morale, vol. I, pp, 58, 65, 369; vol. III, pp. 79–80.

69. Pascal, *Pensées*, Nos 515, 534, 537, 541, 546, pp. 203, 205–7.

70. Nicole, *Essais de Morale*, vol. IV, pp. 154–66.

71. J. Dedieu, 'L'Agonie du Jansénisme (1715–1790)', *Revue d'histoire de l'Eglise de
France*, 14 (1928), pp. 162–214.

72. On the relationship of the rhetoric of patriotism with Jansenism in the 1750s
and 1760s, see D. Van Kley, *The Religious Origins of the French Revolution: from*

Calvinism to the Civil Constitution, 1560–1791 (New Haven, Conn., 1996), pp. 210–18. One can also consult D. Van Kley, 'The Jansenist Constitutional Legacy in the French Prerevolution, 1750–1789', *Historical Reflections/Réflexions Historiques*, 13 (1986), pp. 393–454; and R. Tavenaux, 'Jansénisme et vie sociale en France au XVIIe siècle', *Revue d'histoire de l'Eglise de France*, 54 (1968).

73. J. J. Duguet, *Institution d'un Prince: ou Traité des Qualitéz, des Vertus et des Devoirs d'un Souverain* (London [Rouen?], 1739), pp. 9–11.

74. Ibid., esp. pp. 232–42, 249–59.

75. Ibid., p. 10.

76. Ibid., p. 233.

77. Ibid., pp. 233–4.

78. P. Riley, *The General Will before Rousseau: the Transformation of the Divine into the Civic* (Princeton, N.J., 1986).

79. Carcassonne, *Montesquieu et le problème de la constitution*, p. 38.

Chapter 2   Sociable Virtue and the Rise of Secular Morality, 1745–54

1. In 1787 Rulhière described 1749 as the year which had marked a 'révolution générale dans les lettres et dans les mœurs': 'Discours de Réception de M. de Rulhière, nommé à l'Académie française', in *Oeuvres posthumes de Rulhière, de l'Académie française* (Paris, 1819).

2. Voltaire, *Discours sur l'homme*, part IV, *Mélanges* (Paris, 1961), pp. 236–9.

3. On the extraordinary impact of these particular works, see D. Mornet, *Les Origines intellectuelles de la Révolution française: 1715–1787* (1933; republished, Paris, 1954), pp. 71–5.

4. See J. S. Spink, 'La Vertu politique selon Diderot, ou le paradoxe du bon citoyen', *Revue des Sciences humaines*, 112 (Oct.–Dec. 1963); R. Mauzi, 'Les Rapports du bonheur et de la vertu dans l'œuvre de Diderot', *Cahiers de l'Association internationale des Etudes françaises*, 13 (1961); J. A. Perkins, 'Diderot's Concept of Virtue', *Studies on Voltaire and the Eighteenth Century*, 23 (1963); C. Blum, *Diderot: the Virtue of a Philosopher* (New York, 1974); and A. W. Wilson, *Diderot* (Oxford, 1972), pp. 50–4.

5. Even amongst artisans there was often a remarkable degree of familiarity with the rhetoric of natural law and they frequently employed it in legal disputes, as has been effectively shown in M. Sonenscher, *Work and Wages: Natural Law, Politics and the Eighteenth-Century French Trades* (Cambridge, 1989).

6. On the complex relationship between 'happiness', 'sociability', 'sensibility' and 'virtue', see R. Mauzi, *L'Idée du bonheur dans la littérature et la pensée française au XVIIIe siècle* (Paris, 1960), esp. pp. 580–634; also P. Hazard, *La Crise de la conscience européenne, 1680–1715* (Paris, 1961), pp. 266–84. On the often ambiguous relationship between moral virtue, sensibility and the passions, see J. Ehrard, *L'Idée de nature en France à tambe des lumières* (Paris, 1970), pp. 218–23.

7. Shaftesbury, *An Inquiry Concerning Virtue or Merit* (1711; Manchester, 1977), p. 110.

8. Denis Diderot, *Principes de la philosophie morale; ou Essai de M. S.*** sur le mérite et la vertu. Avec réflexions*, in *Oeuvres complètes*, ed. J. Assézat and Maurice Tourneux (Paris, 1875–77), vol. I, p. 18.
9. See Spink, 'La Vertu politique selon Diderot', p. 473.
10. Diderot, *Principes de la philosophie morale*, pp. 35–6.
11. Ibid., p. 66.
12. Little work has been done on Shaftesbury's influence in France. A full-length study exists, D. B. Schlegel, *Shaftesbury and the French Deists* (North Carolina, 1956), which is useful in some respects, but its interpretations are unconvincing. On the influence of Shaftesbury's concept of the republic, see F. Venturi, *Utopia and Reform in the Enlightenment* (Cambridge, 1971), pp. 71–3.
13. See Schlegel, *Shaftesbury and the French Deists*, pp. 1–42.
14. Bolingbroke made use of Shaftesbury's ideas, but rejected the notion of an innate moral sense. See I. Kramnick, *Bolingbroke and his Circle: the Politics of Nostalgia in the Age of Walpole* (Cambridge, Mass., 1968), pp. 89–91.
15. There is a passing, not very enthusiastic, reference to Shaftesbury in Rousseau's 'Lettres morales', *Oeuvres complètes de Jean-Jacques Rousseau* (Paris, 1959–70), vol. IV, p. 1091. See also Schlegel, *Shaftesbury and the French Deists*, pp. 99–108.
16. On the reception of this work, see Wilson, *Diderot*, pp. 50–2.
17. Cited and translated in R. R. Palmer, *Catholics and Unbelievers in Eighteenth-Century France* (New York, 1961), p. 186.
18. For Diderot's influence on Toussaint, see Wilson, *Diderot*, pp. 53–4
19. See T. J. Barling, 'Toussaint's *Les Mœurs*', *French Studies*, 12 (1958), pp.14–20, who also examines the popularity of this work – and the attacks against it.
20. F. V. Toussaint, *Les Mœurs* (1748; new edition, Amsterdam, 1749), 'Avertissement', pp. ix–x.
21. Ibid., 'Discours préliminaire sur la vertu', pp. xiv–xv.
22. Ibid., pp. xv–xvi.
23. Ibid., p. xvii.
24. Ibid., pp. 171–3, 177–8, 181,183–4.
25. Ibid., pp. 215, 223–5.
26. *Les Mœurs Appréciés, ou Lettre Ecrite à un bel esprit du Marais à l'occasion de cet ouvrage* (Paris, 1748), cited by Barling, 'Toussaint's *Les Mœurs*', p. 15.
27. See E. J. F. Barbier, *Chronique de la Régence et du règne de Louis XV (1718–1763), ou Journal de Barbier, avocat au parlement de Paris*, 8 vols (Paris, 1857), vol. IV, pp. 300–8.
28. D. Mornet, 'Bibliographie d'un certain nombre d'ouvrages philosophiques du XVIIIᵉ siècle et particulièrement de d'Holbach (jusqu'en 1789)', *Revue d'Histoire Littéraire de la France*, 1933, pp. 278ff.
29. On Montesquieu's indebtedness to Shaftesbury, see R. Shackleton, *Montesquieu: a Critical Biography* (Oxford, 1961), pp. 37–8, 58–9, 133–4.
30. Montesquieu, *De l'Esprit des lois*, in vol. 2 of *Oeuvres complètes*, ed. R. Caillois (Paris, 1949–51), book III, pp. 250–61. The following references are all to this volume.
31. See, for example, ibid., book III, chap. 5, pp. 255–6; book IV, chap. 6, pp. 267–9; book V, chap. 2, p. 274.
32. Ibid., 'Avertissement de l'auteur', pp. 227–8.
33. See the note to the 'Avertissement', ibid., p. 1498.

34. Ibid., book III, chap. 5, p. 255, footnote *a*.
35. Ibid., book IV, chap. 5, p. 267.
36. Ibid., book IV, chap. 4, p. 266.
37. Ibid., book IV, chap. 2, pp. 262–5.
38. Ibid., book III, chap. 7, p. 257. On the influence of Mandeville, see M. Richter, *The Political Theory of Montesquieu* (Cambridge, 1977), pp. 43–4.
39. Montesquieu, *De l'Esprit des Lois*, book IV, chap. 2, p. 265, footnote *a*.
40. Ibid., book II, chap. 3, pp. 244–7; book III, chap. 4, p. 254.
41. Ibid., book III, chap. 5, pp. 255–6.
42. On the *parlements* as the 'dépot des lois', see ibid., book II, chap. 3; on the nobility see book VIII, chaps 6–9; on feudalism, books XXIX, XXX.
43. On Montesquieu's influence see E. Carcassonne, *Montesquieu et le problème de la constitution française* française au XVIIIe siècle (1927; republished, Geneva, 1970), esp. pp. 164–9.
44. Rousseau, *Du Contrat social*, book III, 8, in *Oeuvres complètes*, vol. III, pp. 414–19.
45. Vauvenargues, *Introduction à la connaissance de l'esprit humain* (1746), republished in *Oeuvres complètes de Vauvenargues* (Paris, 1968), vol. I, p. 242.
46. Vauvenargues, 'Critique de quelques maximes du Duc de la Rochefoucauld', in *Oeuvres complètes*, vol. I, p. 173.
47. C. Duclos, *Considérations sur les mœurs de ce siècle*, ed. F. C. Green (Cambridge, 1939), p. 51.
48. Ibid., p. 48.
49. Ibid., p. 53.
50. Ibid., p. 51.
51. Ibid., p. 56.
52. Because the English term 'beneficence' has such an archaic flavour, I have retained the French word, untranslated, throughout this book.
53. On the links between 'les vertus sociales' and Saint-Pierre's concept of 'bienfaisance', see F. Brunot, *Histoire de la langue française* (Paris, 1930), vol. VI, pp. 113–15. On the origins of the concept, see also Catherine Duprat, *Le Temps des philanthropes*, vol. I (Paris, 1993), 'Introduction', pp. xiii–xxxiv.
54. C. I. Castel de Saint-Pierre, *Oeuvres diverses de Monsieur l'Abbé de Saint-Pierre*, 2 vols (Paris, 1730), vol. I, *Un Projet pour perfectionner l'Education*, 'Avertissement'.
55. Duclos, *Considérations*, pp. 54–5.
56. See D. Mornet, *Les Origines intellectuelles de la Révolution française: 1715–1787* (1933; republished, Paris, 1954), pp. 258–66.
57. Denesles, *Les Préjugés du public, avec observations*, 2 vols (Paris, 1747), vol. II, pp. 41–2.
58. Studies of Mandeville's concept of virtue and its influence in Britain include S. Burtt, *Virtue Transformed: Political Argument in England, 1688–1740* (Cambridge, 1992), chap. 7; and M. M. Goldsmith, 'Public Virtues and Private Vices: Bernard Mandeville and English Political Ideologies in the Early Eighteenth Century', *Eighteenth-Century Studies*, 9, 4 (1976), pp. 477–510. On the influence of the debate on 'luxury' in France, see E. Ross, 'Mandeville, Melon, and Voltaire: the Origins of the Luxury Controversy in France', *Studies on Voltaire and the Eighteenth Century*, 161 (1976), pp. 1897–1912.
59. Vauvenargues, *Introduction à la connaissance de l'esprit humain*, pp. 244–5.

60. L. Hooke, *Religionis naturalis et moralis philosophiae principia, methodo scholastica digesta* (Paris, 1752–4), cited and translated by Palmer, *Catholics and Unbelievers*, pp. 40–41; see also, p. 51.
61. For the literature of sensibility before Rousseau one can consult P. Trahard, *Les Maîtres de la sensibilité française au XVIIIe siècle, 1715–1789* (Paris, 1931), vols I and II; G. Atkinson, *The Sentimental Revolution: French Writers of 1690–1740* (Washington, 1965); also A. Wilson, 'Sensibility in France in the Eighteenth-Century: a Study in Word History', *French Quarterly*, 13 (1931).
62. On the moral lessons of novels, see V. Mylne, *The Eighteenth-Century French Novel: Techniques of Illusion* (Manchester, 1965), pp. 4–19; and G. May, *Le Dilemme du roman au XVIIIe siècle* (Paris, 1963).
63. See also Mylne, *The Eighteenth-Century French Novel*, pp. 125–43.
64. On Richardson and the English vogue for novels of sensibility, see R. F. Brissenden, *Virtue in Distress: Studies in the Novels of Sentiment from Richardson to De Sade* (London, 1986); J. Todd, *Sensibility: An Introduction* (London, 1986), chapter 5; J. Mullan, *Sentiment and Sociability: the Language of Feeling in the Eighteenth Century* (Oxford, 1988), chapter 2.
65. Wilson, *Diderot*, pp. 427–8.

Chapter 3   Virtue and Radical Political Theory: Rousseau and Mably

1. C. Blum, *Rousseau and the Republic of Virtue* (New York, 1986), p. 26.
2. All references to Rousseau's works in this chapter are taken from the *Oeuvres complètes* (Paris, 1959–70). For Rousseau's early love of Plutarch, see his *Confessions*, in the *Oeuvres complètes*, vol. I, p. 9.
3. See J. Fabre, 'Deux frères ennemis: Diderot et Jean-Jacques', *Diderot Studies*, III (1961), pp. 155–213; and G. R. Havers, 'Diderot, Rousseau, and the *Discours sur l'inégalité*', *Diderot Studies*, III (1961), pp. 219–62.
4. Of the many works which situate Rousseau's political theory in the context of eighteenth-century thought, see in particular: R. Derathé, *Jean-Jacques Rousseau et la science politique de son temps* (Paris, 1970); N. O. Keohane, *Philosophy and the State in France: the Renaissance to the Enlightenment* (Princeton, N.J., 1980); J. Shklar, *Men and Citizens: a Study of Rousseau's Social Theory* (Cambridge, 1969), esp. chapter 2; R. Grimsley, *Jean-Jacques Rousseau: a Study in Self-Awareness* (Cardiff, 1961); and E. M. Wood, 'The State and Popular Sovereignty in French Political Thought: a Genealogy of Rousseau's "General Will"', in F. Krantz (ed.), *History from Below: Studies in Popular Protest and Popular Ideology* (Oxford, 1985).
5. On this debate, see D. Echeverria, 'The Pre- Revolutionary Influence of Rousseau's "Contrat social"', *Journal of the History of Ideas*, 33 (1972), pp. 543–60.
6. See J. Starobinski, *Jean-Jacques Rousseau: Transparency and Obstruction* (1971; trans., Chicago, 1988), p. 63.
7. The description in Rousseau's *Emile* of a rural idyll is in the *Oeuvres complètes*, vol. IV, book IV, pp. 686–91. On Rousseau's varied concepts of utopia, see Shklar, 'Rousseau's Two Models: Sparta and the Age of Gold', *Political Science Quarterly*, 76 (1961); and J. Charvet, 'Rousseau and the Ideal of Community', *History of Political Thought*, 1 (1980).

8. Rousseau, *Confessions*, vol. 1, book VI, p. 263.
9. Rousseau, *Confessions*, book VIII, pp. 377–80; Denis Diderot, *Le Neveu de Rameau*, in *Oeuvres romanesques* (Paris, 1962), p. 433.
10. Rousseau, *Confessions*, book VIII, p. 351.
11. Rousseau, *Discours sur les sciences et les arts*, in *Oeuvres complètes*, vol. III, p. 8.
12. Ibid., p. 19.
13. Ibid., p. 30.
14. Rousseau, *Confessions*, book VIII, p. 356.
15. On the influence on Rousseau of Jansenist concepts of *l'amour-propre* and their suspicion of virtue, see N. O. Keohane, 'The Masterpiece of Policy in Our Century: Rousseau on the Morality of the Enlightenment', *Political Theory*, 6, 4 (1978), pp. 465–9.
16. Rousseau, *Discours sur l'origine et les fondements de l'inégalité parmi les hommes*, in *Oeuvres complètes*, vol. III, p. 156; *Confessions*, book VIII, p. 389.
17. *Images du peuple au dix-huitième siècle: Colloque d'Aix-en-Provence* (Paris, 1973), pp. 203–4.
18. For Jansenist influences on Rousseau's concept of the 'general will', see the works of P. Riley: 'The General Will before Rousseau', *Political Theory*, VI, 4 (1978); and *The General Will before Rousseau: the Transformation of the Divine into the Civic* (Princeton, N. J., 1986).
19. Rousseau, *Discours sur l'écomomie politique* (1758), in *Oeuvres complètes*, vol. III, p. 252.
20. Ibid., p. 259.
21. Rousseau, *Du Contrat social*, in *Oeuvres complètes*, vol. III, book II, chap. i, pp. 368–9.
22. Ibid., book I, chaps v, vi, pp. 359–62.
23. Ibid., book III, chap. iv, pp. 404–6.
24. Ibid., book III, chap. x, pp. 421–3.
25. Rousseau, *Emile*, book IV, p. 524.
26. Ibid.
27. Ibid., book V, pp. 762–3, 777.
28. Ibid., book II, p. 422.
29. Ibid., book IV, p. 509–10.
30. Ibid., p. 488.
31. Ibid., book V, p. 858.
32. For a discussion of this subject, see Marisa Linton, 'Virtue Rewarded? Women and the Politics of Virtue in Eighteenth-Century France', Parts I and II, *History of European Ideas*, 26, 1 (2001).
33. Rousseau, *Emile*, p. 589.
34. Similarly, Julie, in *La Nouvelle Héloïse*, only becomes truly virtuous by controlling her passionate love for Saint-Preux.
35. Rousseau, *Emile*, book V, pp. 817–18.
36. See R. Mauzi, *L'Idée du bonheur dans la littérature et la pensée française au XVIIIe siècle* (Paris, 1960), pp. 624–34.
37. Rousseau, *Les Rêveries du promeneur solitaire*, in *Oeuvres complètes*, vol. I, Sixth Walk, pp. 1052–3.
38. See Mauzi, *L'Idée du bonheur*, pp. 580–603, esp. 596–8, 632.
39. See C. Vellay, 'Saint-Just et Mably', *Annales Révolutionnaires*, I (1908), who suggests that Saint-Just's interest in Mably's theories on the social organisa-

tion of religion influenced Robespierre's festival of the Supreme Being, p. 345.

40. For an important reevaluation of Mably, see J. K. Wright, *A Classical Republican in Eighteenth-Century France: the Political Thought of Mably* (Stanford, Cal., 1997).

41. See M. Cranston, *The Solitary Self: Jean-Jacques Rousseau in Exile and Adversity* (Chicago, 1997), pp. 103–4.

42. Rousseau, *Confessions*, pp. 280, 287.

43. Mably, *Du Cours et de la marche des passions dans la société*, cited in P. Friedman (ed.), *Mably: sur la théorie du pouvoir politique* (Paris, 1975), pp. 271–4. On Rousseau's and Mably's writings on Poland, see Grimsley, *Jean-Jacques Rousseau*, pp. 128–9. For Rousseau's chequered relations with Mably, see Wright, *A Classical Republican*, esp. pp. 99–100, 121–4.

44. For Montesquieu's influence on Mably, and for the subsequent emergence of his political egalitarianism, see Wright, *A Classical Republican*, esp. pp. 24–5, 90–3.

45. Mably, *Des Droits et des devoirs du citoyen* (this edition, Paris, 1972), Letter V, p. 127.

46. On the political theory of *Des Droits et des devoirs du citoyen*, its publication and its 'revolutionary' content, see K. Baker, 'A Script for a French Revolution: the Political Consciousness of the Abbé Mably', in *Eighteenth-Century Studies*, 14, 3 (1981); republished in K. M. Baker, *Inventing the French Revolution* (Cambridge, 1990), esp. pp. 237–8.

47. Mably, *Des Droits et des devoirs du citoyen*, Letter I, p. 13.

48. Ibid., Letter VI, p. 155.

49. Ibid., Letter VI, p. 159.

50. Ibid., Letter III, p. 69.

51. Ibid., Letter VIII, p. 218.

52. *Entretien de Phocion sur le rapport de la morale avec la politique*, in Mably, *Oeuvres complètes de l'abbé de Mably*, 19 vols (Toulouse, 1791), vol. XIV, 'Quatrième entretien', pp. 155–6.

53. Ibid., pp. 157–68.

54. Ibid., pp. 198–9.

55. Ibid., 'Troisième entretien', pp. 147–51.

56. On the stir caused by the appearance of the *Entretiens de Phocion*, see *Mémoires secrets*, 1–2 (April 1763).

Chapter 4   Making the Man of Virtue, 1755–70

1. On the growing preoccupation (especially after the Seven Years War) of the military nobility with the pursuit of soldierly merit as a quality opposed to courtly 'corruption', see J. M. Smith, *The Culture of Merit: Nobility, Royal Service, and the Making of Absolute Monarchy in France, 1600–1789* (Ann Arbor, Mich., 1996), pp. 227–61.

2. See Chaussinand-Nogaret, *La Noblesse au XVIIIe siècle: de la féodalité aux lumières* (Paris, 1976), esp. pp. 195–6; also pp. 53–4, 57–60.

3. See Pappas, 'La campagne des philosophes contre l'honneur', *Studies on Voltaire and the Eighteenth Century*, 105 (1982), pp. 31–44. See also the nuances

of Saint-Lambert's arguments about nobility, honour and virtue in his article on 'honour' for the *Encyclopédie: Encyclopédie, ou Dictionnaire Raisonné des sciences, des arts et des métiers*, 1781 edition, 36 vols (Berne and Lausanne, 1781), vol. XVII, p. 699.

4. Champdevaux, *L'Honneur considéré en lui-même et relativement au duel* (Paris, 1752), pp. 1–2, 4.
5. Ibid., pp. 86–93.
6. Ibid., pp. 48–52.
7. Ibid., pp. 283–7.
8. Ibid., pp. 295–303.
9. Ibid., pp. 343–70.
10. See F. Brunot, *Histoire de la langue française*, vol. VI, pp. 1274–81.
11. On the readership of the *Encyclopédie*, see R. Darnton, *The Business of Enlightenment: a Publishing History of the Encyclopédie, 1775–1800* (Cambridge, Mass., 1979).
12. Denis Diderot, *Oeuvres complètes*, ed. J. Assézat and M. Tourneux (Paris, 1875–7), vol. XIV, pp. 462–3.
13. *Encyclopédie, ou Dictionnaire Raisonné*, vol. XXXV, p. 516. There are several articles on 'vertu' in the *Encyclopédie*. The references here are all to the first and longest, which was by Jean Edmé Romilly. See J. Lough, *The Encyclopédie* (London, 1971), pp. 51–2.
14. Ibid., pp. 517, 519, 522.
15. Ibid., vol. XVIII, p. 585; vol. XXV, pp. 543–5.
16. On the links between virtue, *bienfaisance* and happiness, see R. Mauzi, *L'Idée du bonheur dans la littérature et la pensée française au XVIIIe siècle* (Paris, 1960), pp. 605–13.
17. Voltaire, *Dictionnaire philosophique* (Paris, 1967), pp. 413–14.
18. On Richerism, see the article by E. Préclin, *Les jansénistes du XVIIIe siècle et la constitution civile du clergé: le développement du richerisme, sa propagation dans le bas clergé, 1713–1791* (Paris, 1929). On the political involvement of parish priests, see M. Hutt, 'The Curés and the Third Estate: Ideas of Reform in the Pamphlets of the French Lower Clergy in the Period 1787–1789', *Journal of Ecclesiastical History*, 8 (1957).
19. Diderot, *Oeuvres complètes*, vol. VII, p. 66. J.-J. Rousseau, *Confessions*, in *Oeuvres Complètes* (Paris, 1959–70), book IX, p. 455 (1757). Also, Diderot's letter to Sophie Volland, 2 June 1759, in *Diderot's Letters to Sophie Volland*, ed. and trans. Peter France (Oxford, 1972). See also C. Blum's illuminating comparison between Rousseau's and Diderot's concepts of virtue, *Diderot: the Virtue of a Philosopher* (New York, 1974), esp. pp. 3–4, 56–60, 91–3.
20. C. Duclos, *Considérations sur les mœurs*, ed. F. C. Green (Cambridge, 1939), pp. 55–6.
21. K. Racevskis, 'The French Academy as a Proponent of Egalitarianism', in R. Runte (ed.), *Studies in Eighteenth-Century Culture*, 7 (Madison, Wis., 1978), pp. 105–16.
22. L. Brunel, *Les Philosophes et l'Académie française* (Geneva, 1967), pp. 130–2.
23. C. I. Castel de Saint-Pierre, *Projet pour rendre l'Académie des bons écrivains plus utile à l'Etat*. See also Brunel, *Les Philosophes et l'Académie française*, pp. 58–67.
24. Roche, *Les Républicains des lettres* (Paris, 1988), pp. 189–94, 199–202; on the choice of subjects for the eulogies, see G. Kelly, 'The History of the New Hero:

Eulogy and its New Sources in *Eighteenth-Century France', Eighteenth-Century Theory and Interpretation, 21 (Winter 1980), pp. 3–25.*

25. See M. Linton, 'The Concept of Virtue in Eighteenth-Century France, 1745–1788' (DPhil, University of Sussex, 1993), chapter 5. On the politics of the Fénelon contest and the subsequent suppression of the winning eulogies by La Harpe and Maury, see pp. 149–52.

26. Thomas's many prize essays are collected in, *Oeuvres de M. Thomas de l'Académie Françoise. Nouvelle édition revue, corrigée et augmentée,* 4 vols (Amsterdam, 1773). On the influence of Thomas's style of eulogy and his championship of virtue, see especially Brunel, *Les Philosophes et l'Académie française,* pp. 62–3, 123–7.

27. A. L. Thomas, *Essai sur les Eloges, ou Histoire de la Littérature et de l'Eloquence, appliquès à ce genre d'ouvrage,* in *Oeuvres de M. Thomas,* vol. II, p. 284.

28. A. L. Thomas, *Eloge de Henri-François Daguesseau,* ibid., vol. III, pp. 61–4.

29. A. L. Thomas, *Eloge de Maximilien de Béthune, Duc de Sully,* ibid., vol. III, pp. 271–2. See also, Mlle de Mascarany, *Eloge historique de Maximilien de Béthune, Duc de Sully* (The Hague, 1763), esp. pp. 60–7.

30. Cited by Brunel, *Les Philosophes et l'Académie française,* p. 125.

31. Ibid., pp. 125–7.

32. See F. Gaiffe, *Le Drame en France au XVIIIᵉ siècle* (Paris, 1910); M. Lioure, *Le Drame* (Paris, 1963). Also R. Lewinter, 'L'Exaltation de la vertu dans le théâtre de Diderot', *Diderot Studies,* VIII (1966), pp. 119–69; and A. Guedj, 'Les Drames de Diderot', *Diderot Studies,* XIV (1971), pp. 15–95.

33. Diderot, *Oeuvres complètes,* vol. VII, p. 19.

34. Ibid., p. 86.

35. Ibid., pp. 150–1.

36. Ibid., p. 149.

37. Ibid., pp. 127–8.

38. Ibid., p. 168.

39. On Diderot's plays and their impact, see A. M. Wilson, *Diderot* (Oxford, 1972), esp. pp. 260–74, 313–16, 322–6, 403–13.

40. On the *philosophes'* practice of 'packing' the parterre, see J. Lough, *Paris Theatre Audiences in the Seventeenth and Eighteenth Centuries* (Oxford, 1957), pp. 178–81.

41. M. J. Sedaine, *Le Philosophe sans le savoir* (1765; this edition, Paris, 1936), Act II, scene 4, p. 31.

42. Ibid., Act III, scene 12, p. 48.

43. For example, R. Niklaus, *A Literary History of France: The Eighteenth Century, 1715–1789* (London, 1970), p. 319, sees the work in these terms, and finds the presence of a nobleman as the *philosophe* to be 'inconsistent' with the general bourgeois direction of the play. This is contested in Haydn Mason, 'An Aristocratic *Drame Bourgeois: Le Philosophe sans le savoir', French Studies,* 30 (1976), pp. 404–18. For an important new evaluation of Sedaine and the politics of the *drame bourgeois,* see M. Ledbury, *Sedaine, Greuze and the Boundaries of Genre, Studies on Voltaire and the Eighteenth Century,* vol. 380 (The Voltaire Foundation, May 2000).

44. Sedaine, *Le Philosophe sans le savoir,* Act V, scene 2, p. 65.

45. On the politics of the censors' action, see Ledbury, *Sedaine, Greuze.*

46. For Sedaine's comments, see *Le Philosophe sans le savoir,* p. 69.

47. For David, see T. Crow, *Painters and Public Life in Eighteenth-Century Paris* (New Haven, Conn., 1985), chap. 7.
48. A. Hytier, 'The Decline of Military Values: the Theme of the Deserter in Eighteenth-Century French Literature', *Studies in Eighteenth-Century Culture*, 11 (University of Wisconsin, 1982).
49. A. Corvisier, *L'Armée française à la fin du XVIIᵉ siècle au ministère du Choiseul*, 2 vols (Paris, 1964), vol. II, pp. 699–700. For an intriguing account of subsequent attempts by Mercier and other journalists to appropriate the language of patriotism, see N. R. Gelbart, '"Frondeur" Journalism in the 1770s', *Eighteenth-Century Studies*, 17, 4 (1984), pp. 493–514. On Beaumarchais's plays and their ambiguity towards virtue, see S. Maza, *Private Lives and Public Affairs: the Causes Célèbres of Prerevolutionary France* (Berkeley, Cal., 1993), pp. 289–95.
50. On the philosophic debate over the education of the poor, see H. Chisick, *The Limits of Reform in the Enlightenment: Attitudes toward the Education of the Lower Classes in Eighteenth-Century France* (Princeton, N.J., 1981), pp. 245–77.
51. For a discussion of educational projects to instil patriotic citizenship, see ibid., pp. 205–44; and C. R. Bailey, 'Attempts to Institute a "System" of Secular Secondary Education in France, 1762–1789', *Studies on Voltaire and the Eighteenth Century*, 167 (1977), pp. 105–24.
52. The foremost work on the politics of this event is D. Van Kley, *The Jansenists and the Expulsion of the Jesuits from France, 1757–1765* (New Haven, Conn., 1975).
53. See R. R. Palmer, *Catholics and Unbelievers in Eighteenth-Century France* (New York, 1961), p. 9.
54. L. R. Caradeuc de La Chalotais, *Essai d'éducation nationale, ou Plan d'études pour la jeunesse* (n.p., 1763), prefatory passage; and pp. 2, 5–6, 12–3, 132–3. On La Chalotais, see Van Kley, *The Jansenists*, chap. 6.
55. La Chalotais, *De l'Education publique* (Amsterdam (Paris?), 1762), preface, pp. vi–vii. This was published together with La Chalotais's *Essai d'éducation nationale*. The 'post-scriptum' attached to this work by La Chalotais throws no light on its provenance. According to Barbier it may equally well have been written by Diderot, or by a Jansenist, J. B. L. Crévier. On the authorship of *De l'Education publique*, see Wilson, *Diderot*, pp. 447–8; also R. Mortier, 'The "Philosophes" and Public Education', *Yale French Studies*, 40 (1968). For debates on education, see R. Chartier, M.-M. Compère and D. Julia, *L'Education en France du XVIᵉ au XVIIIᵉ siècle* (Paris, 1976).
56. L. de Beausobre, *Essai sur le bonheur, ou Réflexions philosophiques sur les biens et les maux de la vie humaine* (Berlin, 1758), pp. 4–5; G. Dragonetti, *Traité des vertus et des récompenses... Traduit de l'Italien, par M. Pingeron* (Paris, 1768), pp. 1–4 and 11; J. L. Castilhon, *Traité de l'Influence de la Vertu et du Vice sur le Bonheur et le Malheur*, in *Essais de philosophie et de morale, en partie traduits librement, et en partie imités de Plutarche* (1770), pp. 350–8; *Le Temple du Bonheur, ou Recueil des plus excellens traités sur le bonheur, extraits des meilleurs auteurs anciens et modernes*, 3 vols (Bouillon, 1769).
57. See Mauzi, *L'Idée du bonheur*, p. 623.
58. Castilhon, *Essais de philosophie et de morale*, 'Réflexions préliminaires', pp. xxxii–xxxiii.
59. Pocock calls this idea the 'liberal' paradigm; see his 'Cambridge Paradigms and Scotch Philosophers', in I. Hont and M. Ignatieff (eds), *Wealth and Virtue:*

the Shaping of Political Economy in the Scottish Enlightenment (Cambridge, 1983). See also A. Hirschman, *The Passions and the Interests: Political Arguments for Capitalism Before its Triumph* (Princeton, N.J., 1977).
60. On this controversy in France, see E. Ross, 'Mandeville, Melon, and Voltaire: the Origins of the Luxury Controversy in France'; and R. Galliani, 'Le Débat en France sur le luxe: Voltaire ou Rousseau?', *Studies on Voltaire and the Eighteenth Century*, 161 (1976), pp. 205–17.
61. C. A. Helvétius, *De l'Esprit* (Paris, 1758; reprinted, Verviers, 1973), pp. 328–9.
62. Diderot, *Oeuvres complètes*, vol. VI, pp. 438–9. See also R. Mauzi, 'Les Rapports du bonheur et de la vertu dans l'œuvre de Diderot', *Cahiers de L'Association internationale des Etudes Françaises*, 13 (1961), esp. p. 263.
63. See Wilson, *Diderot*, pp. 659–67; also 682–4, 700–2.
64. Diderot, *Letters to Sophie Volland*, 31 August 1769, pp. 194–5.
65. Beausobre, *Essai sur le bonheur*, pp. 221–2.
66. G. F. Coyer, *Dissertations pour être lues: la première sur le vieux mot de patrie; la seconde sur la nature du peuple* (1755; this edition, The Hague, 1765), pp. 35–6, 44–5, 51–3.

Chapter 5   The Virtuous King: a Rhetoric Transformed

1. There are several recent studies of 'desacralisation', including J. Merrick, *The Desacralization of the French Monarchy in the Eighteenth Century* (Baton Rouge, La, 1990); see also R. Chartier, *The Cultural Origins of the French Revolution* (Durham and London, 1991), chap. 6.
2. L. Petit de Bachaumont (attrib.), *Mémoires secrets pour servir à l'histoire de la République des Lettres en France depuis 1762 jusqu' à nos jours*, 36 vols (London, 1780–9; republished, Farnborough, 1970). The *Mémoires secrets* was a voluminous compendium of news and gossip, derived from newssheets (*nouvelles à la main*) which circulated from 1762 to 1787, although they were not published until 1777 to 1789. For further information, see R. S. Tate, 'Petit de Bachaumont: his Circle and the "Mémoires secrets"', *Studies on Voltaire and the Eighteenth Century*, 65 (Geneva, 1968); L. A. Olivier, 'Bachaumont the Chronicler: a Questionable Renown', *Studies on Voltaire and the Eighteenth Century*, 143 (Geneva, 1975), pp. 161–79; also J. Merrick, 'Sexual Politics and Public Order in Late Eighteenth-Century France: the *Mémoires secrets* and the *Correspondance secrète*', *Journal of the History of Sexuality*, ɪ, 1 (1990), pp. 68–84.
3. The seminal book on this subject is R. Darnton, *The Literary Underground of the Old Regime* (Cambridge, Mass., 1982). On the language of the *Mazarinades*, see Christian Jouhaud, *Mazarinades: La Fronde des mots* (Paris, 1985). For the earlier period one can consult: Jeffrey K. Sawyer, *Printed Poison: Pamphlet Propaganda, Faction Politics, and the Public Sphere in Early Seventeenth-Century France* (Berkeley, Cal., 1990).
4. See D. Van Kley, *The Damiens Affair and the Unravelling of the Ancien Régime, 1750–1770* (Princeton, N.J., 1984).
5. See Kaiser, who argues both that Louis's reputation had already been precarious prior to 1744, and that the attempt to give Louis a soubriquet (and consequently a public reputation) which he could not sustain, was very damaging to the monarchy: T. E. Kaiser, 'Louis *le Bien-Aimé* and the Rhetoric

of the Royal Body', in S. Melzer and K. Norberg (eds), *From the Royal to the Republican Body: Incorporating the Political in Seventeenth and Eighteenth-Century France* (Berkeley, Cal., 1998).

6. J. J. Duguet, *Institution d'un Prince: ou Traité des Qualitéz, des Vertus et des Devoirs d'un Souverain* (London [Rouen?], 1739), pp. 84–6.
7. R. Mauzi, *L'Idée du bonheur dans la littérature et la pensée française au XVIIIᵉ siècle* (Paris, 1960), p. 609.
8. See J. Merrick, 'Politics in the Pulpit: Ecclesiastical Discourse on the Death of Louis XV', *History of European Ideas*, 1, 2 (1986), pp. 149–60.
9. Stanislas Leczinski, 'Réponse au Discours qui a remporté le Prix de l'Académie de Dijon', in *Oeuvres du philosophe bienfaisant*, 4 vols (Paris, 1763), vol. IV, pp. 317–46. Rousseau claimed that a large part of this text for which the king took the credit had been written by a Jesuit, Père le Menou. See J. J. Rousseau, *Confessions, Oeuvres complètes* (Paris, 1959–70), book 8, pp. 365–6.
10. Leczinski, *Oeuvres du philosophe bienfaisant*, vol. I, pp. 218–19.
11. Stanislas's most important political work, *La Voix libre du citoyen, ou observations sur le gouvernement de la Pologne* (1749), was republished in the *Oeuvres du Philosophe bienfaisant*.
12. *Journal des Dames*, January 1764, pp. 48–73, esp. pp. 51, 56–7, together with the comments in N. R. Gelbart, *Feminine and Opposition Journalism in Old Regime France: le Journal des Dames* (Berkeley, Cal., 1987), pp. 133–8. See also, *Mémoires secrets*, I, 11 October 1763. A few days later the *Mémoires* published a poem on Stanislas's kingly virtues, I, 20 October 1763, p. 289.
13. J. Boisgelin, 'Oraison funèbre du Stanislas Iᵉʳ, Roi de Pologne', in *Oeuvres oratoires du Cardinal de Boisgelin*, reprinted in J. P. Migne, *Collection intégrale et universelle des orateurs sacrés* (Paris, 1844–66), vol. 72, cols 199–200.
14. Ibid., p. 206.
15. See, for example: N. Thirel de Boismont, 'Oraison funèbre de…Louis Dauphin', reprinted in Migne, *Collection…des orateurs sacrés*, vol. 65, cols 795, 799–801, 803; J. S. Maury, 'Eloge funèbre de…Louis, Dauphin de France', reprinted in Migne, *Collection…des orateurs sacrés*, vol. 67, cols 1085, 1087, 1090; J. A. J. Cerutti and the duc de La Vauguyon, *Portrait de feu Monseigneur le Dauphin* (Paris, 1766), pp. 4–7, 14–15, 21–3.
16. Maury, 'Eloge funèbre de…Louis, Dauphin de France', col. 1089.
17. A. L. Thomas, *Eloge de Louis, Dauphin de France* (Paris, 1766), pp. 6–7, 28–32.
18. Ibid., p. 32.
19. Ibid., pp. 16–17.
20. Ibid., pp. 32–3, 62.
21. Denis Diderot, *Oeuvres complètes*, ed. J. Assézat and M. Tourneux (Paris, 1875–7), vol. VI, pp. 347–8
22. L. Brunel, *Les Philosophes et l'Académie française*, p. 177.
23. *Mémoires secrets*, III, 27 March 1766.
24. See T. E. Kaiser, 'Madame de Pompadour and the Theaters of Power', *French Historical Studies*, 19 (1996), pp. 1025–44.
25. On the influence of his father's virtuous image on Louis XVI, see E. Lever, *Louis XVI* (Paris, 1985), pp. 39–40; and J. Hardman, *Louis XVI* (New Haven, Conn., 1993), pp. 17–26, esp. pp. 22–3.

26. *Maximes morales et politiques tirées de Télémaque; imprimées par Louis-Auguste, Dauphin* (Versailles, 1766), Maximes II–IV, VIII, X–XIII, XVIII.
27. Cited by J. Thompson, *The French Revolution* (Oxford, 1943), p. 3.
28. See D. Mornet, *Les Origines intellectuelles de la Revolution Française· 1715–1787* (1933; republished, Paris, 1954), pp. 270–1.
29. Elisée, 'Compliment au Roi', *Sermons du R. Père Elisée, carmé déchaussé, prédicateur du Roi*, 4 vols (Paris, 1785), vol. IV, pp. 474–6.
30. *Mémoires secrets*, II, 2 February 1765, pp. 150–2.
31. See J. A. Rigoley de Juvigny, *De la Décadence des lettres et des mœurs, depuis les Grecs et les Romains jusqu'à nos jours* (Paris, 1787), p. 306.
32. Abbé de Sambucy, *Vie de Monseigneur de Beauvais, ancien évêque de Senez* (Paris, 1842), pp. 28–34, 41, 45–8.
33. J. B. C. M. de Beauvais, 'Sur la pudeur', in *Oeuvres complètes de Messire Jean-Baptiste-Charles-Marie de Beauvais, évêque de Senez*, reprinted in Migne, *Collection... des orateurs sacrés*, vol. 71, esp. cols 292–3, 301.
34. Ibid., col. 306.
35. Beauvais, 'Sur la dispensation des bienfaits', Migne, *Collection... des orateurs sacrés*, vol. 71, col. 267.
36. Ibid., col. 262.
37. Ibid., col. 268.
38. Ibid., col. 269.
39. Beauvais, 'Sur l'immortalité de l'âme', Migne, *Collection... des orateurs sacrés*, vol. 71, col. 97; see also, Sambucy, *Vie de Mgr de Beauvais*, pp. 47–8.
40. *Mémoires secrets*, VI, 26 March, 13 April 1773; Pidansat de Mairobert, *Journal Historique de la Révolution opérée dans la Constitution de la Monarchie Françoise, par M. de Maupeou, Chancelier de France*, 7 vols ('Londres', 1775), vol. IV, 16 March 1773.
41. *Mémoires secrets*, VI, 5 and 28 May 1773; vol. VII, 17 April 1774.
42. Cited in Sambucy, *Vie de Mgr de Beauvais*, who gives a detailed account of the court politics surrounding Beauvais's contentious appointment, pp. 48–56.
43. *Mémoires secrets*, VII, 17 April 1774, pp. 160–1.
44. Beauvais, who was still alive, had resigned his bishopric in 1783.
45. Cited in Sambucy, *Vie de Mgr de Beauvais*, p. 60.
46. *Mémoires secrets*, VII, 4 and 17 April 1774, pp. 160–1.
47. Ibid., 17 April, p. 160.
48. On powerful myths of kingship, especially Henri IV and Louis XII, see R. Pillorget, 'Le Recours à l'imaginaire étranger en France au cours des décennies précédant la révolution de 1789', *Revue historique, diplomatique*, 98, 1–2 (1984), pp. 7–30, esp. pp. 18–22. On the cult of Henri IV, see J. Meyer, 'Mythes monarchiques: le cas Henri IV aux XVIIe et XVIIIe siècles', in *La Monarchie absolutiste et l'histoire de France* (Paris, 1987), pp. 169–96.
49. J. F. La Harpe, *Eloge de Henri IV, Roi de France*, printed in de Buri, *Histoire de la vie de Henri IV, Roi de France et de Navarre*, 4 vols (Paris, 1779), vol. IV, p. 249.
50. N. J. Le Couturier, 'Panégyrique de Saint Louis, Prononcé dans la chapelle du Louvre, en présence de messieurs de l'Académie française, le 25 août 1746', in *Oeuvres complètes de Le Couturier*, reprinted in Migne, *Collection... des orateurs sacrés*, vol. 66, esp. cols 263, 273, 275.

51. See A. Rosne (pseudo.), 'Une cause de la décadence de la chaire au XVIIIe siècle: les prédicateurs du panégyrique de Saint Louis devant l'Académie française', *Revue du clergé français* (1897), pp. 113–34, esp. p. 128.
52. N. Thirel du Boismont, 'Panégyrique de Saint Louis, Roi de France. Prononcé dans la chapelle du Louvre, en présence de MM. de l'Académie française, le 25 août 1750', reprinted in Migne, *Collection...des orateurs sacrés*, vol. 65, esp. cols 779, 789.
53. J. F. R. de La Tour du Pin, 'Panégyrique de Saint Louis, Prononcé dans la chapelle du Louvre, en présence de messieurs de l'Académie française, le 25 août 1751', reprinted in Migne, *Collection...des orateurs sacrés*, vol. 53, col. 45.
54. By the 1780s such deliberately contentious 'political discussions' for the panegyric were the norm, see Abbé de Boulogne, *Panégyrique de Saint Louis*, 25 August 1782, republished in *Oeuvres de M. de Boulogne* (Paris, 1826), p. 5.
55. On the influence of the *Académie française* on the panegyrics of St Louis as a growing forum for political and philosophic ideas, see Rosne, 'Une cause de la décadence', pp. 113–34; also Brunel, *Les Philosophes et l'Académie française*, esp. pp. 186–90.
56. A. J. Bassinet, *Panégyrique de Saint Louis, Roi de France, Prononcé...le 25 août 1767* (Paris, 1768), pp. 5, 7, 31, 51.
57. Ibid., pp. 27–8.
58. *Mémoires secrets*, III, 28 August 1767, pp. 220–1.
59. Rosne, 'Une cause de la décadence', p. 122.
60. Bassinet, *Panégyrique de Saint Louis*, Introductory letter, p. VII.
61. Ibid., p. VIII.
62. N. J. Le Couturier, 'Panégyrique de Saint Louis, Prononcé dans la chapelle du Louvre, en présence de messieurs de l'Académie française, le 25 août 1769', in *Oeuvres complètes de Le Couturier*, reprinted in Migne, *Collection...des orateurs sacrés*, vol. 66, col. 373.
63. Ibid., for example, cols 362, 363, 383.
64. Ibid., col. 375.
65. *Mémoires secrets*, IV, 31 August 1769, pp. 304–5.
66. *Mémoires secrets*, V, 8 November and 10 December 1769, pp. 3–4, 25–6. The reasons why the Archbishop lifted his ban so quickly are unclear, see Rosne, 'Une cause de la décadence', p. 123.
67. L. Michaud, *Biographie universelle* (Paris, 1854–65).
68. *Panégyrique de Saint Louis* (1772), republished in J. S. Maury, *Essai sur l'éloquence de la chaire; panégyriques, éloges et discours...*, 2 vols (Paris, 1810), vol. II, for example, pp. 297–9, 301–2, 375–6.
69. Ibid., pp. 360–2. For Voltaire's sarcastic comments, see Rosne, 'Une cause de la décadence', p. 126.
70. Ibid., pp. 302, 328–30.
71. *Mémoires secrets*, VI, 18 September 1772; see also Michaud, *Biographie universelle*.
72. Examples of clerical language in the funeral orations for Louis XV are uncovered in Merrick, 'Politics in the Pulpit'.
73. J. B. Beauvais, *Oraison funèbre du très-grand, très-haut, très-puissant et très-excellent prince, Louis XV le bien-aimé* (Paris, 1774), p. 22.
74. Ibid., p. 11.

75. There were suggestions that Beauvais was reasserting the primacy of the Church, and that not only was he using the oration to lament the expulsion of the Jesuits and the king's ill-treatment of Christophe de Beaumont, but also both this oration and his sermon of the previous year had been engineered by members of the *dévot* party. This suggests that the *dévots* also approved Beauvais's use of the language of virtue and *bienfaisance* to justify their views. See the *Mémoires secrets*, VIII, 13 June 1775, p. 78; also Merrick, 'Politics in the Pulpit', pp. 152–3; and Sambucy, *Vie de Mgr Beauvais*, pp. 63–5.

76. Beauvais, *Oraison funèbre de Louis XV*, pp. 7–8. For further examples, see: A. G. de Géry, 'Oraison funèbre de Louis XV... Prononcé dans l'église abatiale et paroissiale de Saint-Martin d'Epernay, le 10 juin 1774', in *Oeuvres complètes de André-Guillaume de Géry*, reprinted in Migne, *Collection... des orateurs sacrés*, vol. 63, col. 818; N. T. de Boismont, 'Oraison funèbre de Louis XV... Surnommé le Bien-Aimé, Prononcée dans la chapelle du Louvre, le 30 juillet 1774, en présence de Messieurs de l'Académie française', in *Oeuvres oratoires complètes de l'abbé de Boismont, membre de l'Académie française*, reprinted in Migne, *Collection... des orateurs sacrés*, vol. 65, col. 833; P. A. Torné, *Oraison funèbre de Louis XV... surnommé le bien-aimé* (Tarbes, 1774), pp. 5–6.

77. Torné, *Oraison funèbre de Louis XV*, pp. 58–60.

78. Ibid., pp. 133–9, esp. p. 134.

79. Cited by Hardman, *Louis XVI*, p. 35.

80. On the political circumstances surrounding Louis's decision to recall the *parlement*, see Hardman, *Louis XVI*, pp. 27–38.

81. *Mémoires secrets*, VII, 8, 12 and 22 February 1775.

82. See K. M. Baker, 'French Political Thought at the Accession of Louis XVI', *Inventing the French Revolution* (Cambridge, 1990), pp. 109–27. Examples of the shifting idea of virtuous kingship included: C. Fauchet, *Panégyrique de Saint Louis, Roi de France, prononcé dans la chapelle du Louvre le 25 août 1774* (Paris, 1774), esp. pp. 7–8, 14–15, 17–18, 24–5, 72; abbé J. R. Pétity, *Sagesse de Louis XVI... Ouvrage Moral et Politique, sur les Vertus et les Vices de l'Homme*, 2 vols (Paris, 1775); *L'Effusion du Cœur et la France renaissante, Hommages sincères rendus à Louis XVI par son Peuple* (Paris, 1774), which includes much material on *bienfaisance*; whilst the idea of a 'social pact' between king and people, and an evocation of the words of Fénelon, appeared in M. Morizot, *Le Sacre Royal, ou les droits de la Nation Françoise, Reconnus et confirmés par cette Cérémonie*, 2 vols (Amsterdam, 1776), vol. 1, part 1, p. 2.

83. This was the officially-sanctioned advice of Stanislas to Marie Leczinska, in his *Avis du Roi à la Reine sa Fille lors de son Marriage'*, in the work published under his name, *Oeuvres du Philosophe bienfaisant*, vol. I, esp. pp. 1, 3, 21–2.

84. A characteristic treatment of the 'humble virtues' of the long-suffering wife of Louis XV was given in her funeral oration by Boismont, *Oraison funèbre de la très-haute, très-puissante et très-excellente Princesse Marie Leczinska, Reine de France. Prononcé dans la chapelle du Louvre, le 22 novembre 1768, en présence de Messieurs de l'Académie française*, republished in Migne, *Collection... des orateurs sacrées*, vol. 65, esp. pp. 814–16.

85. On representations of Marie-Antoinette, see in particular: L. Hunt, *The Family Romance of the French Revolution* (London, 1992), chap. 4; J. Revel, 'Marie-Antoinette in her fictions: the staging of hatred', in B. Fort (ed.), *Fictions of the French Revolution*, (Evanstan, Ill., 1991), pp. 111–29. On the political impact

of the Diamond Necklace Affair, see A. Cobban, 'The Affair of the Diamond Necklace', in A. Cobban, *Aspects of the French Revolution*, (first published 1968; this edition, St Albans, 1971) and more recently, S. Maza, 'The Diamond Necklace Affair Revisited (1785–1786): the Case of the Missing Queen', in L. Hunt (ed.), *Eroticism and the Body Politic* (Baltimore, Md., 1991). On the queen's actual role in court politics, see J. Hardman, 'The Political Role of Marie-Antoinette', in J. Hardman, *French Politics, 1774–1789, from the Accession of Louis XVI to the Fall of the Bastille* (London, 1995), pp. 198–215.

Chapter 6   The Maupeou Crisis and the Rise of Patriotic Virtue, 1770–5

1. The classic account is J. Egret, *Louis XV et l'opposition parlementaire, 1715–1774* (Paris, 1970).
2. The literature on the ideology and language of the *parlements* is very wide. Among the most important studies are: K. M. Baker, *Inventing the French Revolution* (Cambridge, 1990); J. Merrick, *The Desacralization of the French Monarchy in the Eighteenth Century* (Baton Rouge, La, 1990); J. H. Shennan, 'The Political Vocabulary of the Parlement of Paris in the Eighteenth Century', *Diritto e potere nella storia europea* (Florence, 1982), pp. 951–64; J. Merrick, 'Subjects and Citizens in the Remonstrances of the Parlement of Paris in the Eighteenth Century', *Journal of the History of Ideas* (1990), pp. 453–60. On the political vocabulary of Jansenism see the works of D. Van Kley, especially *The Damiens Affair and the Unravelling of the Ancien Régime, 1750–1770* (Princeton, N.J., 1984), chap. 4; also, 'The Religious Origins of the Patriot and Ministerial Parties in Pre-revolutionary France: Controversy over the Chancellor's Constitutional *Coup*, 1771–1775', *Historical Reflections/Réflexions Historiques*, 18 (1992), pp. 17–63.
3. On the influence of classical authors on rhetorical training, see P. France, *Rhetoric and Truth in France: Descartes to Diderot* (Oxford, 1972), pp. 3–33. One of the most influential handbooks on legal rhetoric was P. L. Gin, *De l'Eloquence du barreau* (Paris, 1767).
4. These arguments were influenced not only by the writings of Montesquieu, but also by the growing sophistication of Jansenist political theory, most importantly L. A. Le Paige in his *Lettres historiques sur les fonctions essentielles du Parlement; sur les droits des pairs, et sur les loix fondamentales du royaume*, 2 vols (Amsterdam, 1753).
5. Baker, *Inventing the French Revolution*, p. 25.
6. See the introduction to B. Stone, *The Parlement of Paris, 1774–1789* (Chapel Hill, N.C., 1981).
7. This was the view of Egret, and has been further developed by W. Doyle, *The Parlement of Bordeaux and the End of the Old Regime, 1771–1790* (London and Tonbridge, 1974).
8. On *patriote* ideology during the Maupeou coup, the best overall work is D. Echeverria, *The Maupeou Revolution: a Study in the History of Libertarianism* (Baton Rouge, La, 1985), part I; also S. M. Singham, ' "A Conspiracy of Twenty Million Frenchmen": Public Opinion, Patriotism and the Assault on Absolutism during the Maupeou Years' (PhD thesis, University of Princeton, 1991), chap. 2.

9. For the wider historiography of the Maupeou coup, see also W. Doyle, 'The *Parlements* of France and the Breakdown of the Old Regime', *French Historical Studies*, 6 (1970), pp. 415–58; also M. G. S. Mansergh, 'The Revolution of 1771, or the Exile of the *Parlement* of Paris' (DPhil, University of Oxford, 1973). On the lawyers attached to the *parlement* of Paris, see D. A. Bell, 'Lawyers into Demagogues: Chancellor Maupeou and the Transformation of Legal Practice in France', *Past and Present*, 130 (1991), pp. 107–41.
10. For evidence of ideologies in the 1730s, see P. R. Campbell, 'Aux origines d'une forme de lutte politique: avocats, magistrats et évêques. Les crises parlementaires et les jansénistes', *Jansénisme et Révolution* (Paris, 1990); and J. Merrick, '"Disputes over Words": a Constitutional Conflict in France, 1730–32', *French Historical Studies*, 14, 4 (1985–6), pp. 497–520.
11. See F. Bluche, *Les Magistrats du parlement de Paris au XVIIIᵉ siècle* (Paris, 1986), pp. 201–4.
12. D'Aguesseau, *1st mercuriale* (1698), cited by Bluche, *Les Magistrats du parlement de Paris*, p. 202.
13. A shortened version of Duguet's work, containing lengthy extracts on the importance of political virtue, appeared in Abbé André, *L'Esprit de M. Duguet, ou Précis de la Morale Chrétienne tiré de ses Ouvrages* (Paris, 1764), esp. pp. 119–60, 195–6. Bolingbroke's translations included one in the midst of the Maupeou coup: *Pensées de Milord Bolingbroke sur différents sujets d'histoire, de philosophie, de morale, etc....recueillies par L. Laurent Prault* (Amsterdam, 1771).
14. See R. Bickart, *Les Parlements et la notion de souveraineté nationale au XVIIIᵉ siècle* (Paris, 1932), pp. 278–9.
15. *Recueil des réclamations, remontrances, lettres, arrêts, arrêtés, protestations des parlemens, cour des aides, chambre des comptes, baillages, présidiaux, élections, au sujet de l'édit de décembre 1770*, 2 vols (London, 1773), vol. I, 'Remontrance du 16 janvier', Parlement de Paris, 1771, p. 34.
16. Ibid., vol. II: 'Lettre du Parlement de Rouen au Roi, du 8 février', pp. 209–10; 'Lettre du Parlement de Dijon au Roi, du 6 février 1771', p. 457; 'Lettre du Parlement de Bretagne au Roi, du 24 avril', p. 304; 'Très-humbles et très-respectueses Remontrances du Parlement de Bordeaux au Roi, du 25 Février 1771', p. 429; 'Très-Humbles et Très-Respectueuses Remontrances du Parlement de Provence au Roi, du 18 février 1771', p. 486.
17. Lettre du Parlement de Toulouse au Roi, du 19 février', ibid., vol. II, pp. 322–3.
18. 'Remontrances du Parlement Séant à Rouen', 19 mars 1771', ibid, vol. II, pp. 230–1.
19. 'Très humbles et très respectueuses remontrances de la Cour des Aides de Paris, du 18 février 1771, sur l'édit de décembre 1770, et l'état actuel du Parlement de Paris', reprinted in *Les 'Remontrances' de Malesherbes, 1771–1775*, ed. E. Badinter (1985), p. 157. On the language of Malesherbes, see Badinter's introduction, also K. M. Baker, 'French Political Thought at the Accession of Louis XVI', *Inventing the French Revolution*, pp. 117–20.
20. 'Remontrances de la Cour des Aides de Paris, du 18 février 1771', p. 152.
21. Ibid., p. 153.
22. Ibid., p. 155.
23. Ibid., p. 158.

24. Thus wrote Morellet to Condorcet, cited in J. M. S. Allison, *Lamoignon de Malesherbes* (New Haven, Conn., 1938), p. 17; see also Badinter's comments on the impact of these remonstrances in *Les Remontrances de Malesherbes*, pp. 91–6.

25. Bachaumont (attrib.), *Mémoires secrets*, v, 26 February 1771, p. 221 (see Chapter 5, note 2). It seems highly likely that much of this work at the time of the Maupeou coup was being compiled by the pro-parlement polemicist, Pidansat de Mairobert.

26. D. Van Kley, 'The Jansenist Constitutional Legacy in the French Prerevolution, 1750–1789', *Historical Reflections/Réflexions Historiques*, 13 (1986), pp. 417–18. For Target, see P. Boulloche, *Un avocat du XVIIIᵉ siècle* (1893).

27. G. J. B. Target, *Lettre d'un homme à un autre homme sur l'extinction de l'ancien Parlement et la création du nouveau* (n.p., 1771), p. 14.

28. On the political resonances of Target and J. V. Delacroix's *mémoires* in 1774 in defence of the *rosière* festival, which rewarded virtuous peasant girls, see S. Maza, 'The Rose-Girl of Salency: Representations of Virtue in Prerevolutionary France', *Eighteenth-Century Studies*, 22, 3 (1989), pp. 395–412, now republished in S. Maza, *Private Lives and Public Affairs: the Causes Célèbres of Prerevolutionary France* (Berkeley, Cal., 1993).

29. C. Mey, *Maximes du droit public français*, 2 vols (Amsterdam, 1775), vol. II, 'Dissertation sur le droit de convoquer les Etats-généraux'. This did not appear in the first edition of 1772.

30. Ibid., vol. I, p. 231.

31. See the illuminating account in K. M. Baker, 'A Classical Republican in Eighteenth-Century Bordeaux: Guillaume-Joseph Saige', in *Inventing the French Revolution*.

32. G. J. Saige, *Caton, ou Entretien sur la liberté et les vertus politiques* (originally published 1770; this edition, Paris, 1795), p. 349.

33. Ibid., pp. 397–8.

34. See, for example, the anonymous pro-*parlementaire* pamphlet, *Le Patriote Parisien* (n.p., 1774), esp. p. 3. Much of the material on Madame du Barry was afterwards published in Pidansat de Mairobert (attrib.), *Anecdotes sur Madame la Comtesse du Barry* (Amsterdam, 1776).

35. *Maupeouana, ou correspondance secrette et familière du Chancelier Maupeou avec son cœur Sorhouet...Nouvelle édition sur le manuscrit original*, 2 vols (n.p., 1773), vol. I, pp. 2, 4–6.

36. *Mémoires secrets*, V, 5 and 9 July 1771, pp. 276–8.

37. On the attempts of the government to influence public opinion, see Echeverria, *The Maupeou Revolution*, part II; also D. Hudson, 'In Defence of Reform: French Government Propaganda during the Maupeou Crisis', *French Historical Studies*, 8 (1973), pp. 51–76.

38. J. B. Moreau, *Leçons de morale, de politique et de droit public, puisées dans l'histoire de notre monarchie* (Versailles, 1773), p. 15; see also K. M. Baker, 'Controlling French History: the Ideological Arsenal of Jacob-Nicolas Moreau', in *Inventing the French Revolution*.

39. One such appeal was contained in an anonymous pamphlet, *Ego*, which, mindful of the recent defection of the Princes of the Blood, used the example of Cicero to remind wavering magistrates that they should remain true to their honour and their virtue, see Pidansat de Mairobert (attrib.), *Journal*

historique de la Révolution opérée dans la Constitution de la Monarchie Françoise, par M de Maupeou, Chancelier de France; 'Nouvelle édition, revue, corrigée et augmentée', 7 vols (London, 1775), vol. IV, 14 March 1773, pp. 108–10.

40. P. P. N. Henrion de Pansey, *Discours prononcé à la rentrée de la conférence publique de Messieurs les Avocats du Parlement de Paris, le 13 janvier 1775* (Paris, 1775), pp. 7–8.

41. Ibid., p. 4.

42. On the Molé family, see J. Félix, *Les Magistrats du parlement de Paris, 1771–1790* (Paris, 1990), pp. 203–4. In 1773 Henrion de Pansey dedicated his *Traité des fiefs du Dumoulin* to François Molé, son of a *président à mortier* of the exiled *parlement*; a gesture which had annoyed Maupeou to the extent of his having it banned, although an edition of the book appeared in Geneva in 1774.

43. On the politics of the painting of Molé confronting the *frondeurs*, by F. A. Vincent, which had such a success at the 1779 Salon, and which was commissioned by d'Angiviller, himself a defender of monarchy rather than the *parlements*, see T. E. Crow, *Painters and Public Life in Eighteenth-Century Paris* (New Haven, Conn., 1985), pp. 193–5.

44. Henrion de Pansey, *Discours prononcé à la rentrée . . . de Messieurs les Avocats du Parlement de Paris*, p. 8.

45. Ibid., p. 30.

46. Ibid., pp. 22–3.

47. Ibid., p. 34. Molé's 'virtues' are also discussed on pp. 8–11, 16–19, 25 and 35.

48. Ibid., pp. 21 and 25.

49. Henrion de Pansey himself was not a political radical. But he was also an expert on feudal law, and a few months before delivering this eulogy he had brought his knowledge to bear in the service of the comte de Rennepont, whose peasants had taken him to court over wood and pasture rights. With an extraordinarily poor sense of timing, Pansey published his massive and long-awaited treatise on feudal law at the beginning of August 1789, see L. Michaud, *Biographie universelle* (Paris, 1854–65).

50. *Mémoires secrets*, VII, 7 February 1775, pp. 281–2.

51. Ibid.

52. P. A. Robert de Saint-Vincent, *Mémoires*, unpub., typed copy in the possession of Dale Van Kley, p. 333.

53. For the evidence that Jansenist ideas drew some women into active political support of the patriot cause, see S. M. Singham, 'Vox populi vox Dei: les jansénistes pendant la révolution Maupeou', *Jansénisme et Révolution* (Paris, 1990), pp. 189–90.

54. A. McClellan, 'D'Angiviller's "Great Men" of France and the Politics of the Parlements', *Art History*, 13, 2 (June 1990), pp. 175–92.

55. See N. R. Gelbart, ' "Frondeur" journalism in the 1770s', *Feminine and Opposition Journalism, in Old Regime France* (Berkeley, Calif., 1987).

56. *Journal des dames*, August 1775, pp. 251–5; Henrion was at this time Mercier's own lawyer, see Gelbart, *Feminine and Opposition Journalism*, p. 228.

57. On the politicisation of lawyers resulting from this crisis, see Bell, 'Lawyers into Demagogues'; and Maza, *Private Lives and Public Affairs*.

58. J. V. Delacroix, *Réflexions sur les Mémoires, par M. de La Croix* (n.p., 1775), p. 7. On Delacroix's text, see also Maza, *Private Lives and Public Affairs*, pp. 116–20.

59. Delacroix, *Réflexions sur les Mémoires*, p. 10.

60. *Journal des dames*, August 1775, pp. 233–40, esp. pp. 233–6.
61. Denis Diderot, 'Sur l'histoire du Parlement de Paris par Voltaire', *Oeuvres complètes*, ed. J. Assézat and M. Tourneux (Paris, 1875–7), vol. VI, p. 404.
62. L. S. Mercier, *Le Tableau de Paris*, '*Nouvelle édition*', 8 vols (Amsterdam, 1782–3), vol. IV, p. 235.
63. See Doyle, 'The *Parlements* of France', p. 453.
64. On the effect of these polemics on public opinion as a social phenomenon, see Echeverria, *The Maupeou Revolution*, pp. 22–33, 38–9; and Singham, '"A Conspiracy of Twenty Million Frenchmen"', esp. chap. 3.

Chapter 7   The Triumph of Virtue, 1774–88

1. Cited in G. A. Kelly, *Victims, Authority, and Terror* (Chapel Hill, N.C., 1982), p. 308, note 89.
2. Work done by historians on political language generally in the prerevolutionary period shows that there was a remarkable degree of consensus about its use by participants: see, for example, Darnton's findings, especially on the use of the discourse of virtue in the pamphlets in the Kornmann affair, R. Darnton, 'Trends in Radical Propaganda on the Eve of the French Revolution, 1782–1788' (Dphil, Oxford, 1964), pp. 316–56. On the marked consistency in political consciousness and language amongst the members of the first Assembly of Notables, see V. R. Gruder, 'Paths to Political Consciousness: the Assembly of Notables of 1787 and the "Pre-Revolution" in France', in *French Historical Studies*, 13, 3 (1984), pp. 323–55. The phrase 'idiom of virtue' is used by Thomas Crow when describing public familiarity with the values disclosed in David's 'Oath of the Horatii', in *Painters and Public Life in Eighteenth-Century Paris* (New Haven, Conn., 1985) p. 228.
3. Darnton, 'Trends in Radical Propaganda', p. 24.
4. D. Mornet, *Les Origines intellectuelles de La Revolution Française: 1715–1787* (1933; republished, Paris, 1954), pp. 258–66.
5. J. P. Costard, *Dictionnaire universel, historique et critique des mœurs … des peuples des quatres parties du monde*, 4 vols (Paris, 1772), article on 'virtue', vol. IV, p. 505. Contrast this with the straightforward accounts under 'vertu' in the *Dictionnaire Universel, François et Latin* (1704); and in A. Furetière, *Dictionnaire Universel, 'Revû, corrigé et considérablement augmenté par M. Brutel de La Rivière'*, 4 vols (The Hague, 1727).
6. See, for example, the linguistic connection between nobility and honour made by L. G. Buat-Nançay, *Eléments de la Politique, ou Recherche des vrais Principes de l'Economie sociales* (London, 1773), esp. pp. 184–5.
7. H. L. La Tour du Pin (marquise de), *Memoirs of Madame de La Tour du Pin* (this edition, ed. and trans. F. Harcourt; London, 1985), pp. 26–7.
8. Cited in J. Charrier, *Claude Fauchet: Evêque constitutionnel du Calvados*, 2 vols (Paris, 1909), vol. I, p. 22. See also Ruth Graham, 'The Revolutionary Bishops and the *Philosophes*', *Eighteenth-Century Studies*, 16, 2 (Winter 1982/3), pp. 117–40.
9. Charrier, *Claude Fauchet*, vol. I, pp. 11–21; p. 19.
10. On the political fragmentation of the *parlementaires* at the outbreak of the Revolution, see W. Doyle, *The Parlement of Bordeaux and the End of the Old*

Regime, 1771–1790 (1974); also D. L. Wick, *A Conspiracy of Well-Intentioned Men: the Society of Thirty and the French Revolution* (New York, 1987).

11. Chaussinand-Nogaret, *La Noblesse au XVIIIe siècle: de la féodailité aux lumières* (Paris, 1976), pp. 192–200.

12. For a good example of the tactical exploitation of the language of patriotism and constitution during disputes over the elections of nobles to the Estates General in Artois, see N. Hampson, 'The Enlightenment and the Language of the French Nobility in 1789: the Case of Arras', in D. J. Mossop, G. E. Rodmell and D. B. Wilson (eds), *Studies in the French Eighteenth Century, Presented to John Lough* (Durham, 1978).

13. On the court nobility and the Party Patriot, see Wick, *A Conspiracy of Well-Intentioned Men*.

14. See Mornet, *Les Origines intellectuelles*, pp. 270–7.

15. On the points at which Rousseau and the Jansenists converged, see D. Van Kley, *The Religious Origins of the French Revolution: From Calvinism to the Civil Constitution, 1560–1791* (New Haven, Conn., 1996), pp. 295–97. On *L'Ecclésiastique citoyen*, see pp. 338–41.

16. On Fauchet's interpretation of Rousseau's ideas for the *Cercle Social*, the educational society that he helped to set up during the Revolution, see J. McDonald, *Rousseau and the French Revolution, 1762–1791* (London, 1965), pp. 76–80.

17. Charrier, *Claude Fauchet*, vol. I pp. 37–41.

18. On Elisée's life, see the biographical notice in the *Oeuvres choisies du P. Elisée, précédées d'une notice biographique* (Paris, 1828), pp. 5–9.

19. Elisée, *Premier Sermon sur la Fausseté de la Probité sans la Religion*, in *Sermons du R. Père Elisée, carmé déchaussé, prédicateur du Roi*, 4 vols (Paris, 1785), vol. I, pp. 149–50. He devoted two further sermons to this same subject, also the *Sermon sur l'excellence de la morale Chrétienne*, ibid.

20. Ibid., I, p. 181.

21. F. G. Cormeaux, *Discours sur les charmes de la vertu*, in *Oeuvres oratoires complètes de Cormeaux*, reprinted in J. P. Migne, *Collection intégrale et universelle des orateurs sacrés* (Paris, 1844–66), vol. 72, cols, 134–5.

22. C. L. Richard, *Défence de la religion, de la morale, de la vertu, de la politique et de la société, ou Réfutation du 'système social'* (Paris, 1775); *Annales de la charité et de la bienfaisance chrétienne*, 2 vols (Lille and Paris, 1785).

23. Boismont, *Sermon pour l'Assemblée extraordinaire de Charité, Qui s'est tenu à Paris, à l'occasion de l'établissement d'une maison royale de santé, en faveur des ecclésiastiques et des militaires malades; Prononcé dans l'église des religieux de la Charité, le 13 mars 1782*, in, *Oeuvres oratoires complètes de l'abbé de Boismont*, reprinted in Migne, *Collection . . . des orateurs sacrés*, vol. 65, col. 745.

24. Ibid., cols 750–1.

25. Bachaumont (attrib.), *Mémoires secrets*, XX, 6 April 1782 (see Chapter 5, note 2).

26. Charrier, *Claude Fauchet*, vol. I, pp. 34–7.

27. Cited in ibid., p. 105.

28. Parker argues, however, that the changes insituted by the Oratorians probably did not really make themselves felt until the 1780s. See H. T. Parker, *The Cult of Antiquity and the French Revolutionaries* (1937; republished, New York, 1965), pp. 31–2.

29. L. B. Proyart, *L'Ecolier vertueux, ou vie édifiante d'un Ecolier de l'Université de Paris, mort le 23 décembre de l'année 1768. Par M. l'Abbé *** (Paris, 1772).
30. J. M. Thompson, *Robespierre* (1935; Oxford, 1988), pp. 11–12. Proyart probably contributed to the earliest biographical work on Robespierre, revealing details from Robespierre's youth to discredit him: ibid., pp. 599–602. For Proyart's stand against religious toleration for Protestants in 1787, see J. Merrick, *The Desacralization of the French Monarchy in the Eighteenth Century* (Baton Rouge, La 1990), p. 145.
31. Examples of the genre include: L. P. Bérenger and E. Guibard, *La Morale en action* (Lyon, 1783); J. L. Carra, *Esprit de la morale et de la philosophie* (The Hague, 1777); S. A. C. Dagues de Clairfontaine, *Bienfaisance françois, ou Mémoires pour servir à l'Histoire de ce Siècle*, 2 vols (Paris, 1778); C. H. Piarron de Chamousset, *Oeuvres complettes* (sic) *de M. de Chamousset, contenant ses projets d'humanité, de bienfaisance et de patriotisme*, 2 vols (Paris, 1783). On the rapid escalation of works on *bienfaisance* and patriotism in the 1780s, see also H. Chisick, *The Limits of Reform in the Englightenment: Attitudes toward the Education of the Lower Classes in Eighteenth-Century France* (Princeton, N.J., (1981), pp. 215–38.
32. J. P. Brissot, *Bibliothèque philosophique de législateur, du politique, du jurisconsulte*, vol. IX (10 vols, Berlin, 1782–5), p. 289.
33. On the growing political interest in the permitted and tolerated press, see J. D. Popkin, 'The Prerevolutionary Origins of Political Journalism' in K. M. Baker (ed.), *The Political Culture of the Old Regime* (Oxford, 1987); also the articles in J. R. Censer and J. D. Popkin (eds), *Press and Politics in Pre-Revolutionary France* (Berkeley, Cal., 1987).
34. For a discussion of the *affiches* and their diffusion of secular morality, see Mornet, *Les Origines intellectuelles*, pp. 349–56. For the possible link between the politicisation of bourgeois readers through the *affiches* and the origins of the Revolution, see the cogent exploration by C. Jones, 'The Great Chain of Buying: Medical Advertisement, the Bourgeois Public Sphere, and the Origins of the French Revolution', *American Historical Review*, 101 (1996), pp. 13–40.
35. See the 'Avis' at the end of vol. II of Dagues de Clairfontaine, *Annales de la bienfaisance* (1778). This work contained stories of virtue and acts of *bienfaisance*, many of which were culled from the press, extending from 1715 to 1774.
36. Ibid., 'Approbation' at the end of vol. III, by Lourdet, Professeur Royal.
37. R. Estienne (attrib.), *Les Etrennes de la vertu* (Paris, Savoye, 1782–92). Members of the public would write in to the *Journal de Paris* and other journals to participate with their own stories of remarkable acts of virtue, and many of their letters were republished in *Les Etrennes de la vertu*, see, for example, the volume for 1782, pp. 23, 27, 29, 31, 40, 54 and 123.
38. Ibid. (1782), 'Avertissement'.
39. Ibid. (1786), pp. 21–3, 37–8, 88–91.
40. Ibid. (1786), p. 91.
41. Ibid. (1788), pp. 80–1.
42. On *bienfaisance* as a social project, see C. Jones, *Charity and Bienfaisance: the Treatment of the Poor in the Montpellier Region, 1740–1815* (Cambridge, 1982); and O. Hufton, *The Poor of Eighteenth-Century France, 1750–1789* (Oxford, 1974). The major study by C. Duprat, *Le Temps des philanthropes*, vol. I

(Paris, 1993), concentrates on the revolutionary era, but Part I focuses on the period from 1780 (the date when the *Société Philanthropique* was established) up to the Revolution.
43. La Tour du Pin, *Memoirs*, p. 16.
44. N. E. Rétif de la Bretonne, *La Vie de mon père*, translated as *My Father's Life* by R. Veasey (Gloucester, 1986), p. 108.
45. Ibid., Preface, p. 1.
46. J. J. Rousseau, *Discours sur les sciences et les arts*, in *Oeuvres complètes* (Paris, 1959–70), p. 25.
47. Bachaumont (attrib.), *Mémoires secrets*, XXIII, 25 August 1783, pp. 137–45. These prizes for 'an act of virtue by a poor Frenchman' had been set up by a noted philanthropist, Auget de Montyon, and were thereafter given annually.
48. The *Etrennes de la vertu* noted and publicised many such prizes for virtue, and festivals set up in imitation of the one at Salency; for *rosière* festivals, for example, see (1782), pp. 85–6; (1783), pp. 28–30; prizes for virtue include (1782), pp. 34–6 (these were the prizes of Auget de Montyon); (1786), pp. 8–9; (1787), pp. 117–20; (1788), pp. 80–1. See also J. B. Nougaret, *Les Rosières* (Paris, n.d., 1820?).
49. See, for example, L. Gershoy, *Bertrand Barère: a Reluctant Terrorist* (Princeton, N.J., 1962), pp. 22–43.
50. W. H. Everdell, 'The Rosières Movement, 1766–1789: a Clerical Precursor of the Revolutionary Cults', *French Historical Studies*, 9, 1 (Spring 1975), pp. 23–36.
51. S. F. Brulart de Genlis (comtesse de), *Mémoires inédits de Madame de Genlis; pour servir à l'histoire des dix-huitième et dix-neuvième siècles*, 8 vols (Paris, 1825–6), vol. I, pp. 203–6.
52. S. Maza, 'The Rose-Girl of Salency: Representations of Virtue in Prerevolutionary France', *Eighteenth-Century Studies*, 22, 3 (Spring 1989), pp. 395–412.
53. Nougaret, *Les Rosières*, pp. 44–87.
54. See M. G. J. Crèvecœur, *Lettres d'un cultivateur américain...depuis l'Année 1770...jusqu'en 1786* (originally translated 1784; this edition, Paris, 1787), p. 28. See also Darnton, 'Trends in Radical Propaganda', pp. 111–20.
55. C. J. Mathon de la Cour, *Discours sur les meilleurs moyens de faire naître et d'encourager le patriotisme dans une monarchie* (Paris, 1789), pp. 12–15.
56. Claude Fauchet, *Discours sur les mœurs rurales prononcé dans l'église de Surenne, le 10 d'août 1788, pour la fête de la rosière* (Paris, 1788), p. 4.
57. Ibid., pp. 17–18.
58. See Charrier, *Claude Fauchet*, vol. I, pp. 55–6. On the general acceptance this extraordinary sermon was accorded, see pp. 52–4. See also Everdell, 'The Rosières Movement', pp. 33–4; and Maza, 'The Rose-Girl of Salency', p. 409.
59. J. S. Maury, *Discours prononcé dans l'Académie Françoise, le jeudi 27 janvier 1785, à la Récéption de M. l'Abbé Maury* (Paris, 1785), pp. 26–7.
60. See, for example, A. J. B. Boucher D'Argis, *De l'Education des Souverains, ou des Princes destinés à l'être* (Geneva, 1783), esp. pp. 5, 16–7, 21–4.
61. P. L. C. Gin, *Les Vrais principes du gouvernement françois, démontrés par la raison et par les faits. Par un François. Nouvelle édition, revue, corrigée et augmentée* (Geneva, 1782), pp. 56–9.

62. P. L. C. Gin, *Eloge de Monseigneur le Dauphin, père de Louis XVI* (1779), republished in P. L. C. Gin, *De la Religion, par un Homme du Monde*, 5 vols (Paris, 1778–80), vol. V (1780), pp. 1–3.
63. Ibid., pp. 8–9.
64. Ibid., pp. 39–40. As Louis's latest biographer Hardman notes, Louis was the only one of the Bourbons not to be accorded an official soubriquet, though the reasons for this appear rather uncertain. See J. Hardman, *Louis XVI* (New Haven, Conn., 1993), Preface, p. vii.
65. For an interesting account of the evidence, see G. A. Kelly, 'The Machine of the Duc D'Orléans and the New Politics', *Journal of Modern History*, 51 (1979), pp. 667–84. On the evolution from closed to open politics, see Kelly, *Victims, Authority, and Terror*, p. 284.
66. Ibid., p. 671.
67. *Mémoires secrets*, xxxi, 15 and 17 February 1786, pp. 111, 114–17.
68. C. Fauchet, *Oraison Funèbre de Louis-Philippe D'Orléans* (Paris, 1786), p. 2.
69. Ibid., p. 3.
70. Ibid., pp. 8–9.
71. Ibid., pp. 15–17.
72. Ibid., pp. 23–4.
73. *Mémoires secrets*, xxxi, 28 February 1786. See also Charrier, *Claude Fauchet*, pp. 29–33.
74. See Kelly, 'The Machine of the Duc D'Orléans and the New Politics', p. 673.
75. *Etrennes de la vertu* (1788), p. 16, pp. 45–6.
76. See V. Wyndham, *Madame de Genlis* (London, 1958), p. 113.
77. J. Necker, *De L'importance des opinions religieuses* (1788), in J. Necker, *Oeuvres complètes* (1820–1; Scientia Verlag Allen, 1971), vol. XII, see esp. pp. 146–62.
78. Ibid., pp. 80–1. On the moral and religious ideas of Necker, see H. Grange, *Les Idées de Necker* (Paris, 1974), pp. 517–53. See also Chisick, *The Limits of Reform*, p. 238.
79. Necker, *De L'importance des opinions religieuses*, pp. 175–80.
80. Ibid., pp. 169–72.
81. Ibid., pp. 173–4.
82. Cited by Grange, *Les Idées de Necker*, p. 546, note 54.

Conclusion: Virtue and the Creation of Revolutionary Politics

1. See G. A. Kelly, *Victims, Authority, and Terror* (Chapel Hill, N.C., 1982), pp. 281–98.
2. See the many works of Dale Van Kley, in particular 'New Wine in Old Wineskins: Continuity and Rupture in the Pamphlet Debate of the French Pre-revolution, 1787–1789', *French Historical Studies*, 17, 2 (1991).
3. On the continuing influence on the revolutionaries of their classical education and the ways this changed between 1789 and 1794, see H. T. Parker, *The Cult of Antiquity and the French Revolutionaries* (1937; republished, New York, 1965), pp. 8–36. More recently, the important study by T. Tackett, *Becoming a Revolutionary: the Deputies of the French National Assembly and the Emergence of a Revolutionary Culture (1789–1790)* (Princeton, N.J., 1996), argues that the deputies did not adopt the Enlightenment wholesale but only as needed,

pragmatically, and used many other traditions, including judicial ones (pp. 48–65). He says little about the classical republican tradition, but he does note that in the early months of the Revolution the deputies referred more often to the classics and to history than they did to Rousseau (pp. 65, 304). On the impact of Jansenism, see pp. 65–67.

4. P. Trahard, *La Sensibilité révolutionnaire, 1789–1794* (Paris, 1936); and R. Darnton, *The Kiss of Lamourette: Reflections in Cultural History* (London, 1990), pp. 17–18.

5. Cited by R. Chartier in *The Cultural Origins of the French Revolution* (Durham and London, 1991), pp. 111–13. Chartier also addresses here the changes shown in the language of kingship. On the relative lack of radical political language in the overall grievances of the *cahiers*, first pointed out by Mornet, see the summary of recent research in R. Chartier, 'From Words to Texts: the *Cahiers de doléances* of 1789', in R. Chartier, *The Cultural Uses of Print in Early Modern France* (Princeton, N.J., 1987), pp. 110–44.

6. On the language of kingship, citizenship and *bienfaisance* in the *cahiers*, see the wide-ranging study of the general *cahiers* of the nobility and the Third Estate by G. Shapiro and J. Markoff, *Revolutionary Demands: a Content Analysis of the Cahiers de Doléances of 1789* (Stanford, Cal., 1998), pp. 369–76.

7. Cited and translated by Shapiro and Markoff, *Revolutionary Demands*, p. 373.

8. See, for example, *Les Réflexions et la Résolution d'un Bon Roi* (En France, 1788), esp. pp. 7, 10; and Martin de Mariveaux, *L'Ami des lois, ou les vrais principes de la monarchie française* (Paris, 1775; republished 1788), esp. pp. 19–20 on the need for virtuous ministers.

9. *Les Quarante Vœux principaux de la Nation* (n.p., 1789).

10. Cited by R. Darnton, 'Trends in Radical Propaganda on the Eve of the French Revolution, 1782–1788' (Dhil, Oxford, 1964), pp. 275–6.

11. E. Sieyès, *Qu'est-ce que le Tiers état?* (1789; this edition, Geneva, 1970), chap. 6, p. 195.

12. On the political ideas of Sieyès, one of the most comprehensive studies is that of M. Forsyth, *Reason and Revolution: the Political Thought of the Abbé Sieyès* (Leicester, 1987). For a recent reevaluation of Sieyès' rhetoric as a tactical self-definition of the bourgeoisie, see W. H. Sewell, *A Rhetoric of Bourgeois Revolution: the Abbé Sieyès and What is the Third Estate?* (Durham, N.C., 1994).

13. Sieyès, *Qu'est-ce que le Tiers état?*, chap. 6, p. 196.

14. A recent monograph expresses doubt about the extent of Sieyès' connections with the Society of Thirty, given that most of the latter were working for a union of Orders. See K. Margerison, *Pamphlets and Public Opinion: the Campaign for a Union of Orders in the Early French Revolution* (West Lafayette, Ind., 1998), chapter 5, 'Sieyès and Public Opinion', esp. pp. 94–5. Margerison here also contends that Sieyès' political influence in this pre-revolutionary period was not as intense as has commonly been assumed.

15. On the relations between Sieyès and d'Orléans, see Kelly, *Victims, Authority and Terror*, p. 53.

16. See D. Van Kley, 'From the Lessons of French History to Truths for All Times and All People: the Historical Origins of an Anti-Historical Declaration', in D. Van Kley (ed.), *The French Idea of Freedom: the Old Regime and the Declaration of Rights of 1789* (Stanford, Cal., 1994), pp. 110–11.

17. On the centrality of virtue to the revolutionary concept of citizenship, see P. Rétat, 'The Evolution of the Citizen from the Ancien Régime to the Revolution', in R. Waldinger, P. Dawson and I. Woloch (eds), *The French Revolution and the Meaning of Citizenship* (Westport, Conn., 1993), pp. 3–15. Also the exploration of education for citizenship, in J. L. Labarrière, 'De la vertu du citoyen éclairé', in J. Boulad-Ayoub (ed.), *Former un nouveau peuple? Pouvoir, éducation, révolution* (Paris, 1996), pp. 57–69. Labarrière, however, shows that the rhetoric of virtue was not universally employed during the Revolution, any more than it had been during the *ancien régime*; thus, Condorcet's plans for education mostly avoided the term.

18. In addition to works already mentioned, studies of revolutionary rhetoric and the power of words include: J. Renwick (ed.), *Language and Rhetoric of the Revolution* (Edinburgh, 1990); M. E. Blanchard, *Saint-Just et Cie: la révolution et les mots* (Paris, 1980); N. Parker, *Portrayals of Revolution: Images, Debates and Patterns of Thought on the French Revolution* (Hemel Hempstead, 1990), esp. chap. 1; E. Kennedy, *A Cultural History of the French Revolution* (New Haven, Conn., 1989); B. C. J. Singer, *Society, Theory and the French Revolution: Studies in the Revolutionary Imaginary* (London, 1986).

19. Amongst the studies of revolutionary journalism one should include: C. Hesse, *Publishing and Cultural Politics in Revolutionary Paris, 1789–1810* (Berkeley, Cal., 1991); H. Gough, *The Newspaper Press in the French Revolution* (London, 1988); J. D. Popkin, *Revolutionary News: the Press in France, 1789–1799* (Durham and London, 1990).

20. In a lucid and subtle defence of his position, Furet explicitly rejected the term ('I never use it') as a means of describing the Jacobin government. See his 'A Commentary', *French Historical Studies*, 61, 4 (1990), p. 795.

21. C. Blum, *Rousseau and the Republic of Virtue* (New York, 1986), pp. 147–8.

22. For example, ibid., pp. 150–1, p. 277.

23. A perspective on the relationship between Robespierre's concept of virtue and his pragmatic politics is offered in M. Linton, 'Robespierre's Political Principles', W. Doyle and C. Haydon (eds), *Robespierre: History and Literature* (Cambridge, 1999).

24. On the revolutionary idea of creating 'new men', see M. Ozouf, *L'Homme régénéré: essais sur la Révolution française* (Paris, 1989), pp. 116–57; also, the articles in Boulad-Ayoub (ed.), *Former un nouveau peuple?*

25. Despite its title, P. Higonnet, *Goodness Beyond Virtue: Jacobins during the French Revolution* (Cambridge, Mass. 1998), is not a study of moral politics but a broader, more social analysis: the idea of virtue is not discussed at all, in either its pre-revolutionary or revolutionary forms.

26. E. Radcliffe, 'Revolutionary Writing, Moral Philosophy, and Universal Benevolence in the Eighteenth Century', *Journal of the History of Ideas*, 54, 2 (1993), pp. 221–40. See also, C. Jones, 'Radical Sensibility in the 1790s', in A. Yarrington and K. Everest (eds), *Reflections of Revolution: Images of Romanticism* (London, 1993).